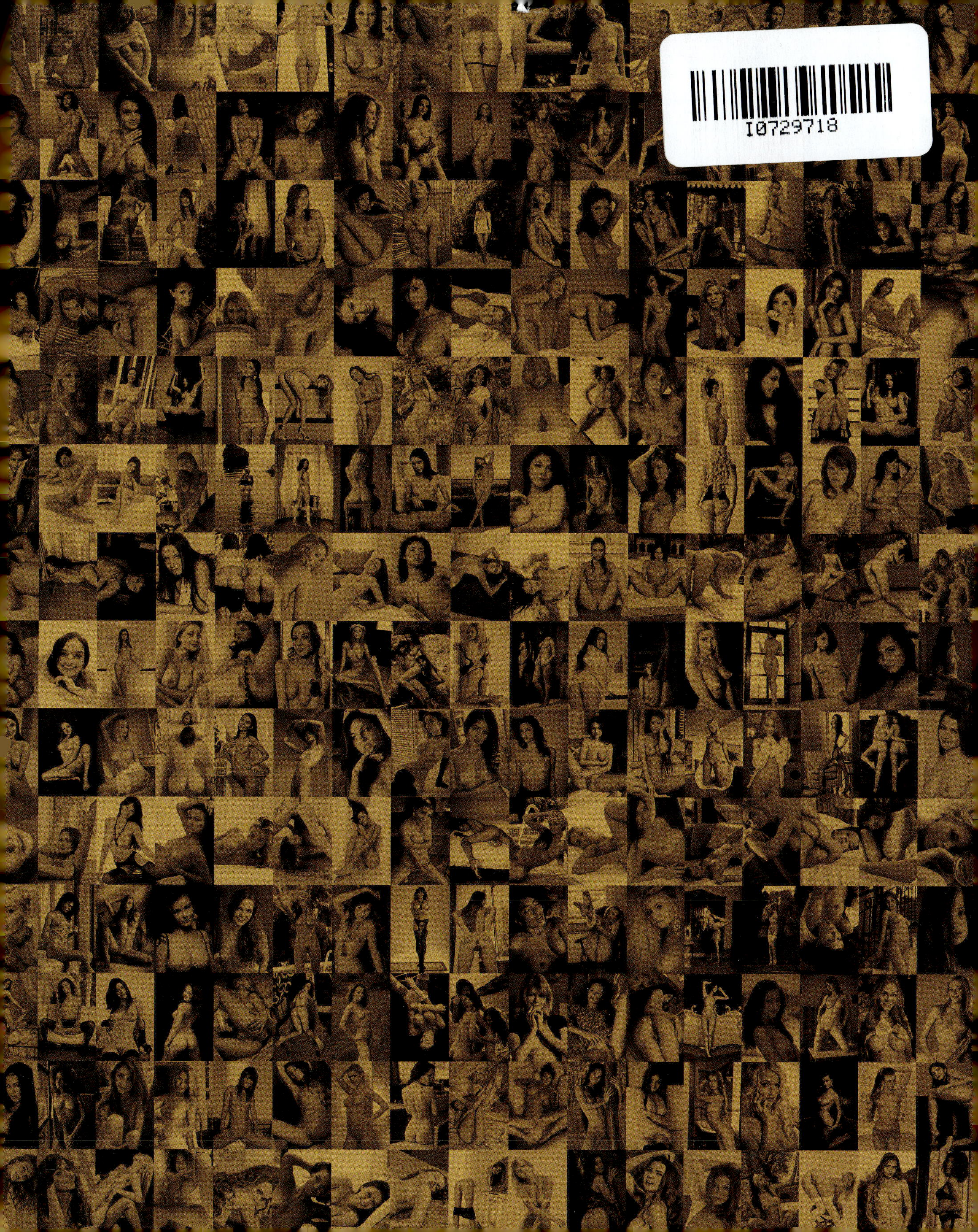

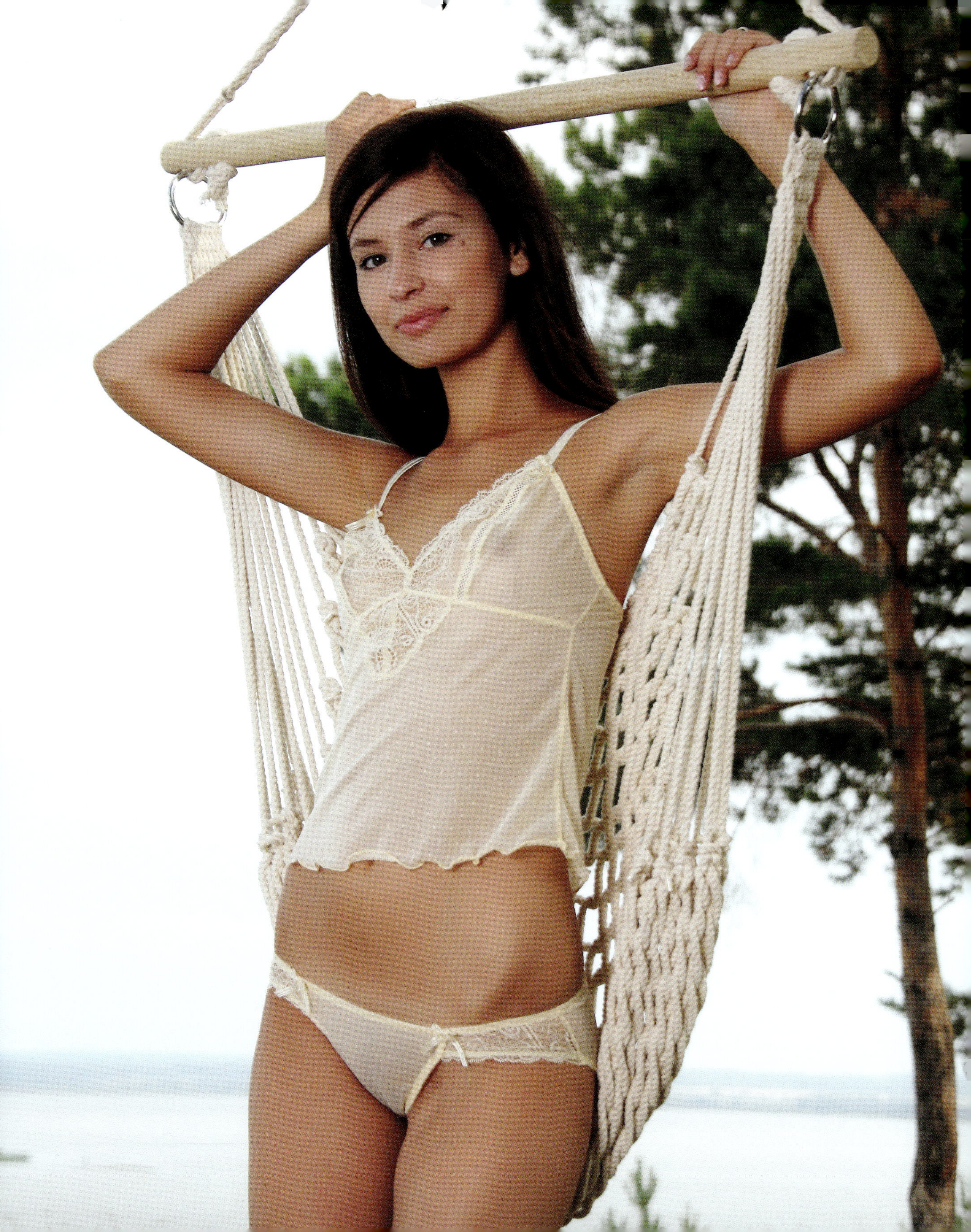

TOP MODELS OF

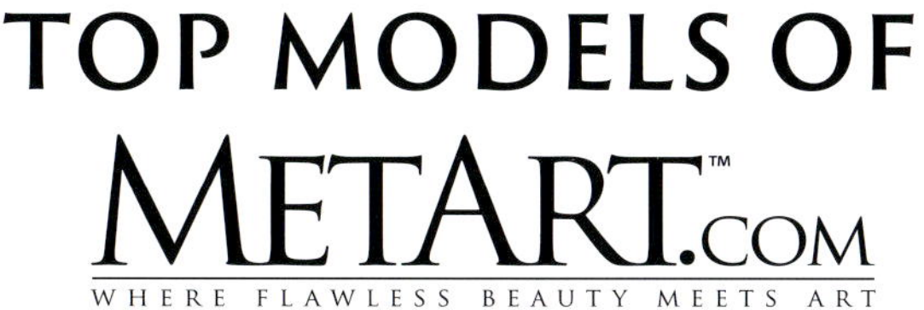

IRINA J

COLLECTED AND EDITED BY ISABELLA CATALINA

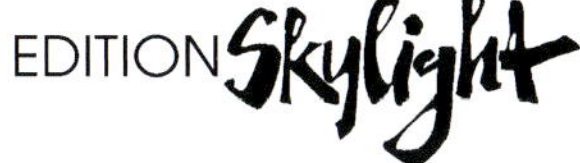

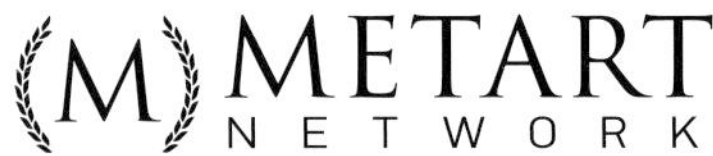

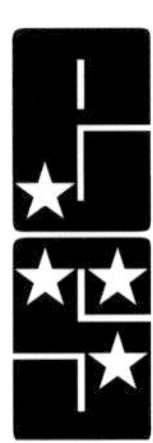

First edition 2025
Copyright © 2025 by Edition Skylight

EDITION SKYLIGHT
Rosengartenstrasse 13B
CH-8608 Bubikon / Zürich
Switzerland
info@edition-skylight.com
www.edition-skylight.com

ISBN 978-3-03766-714-9

Bibliographic information published by Die Deutsche Bibliothek
Die Deutsche Bibliothek lists this publication in the
Deutsche Nationalbibliografie; detailed bibliographic data
are available in the Internet at http://dnb.ddb.de.

Printed in Bosnia and Herzegovina

A SLENDER, ATHLETIC FIGURE WITH SMALL BREASTS AND AN AMAZING ASS ...

Seductive Russian beauty **Irina J** is many MetArt members' embodiment of a perfect teen and she's a classic star of our prestigious MetArt 50+ Club, girls so popular they've been featured here at least fifty times during their modeling career. Tall and slender with soulful brown eyes, she remains a perennial favorite well worth browsing the archives to discover.
Gorgeous Irina made her debut on September 15, 2009 at the age of 18. She likes summer, sun and beach and all kind of activities such as horse riding, swimming and aerobics. She loves to show her beauty and getting a lot of attention through her photo sessions. She hates monotony and tries to get experienced by travelling, meeting people, make new friends, and trying out new food.
And what was it about Irina that we all liked so much? Maybe her naturally glamorous demeanor, the lovely face with full lips and a distinctive beauty mark; the slender, athletic figure with small breasts and an amazing ass; the pretty pussy, sometimes shaved, sometimes hairy; the graceful moves and sultry smile; no wonder so many members claim her as their "all time favorite". In her bio, Irina revealed that she was studying to be an architect – brains as well as beauty!

DIESE SCHLANKE, ATHLETISCHE FIGUR MIT KLEINEN BRÜSTEN UND EINEM UNGLAUBLICHEN HINTERN ...

Die verführerische russische Schönheit **Irina J** verkörpert für viele MetArt-Mitglieder den perfekten Teenager und ist ein klassischer Star unseres renommierten MetArt 50+ Clubs. Die Models sind so beliebt, dass sie im Laufe ihrer Modelkarriere mindestens fünfzig Mal hier vorgestellt wurden. Groß und schlank mit gefühlvollen braunen Augen ist sie ein absoluter Dauerbrenner und es lohnt sich, in den Archiven zu stöbern, um mehr von ihr zu entdecken.
Die wunderschöne Irina feierte ihr Debüt am 15. September 2009 im Alter von 18 Jahren. Sie mag den Sommer, Sonne und Strand und alle möglichen Aktivitäten wie Reiten, Schwimmen und Aerobic. Sie liebt es, ihre Schönheit zu zeigen und durch ihre Fotosessions viel Aufmerksamkeit zu erregen. Sie hasst Monotonie und versucht, Erfahrungen zu sammeln, indem sie reist, Leute kennenlernt, neue Freundschaften schließt und neue Gerichte probiert.
Und was hat uns allen so an Irina gefallen? Vielleicht liegt es an ihrem natürlich glamourösen Auftreten, dem hübschen Gesicht mit vollen Lippen und einem markanten Schönheitsfleck; der schlanken, athletischen Figur mit kleinen Brüsten und einem umwerfenden Arsch; der hübschen Muschi (für die Shootings mal rasiert, mal behaart); den anmutigen Bewegungen und dem sinnlichen Lächeln. Kein Wunder, dass so viele Mitglieder sie als ihre „Allzeit-Favoritin" bezeichnen. In ihrer Biografie verriet Irina, dass sie Architektur studiert – Köpfchen und Schönheit!

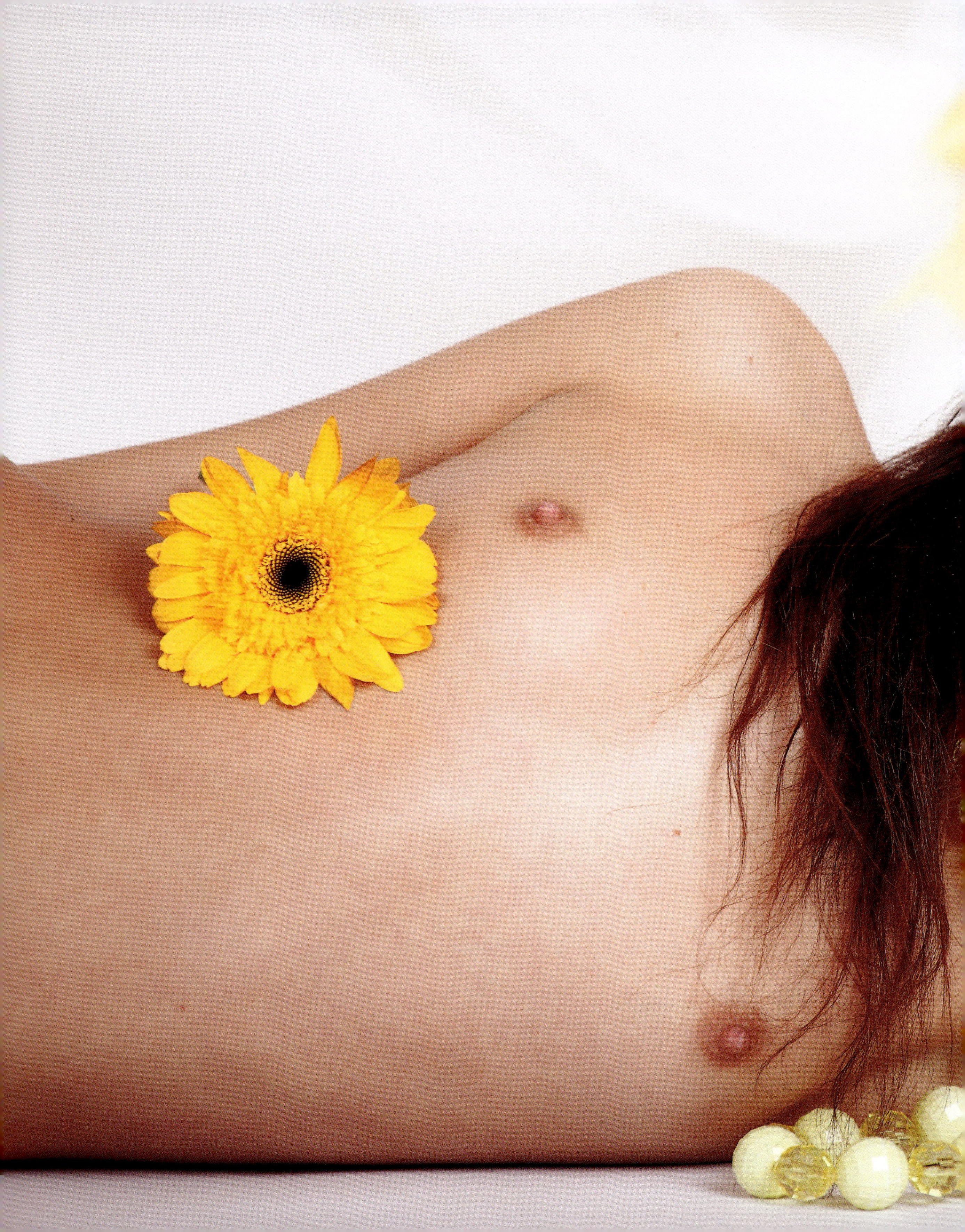

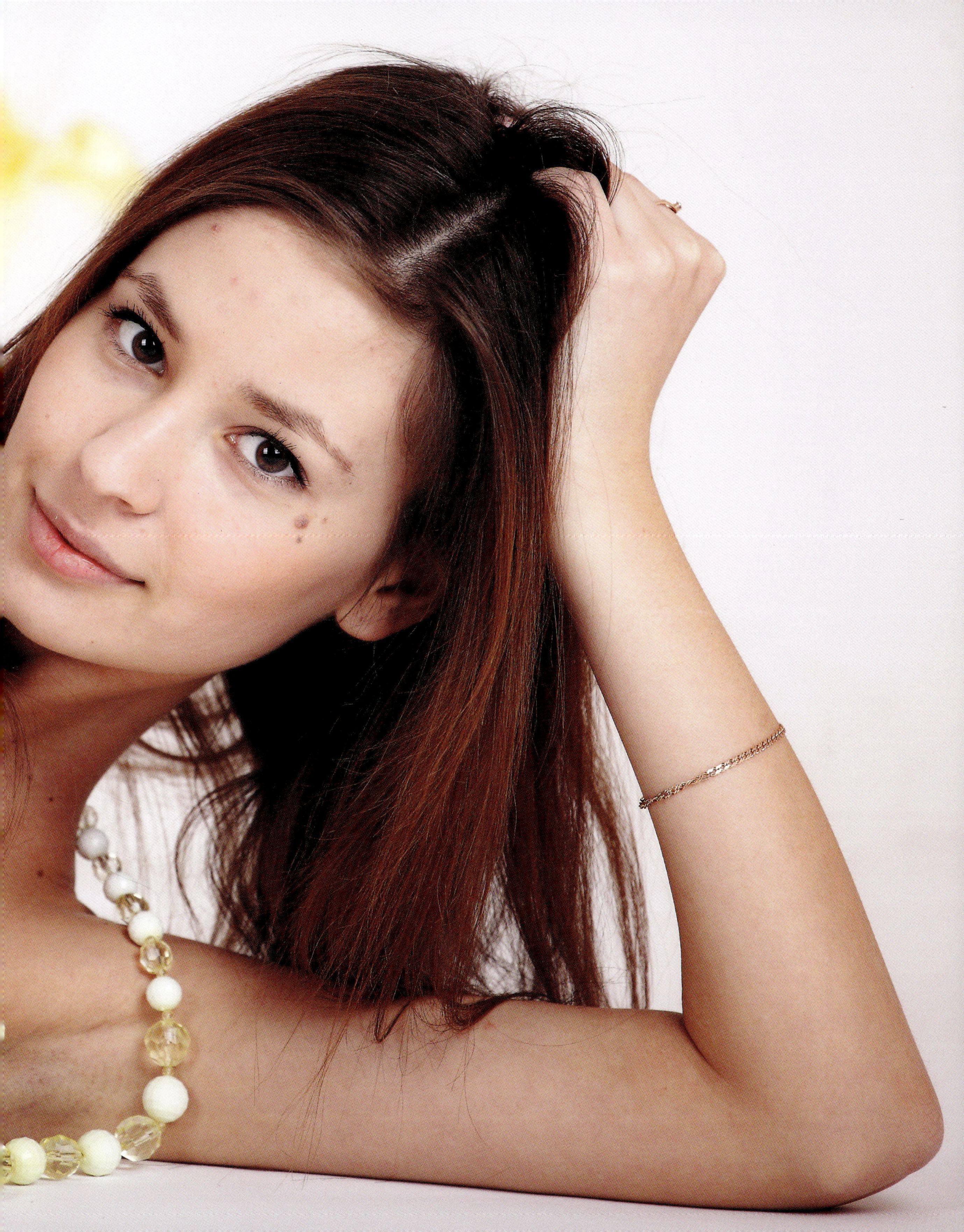

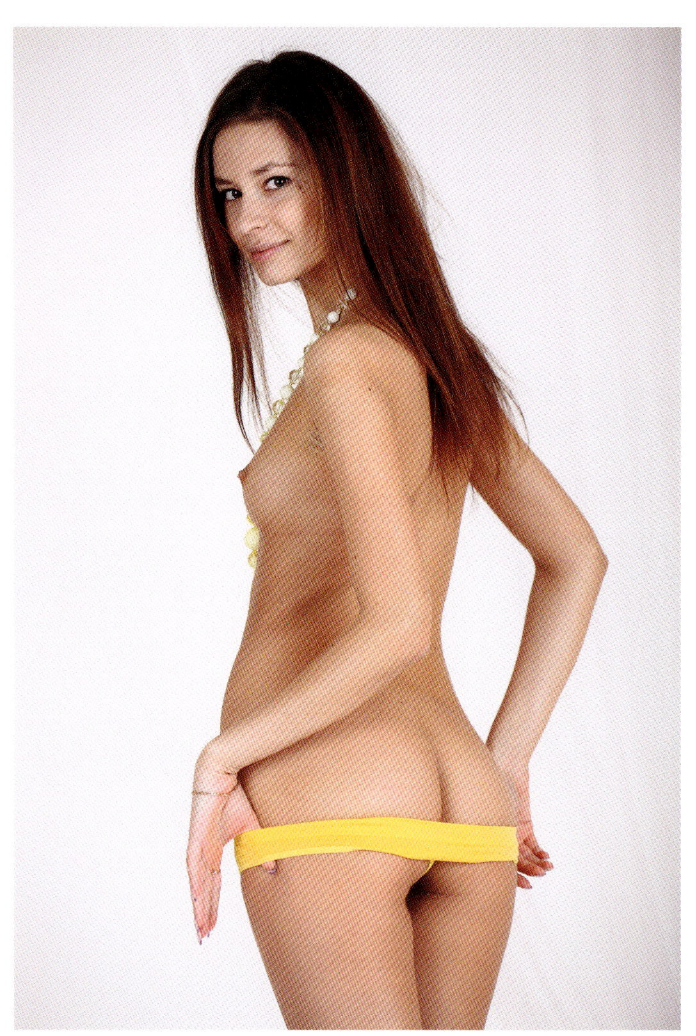

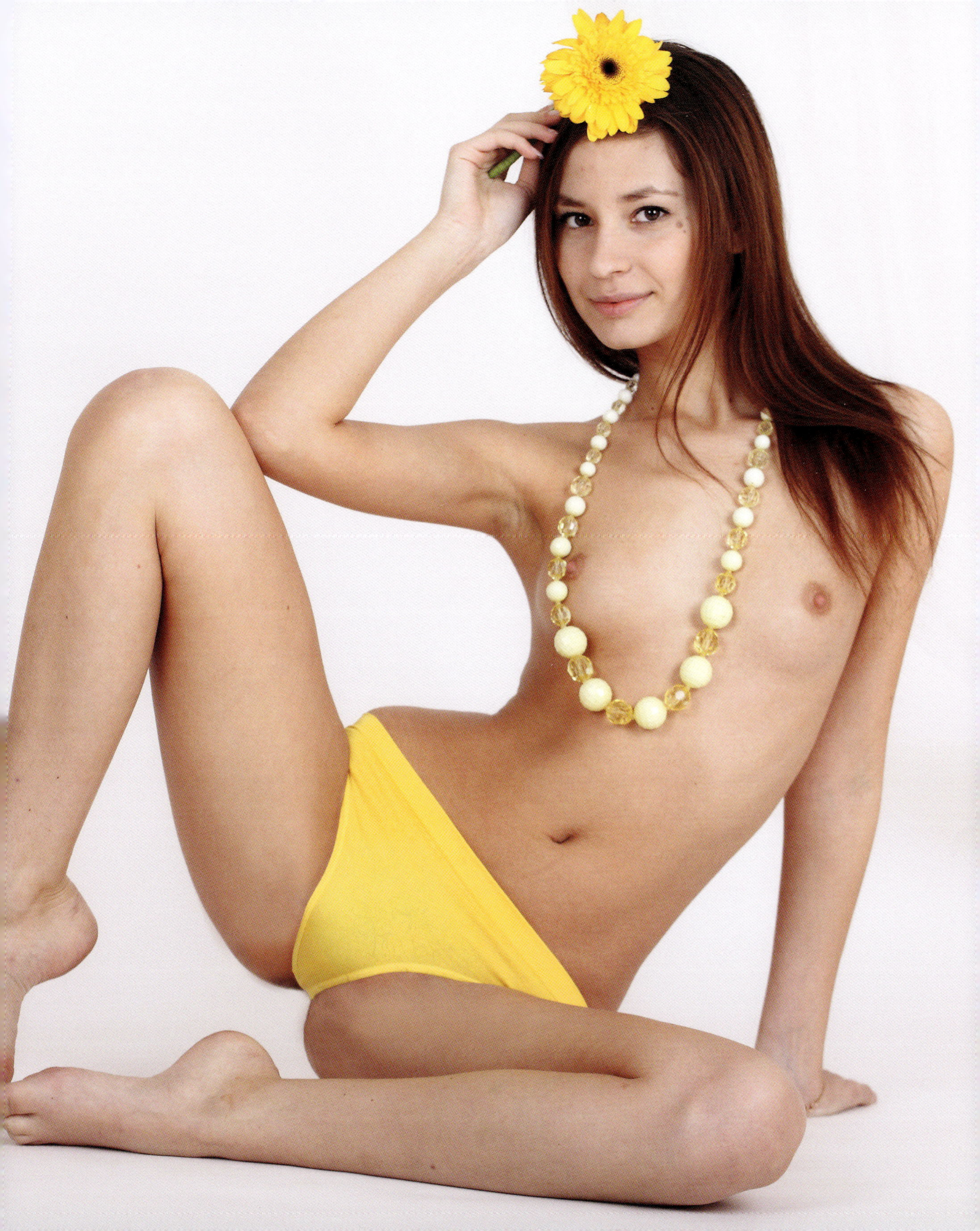

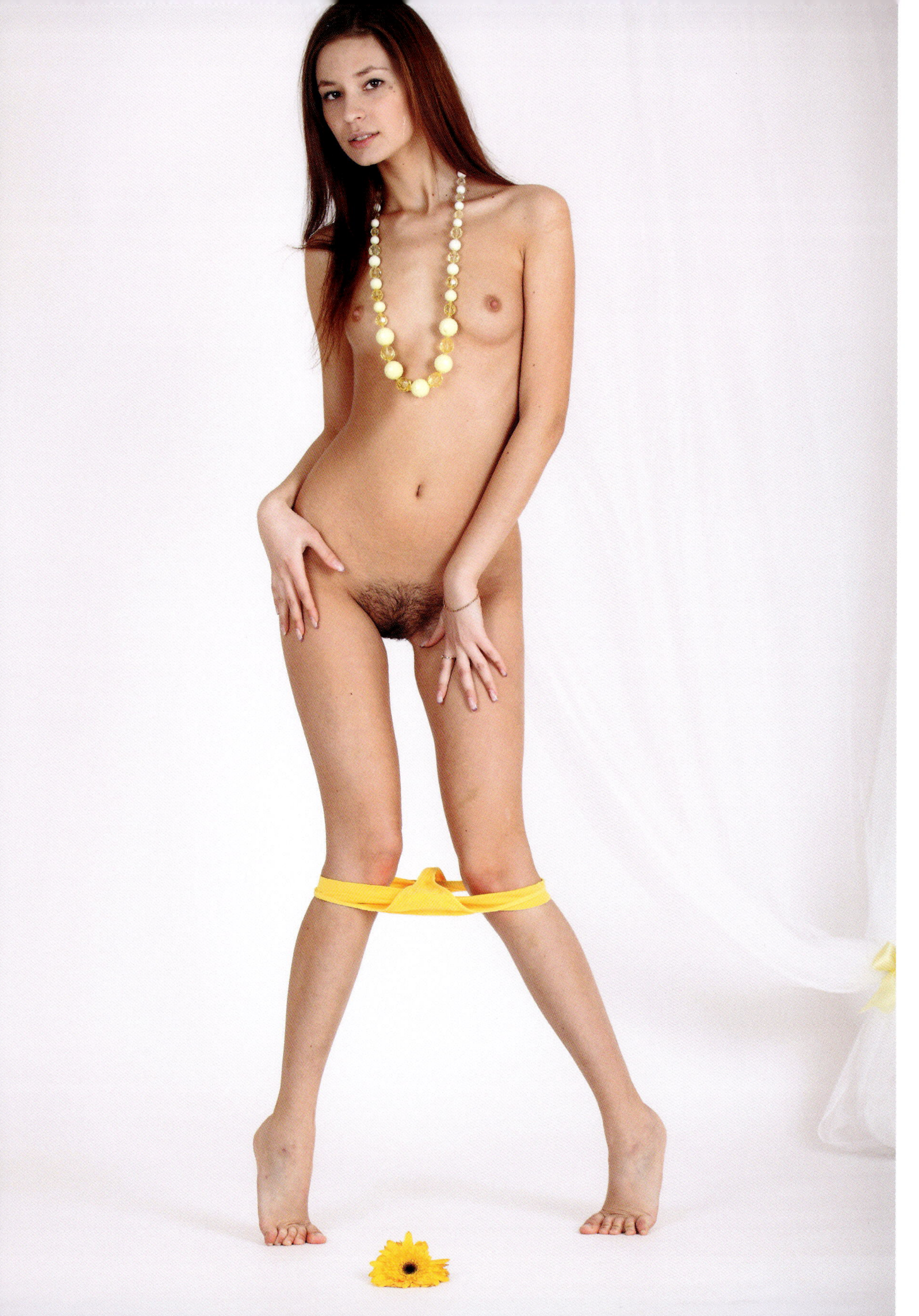

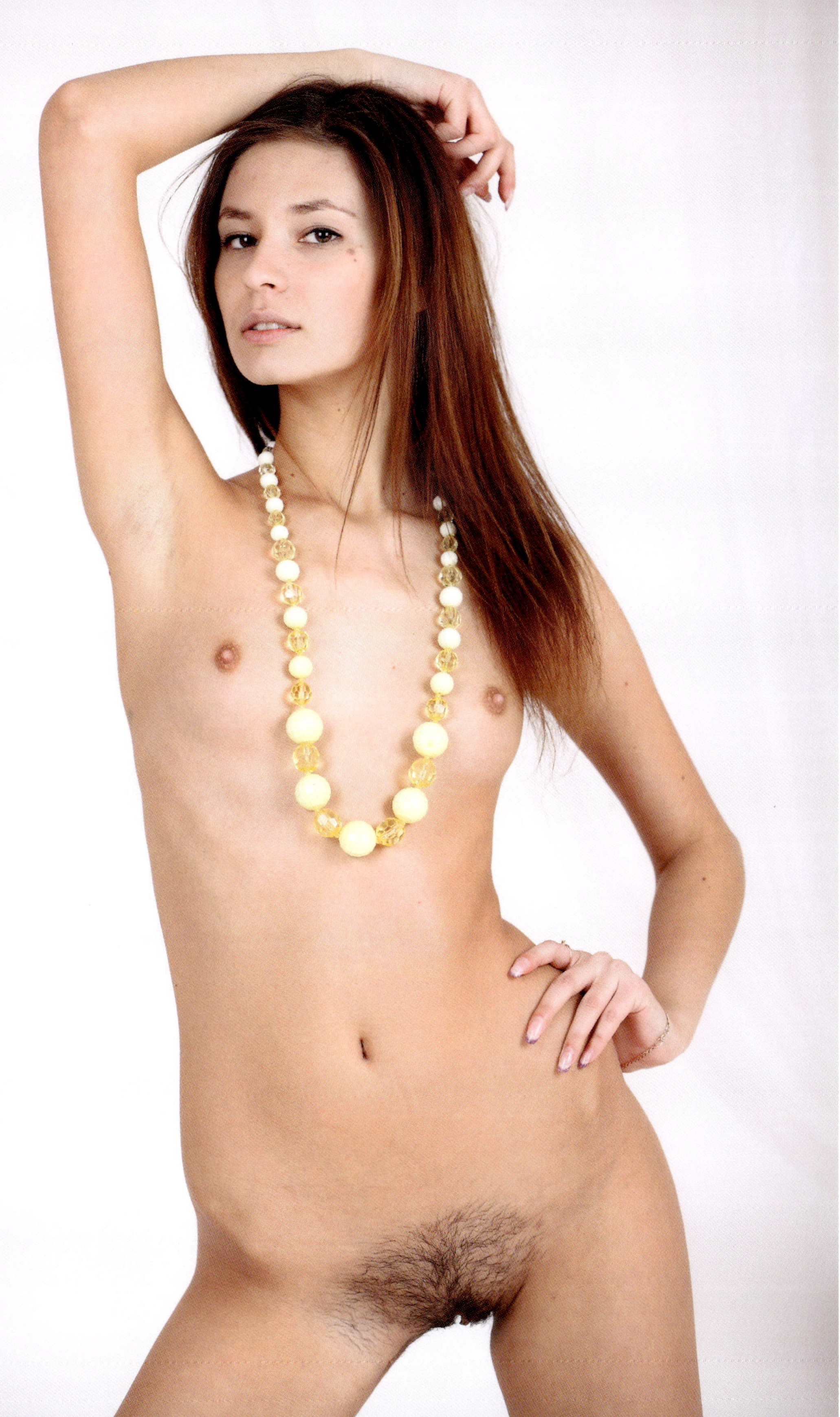

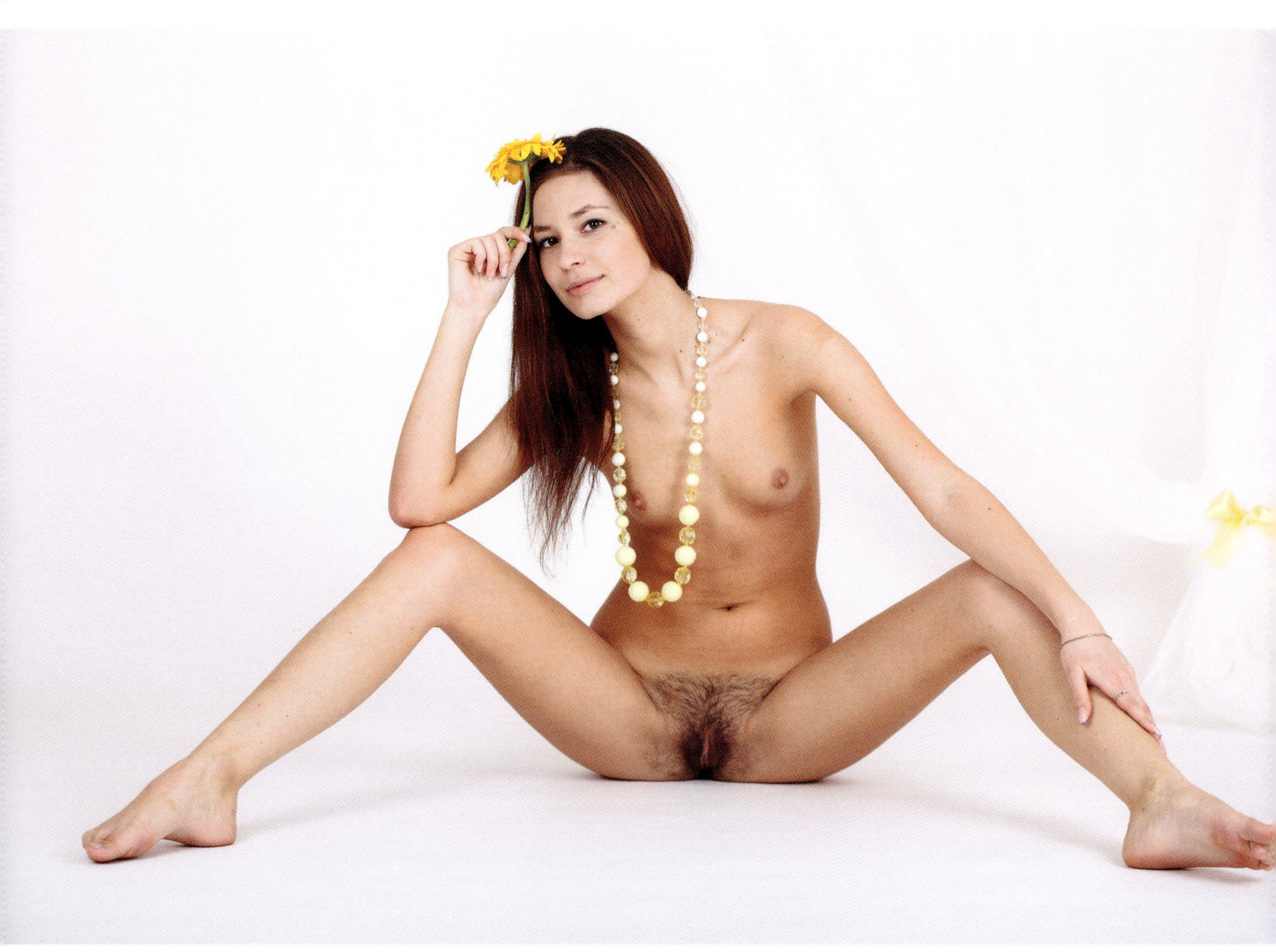

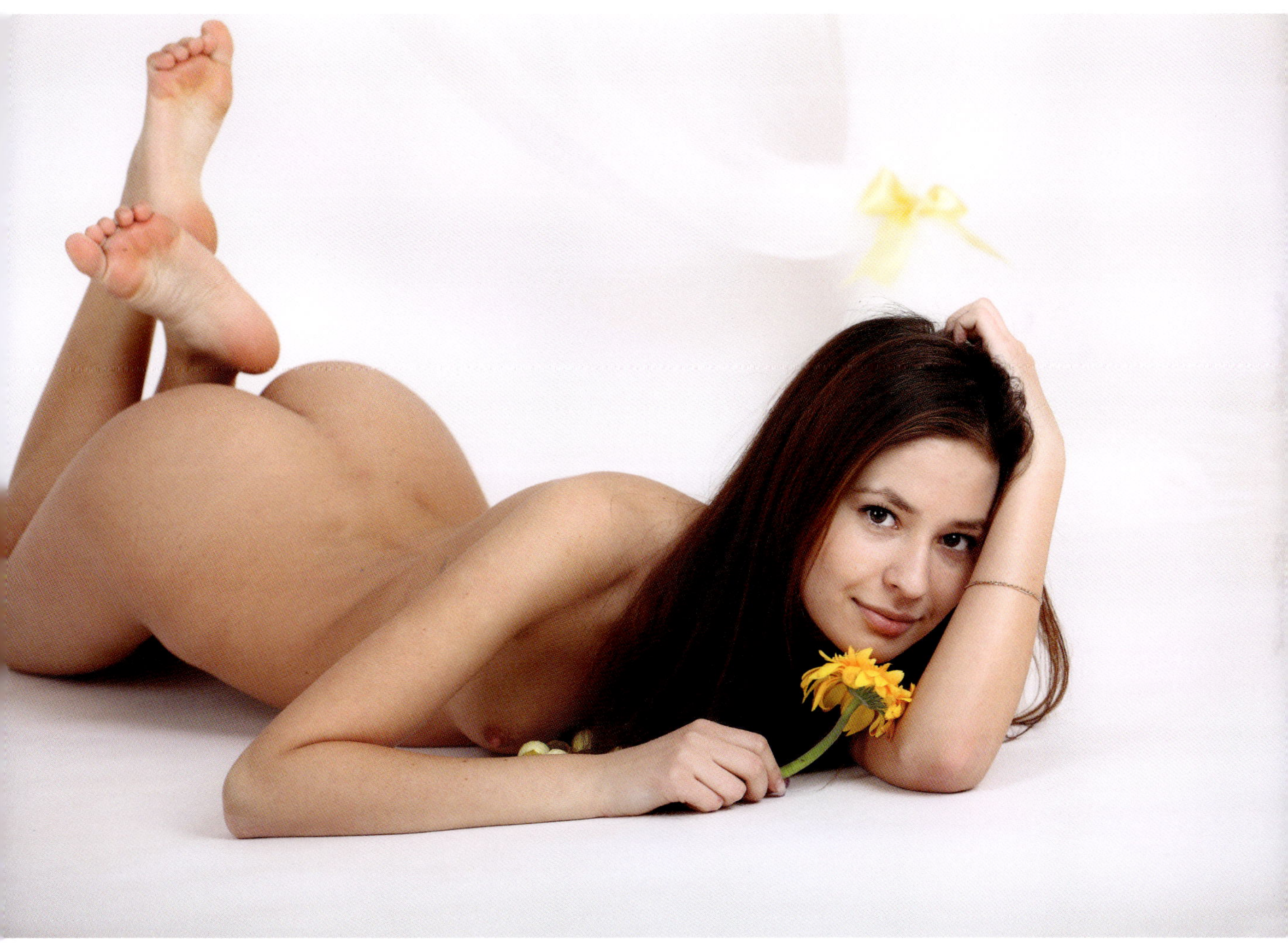

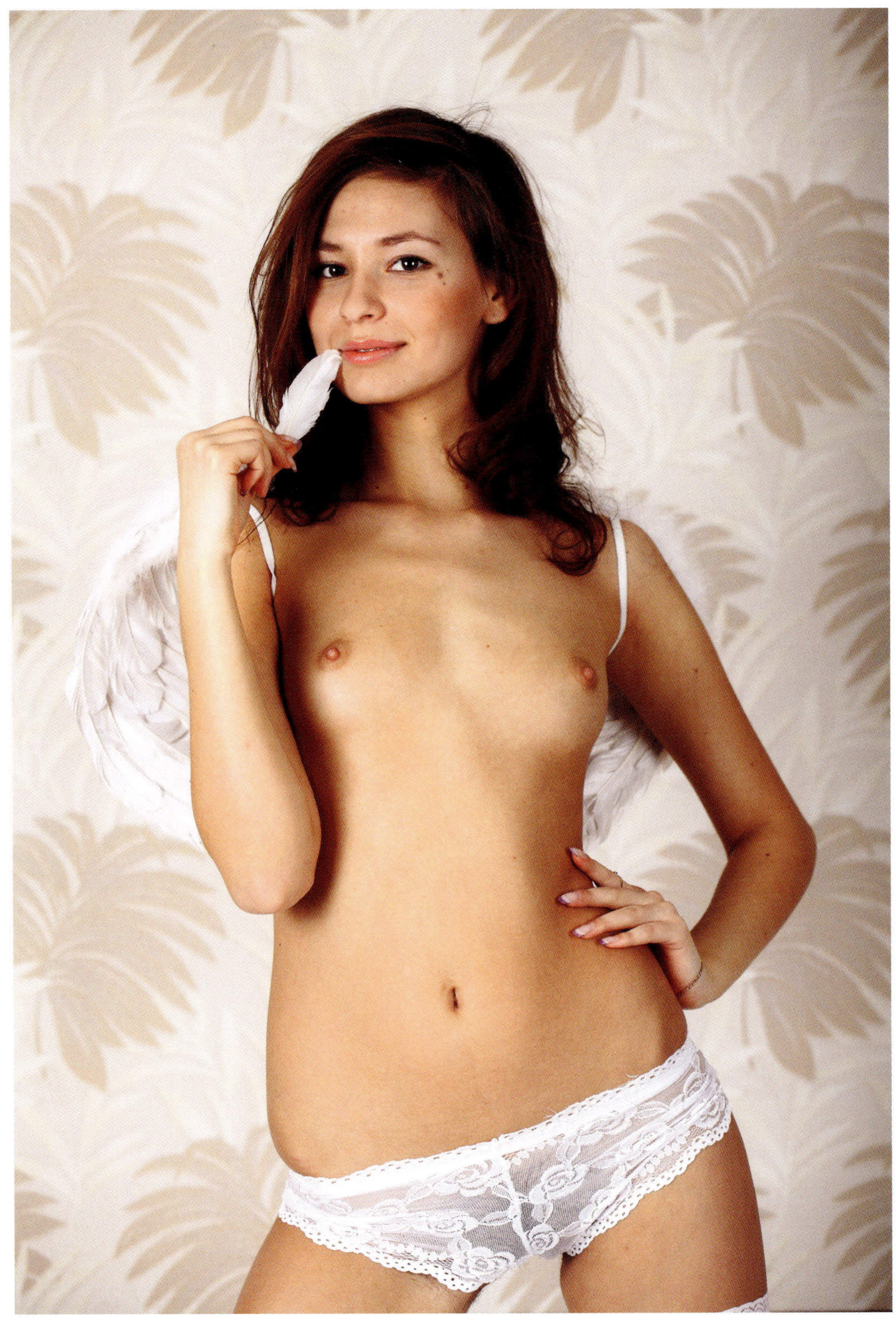

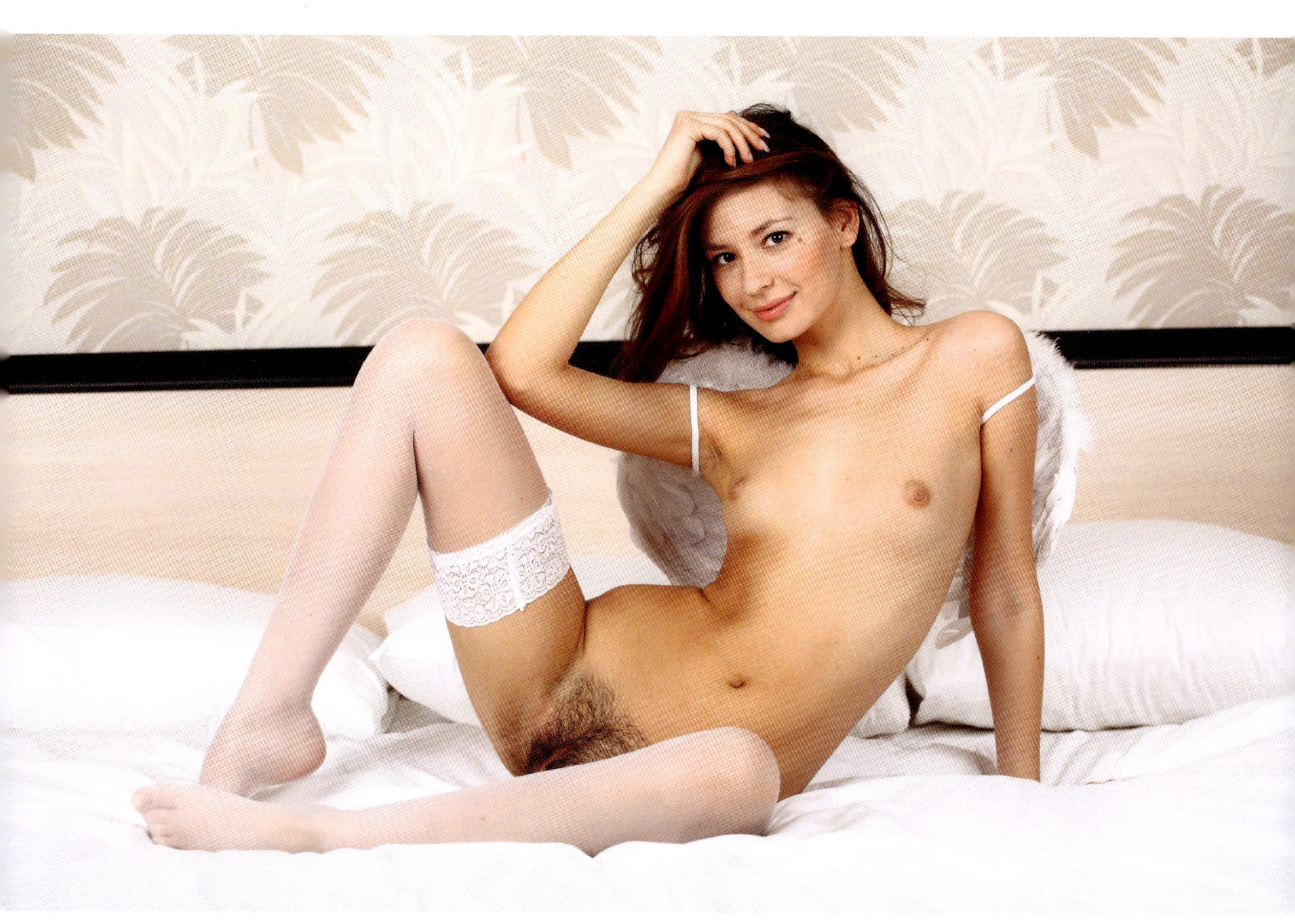

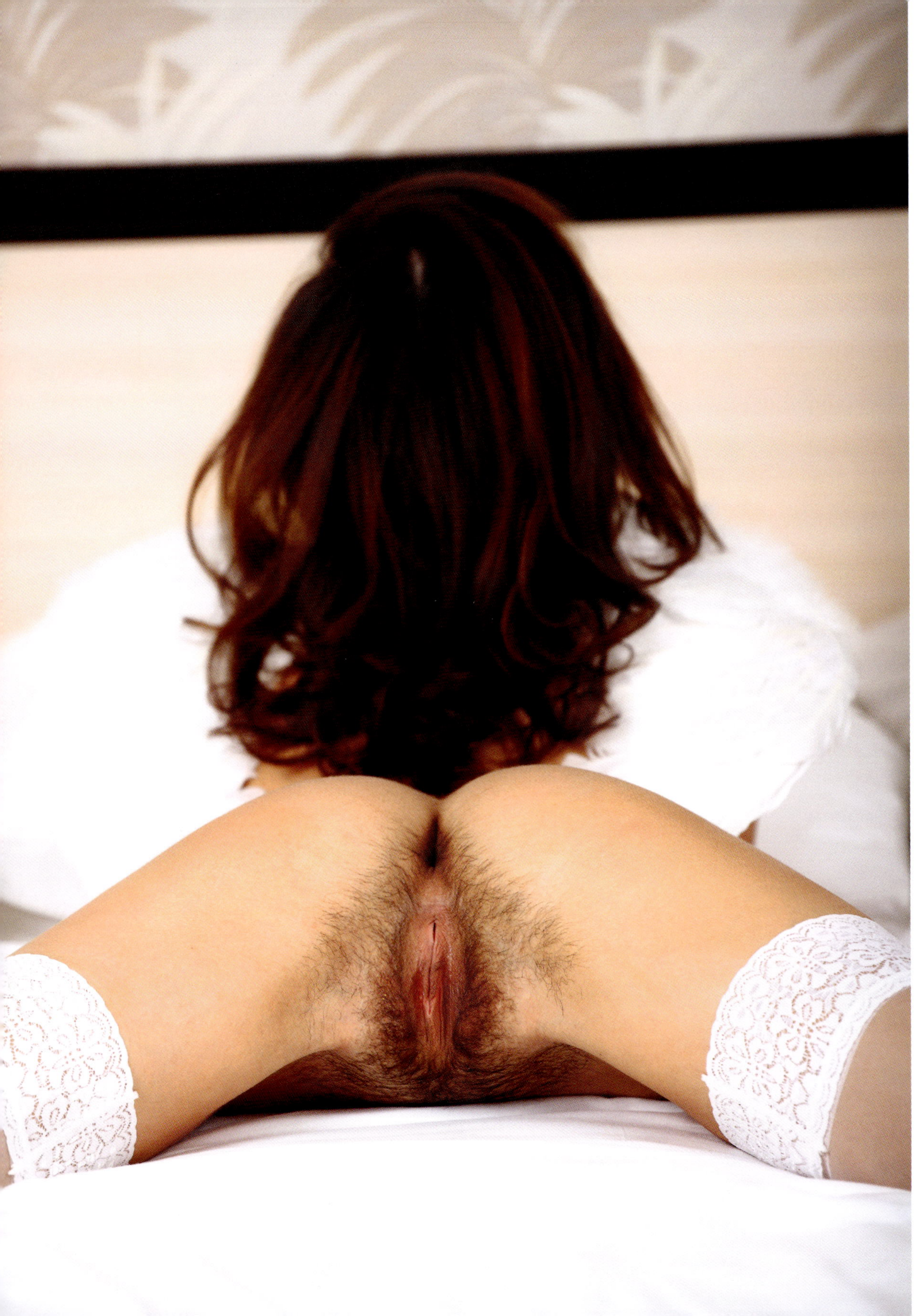

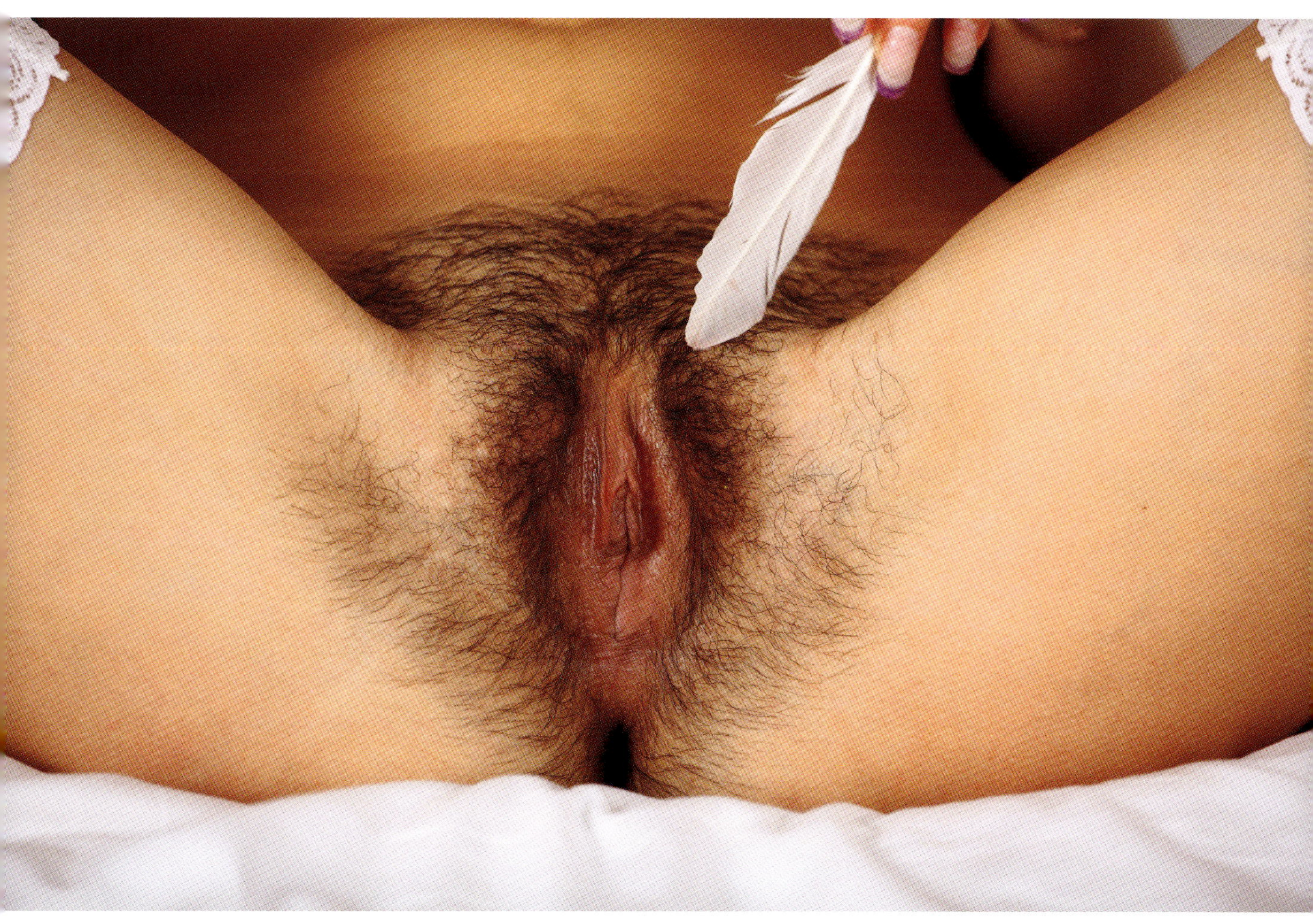

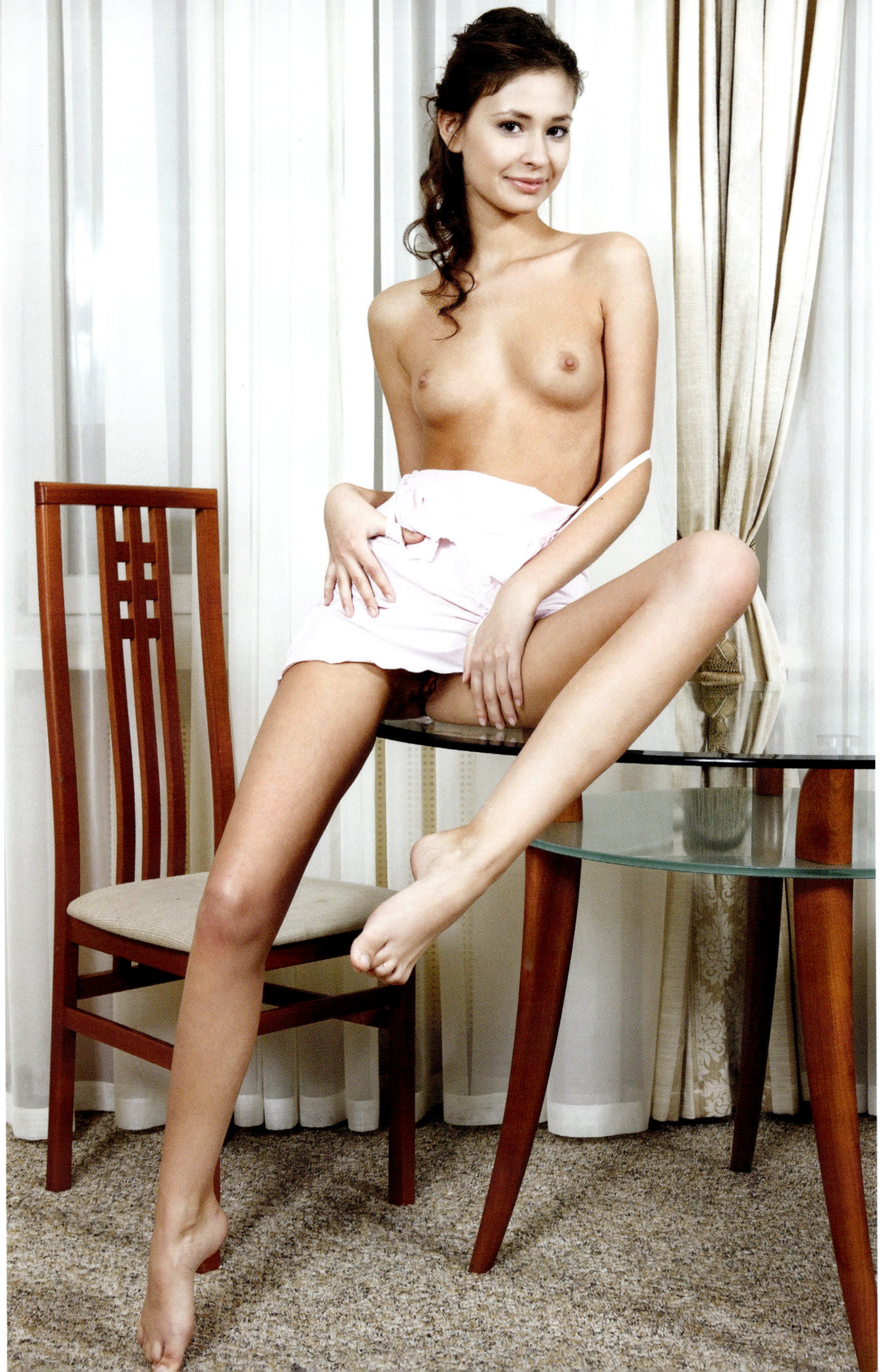

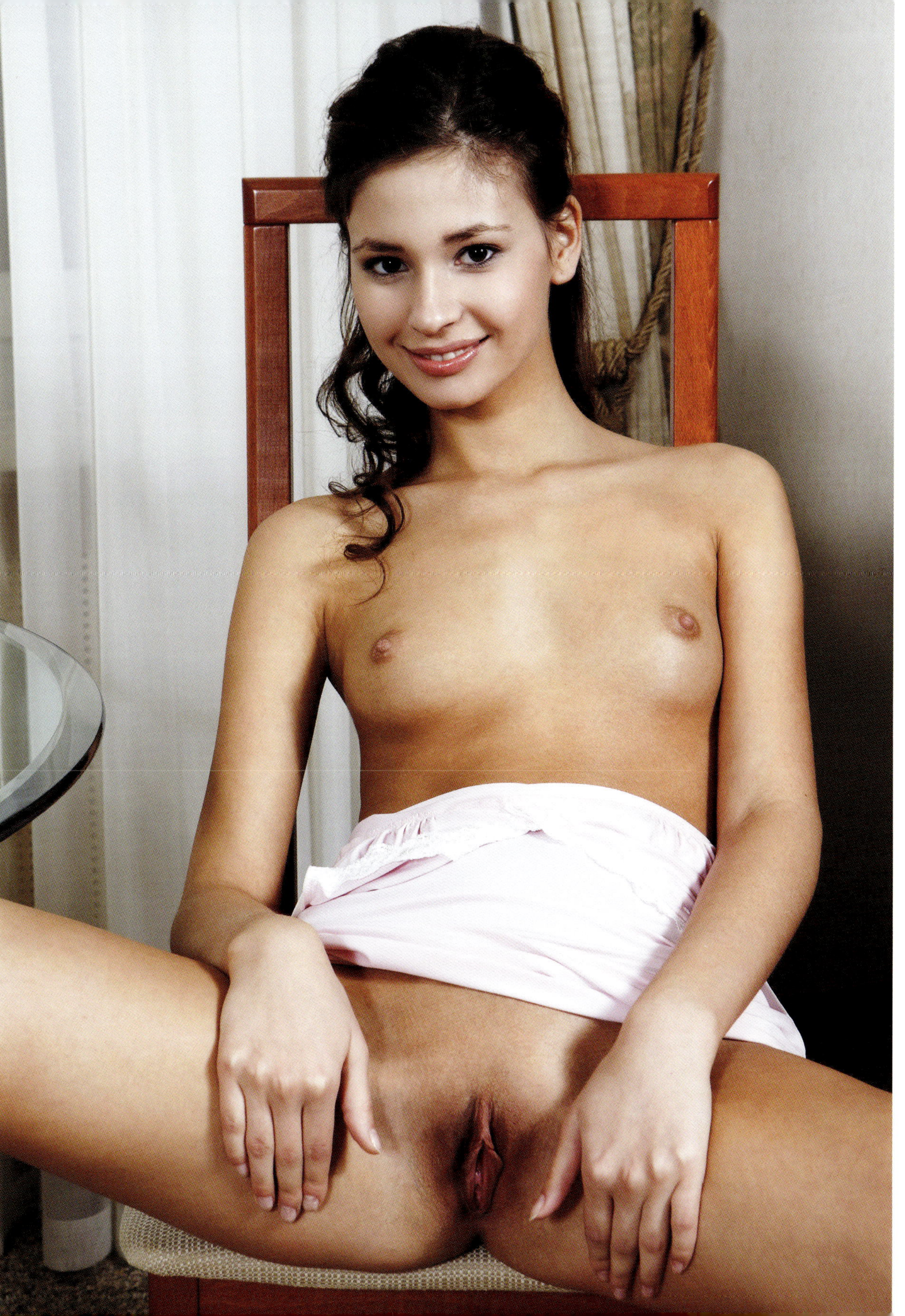

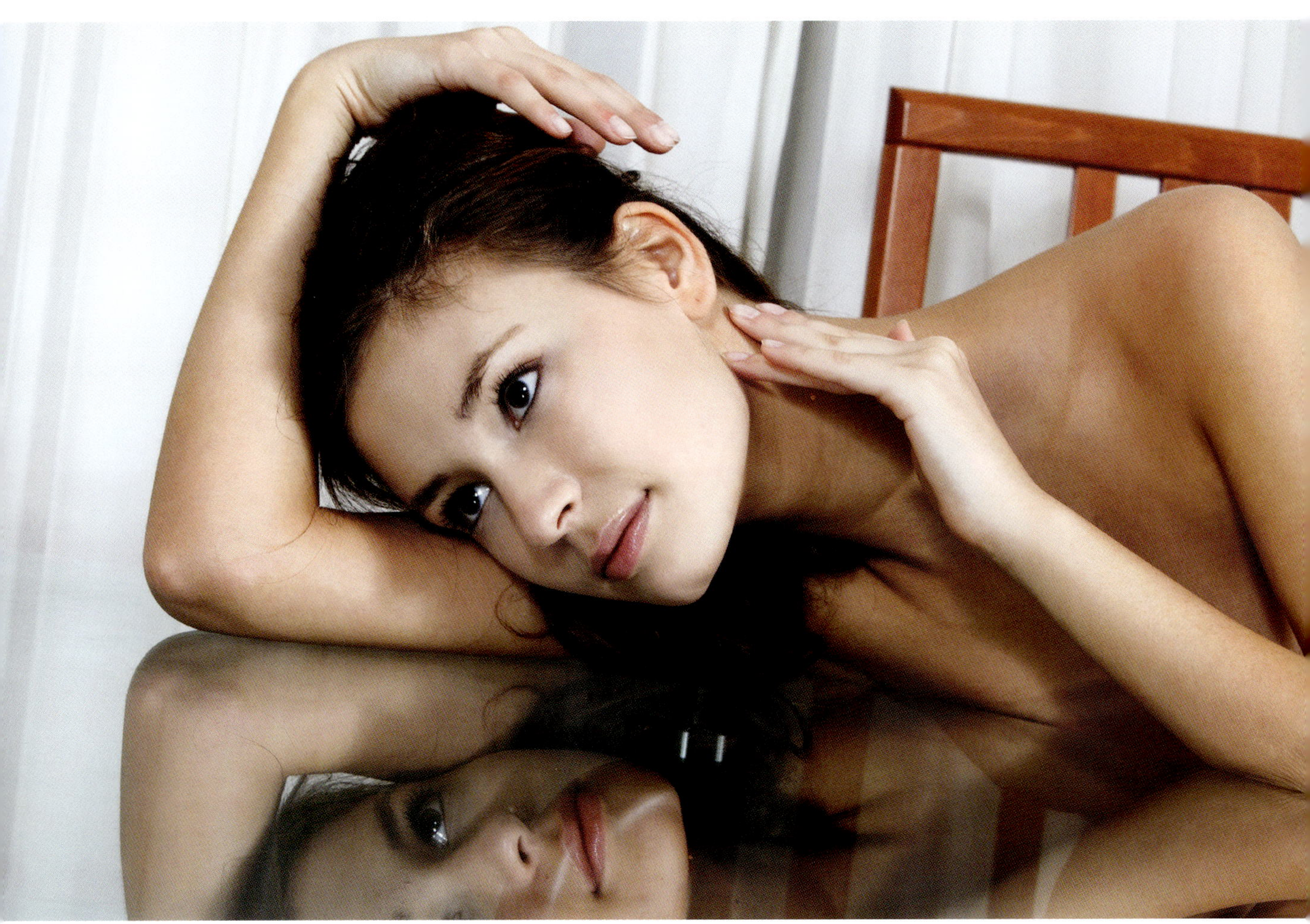

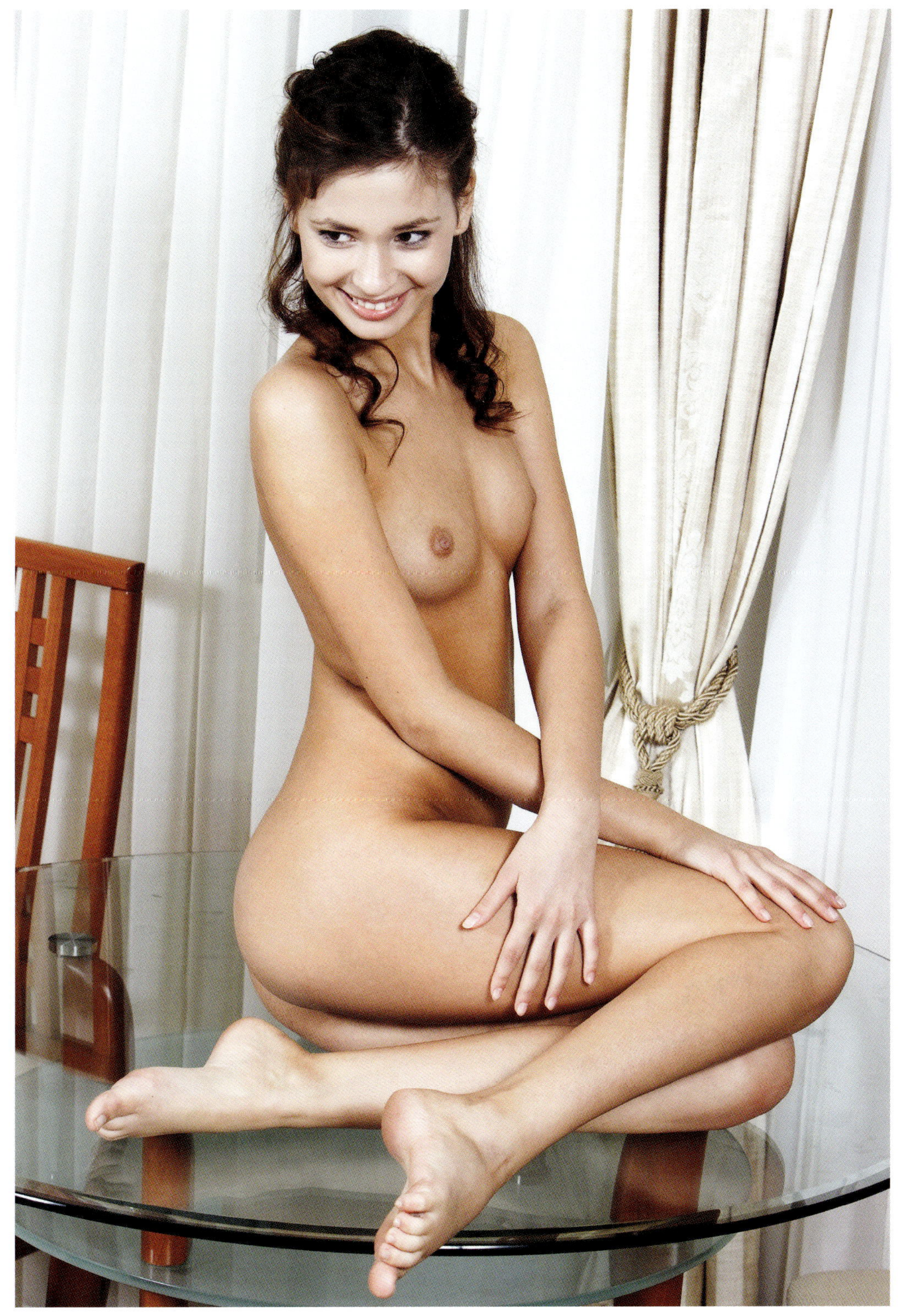

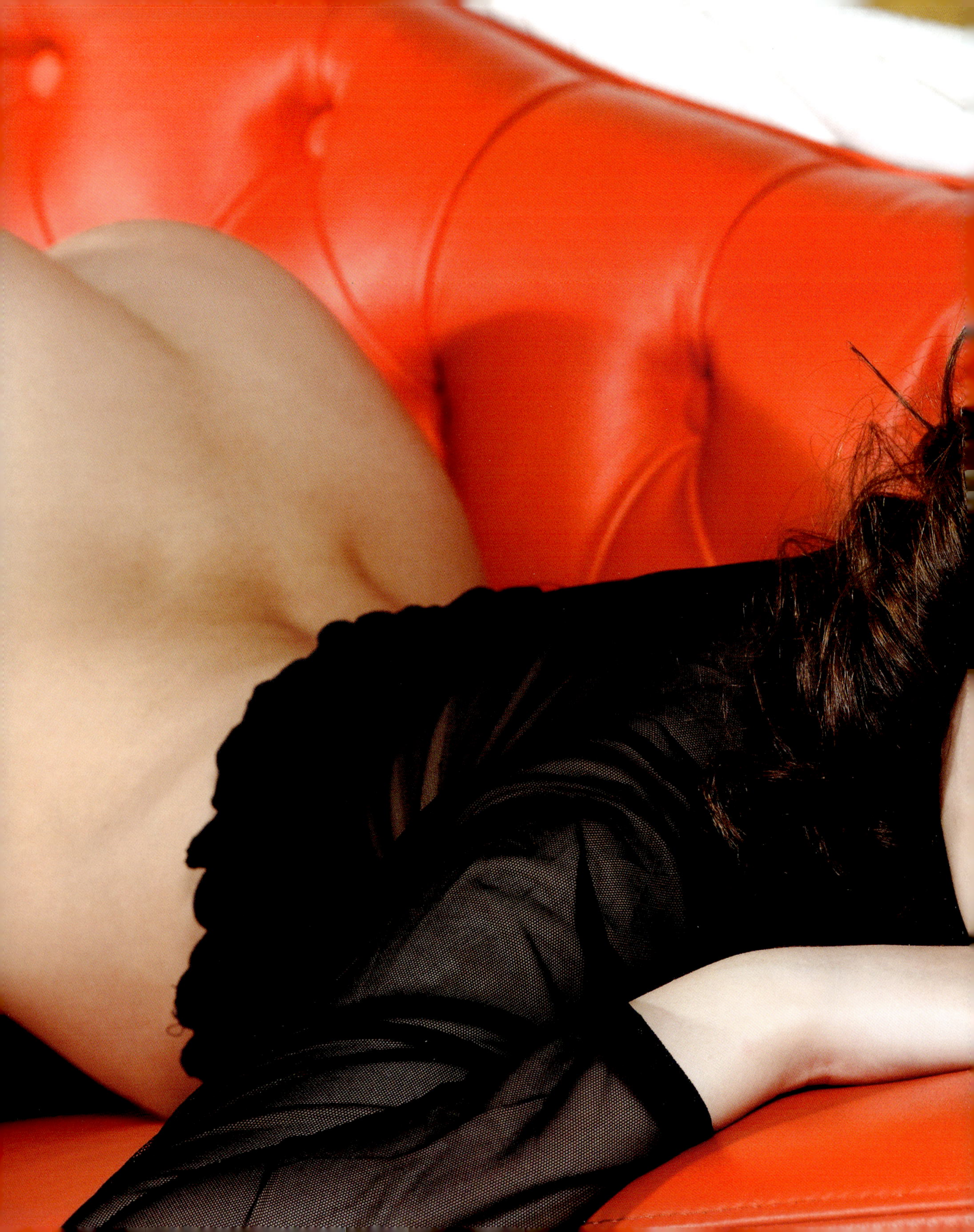

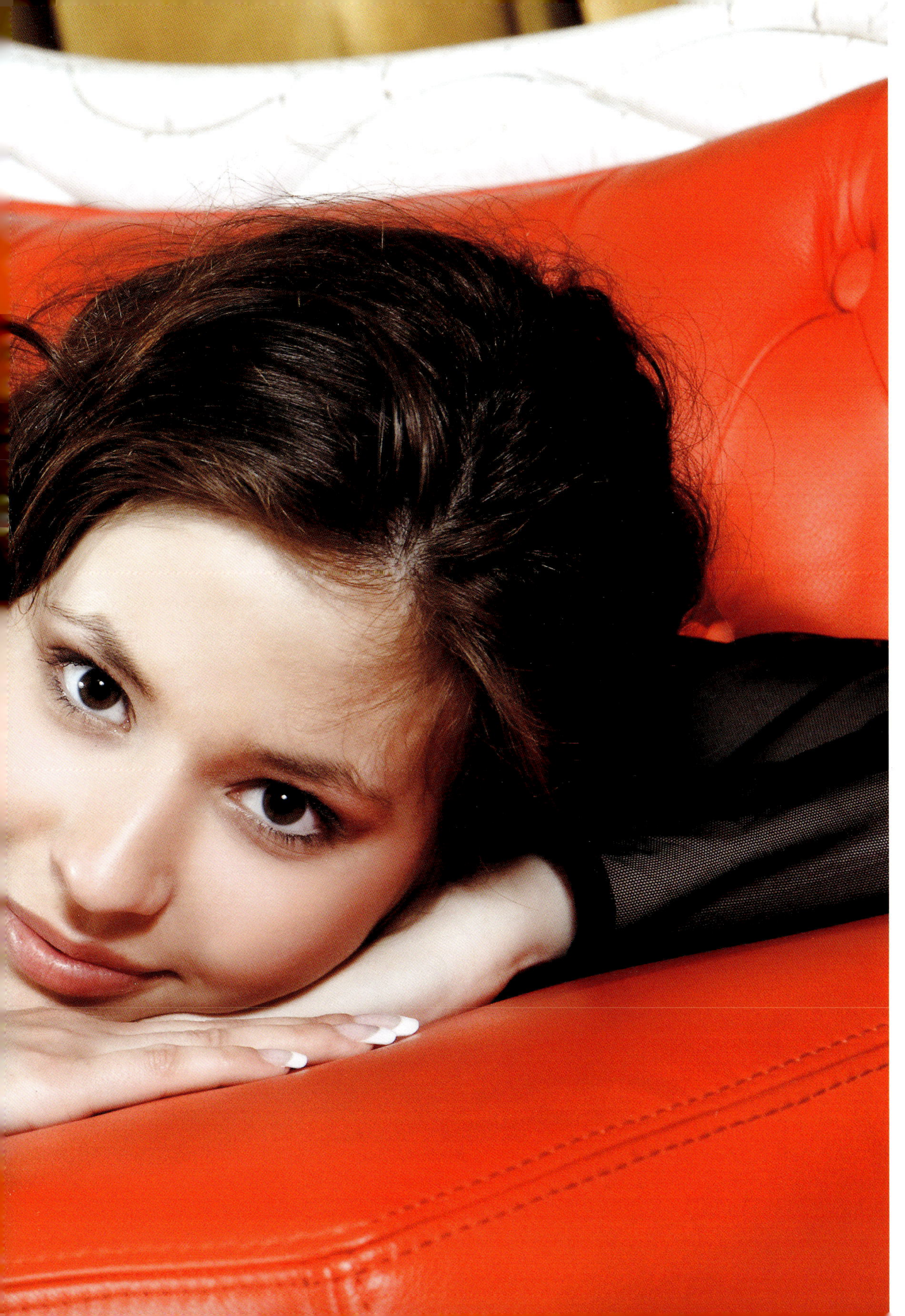

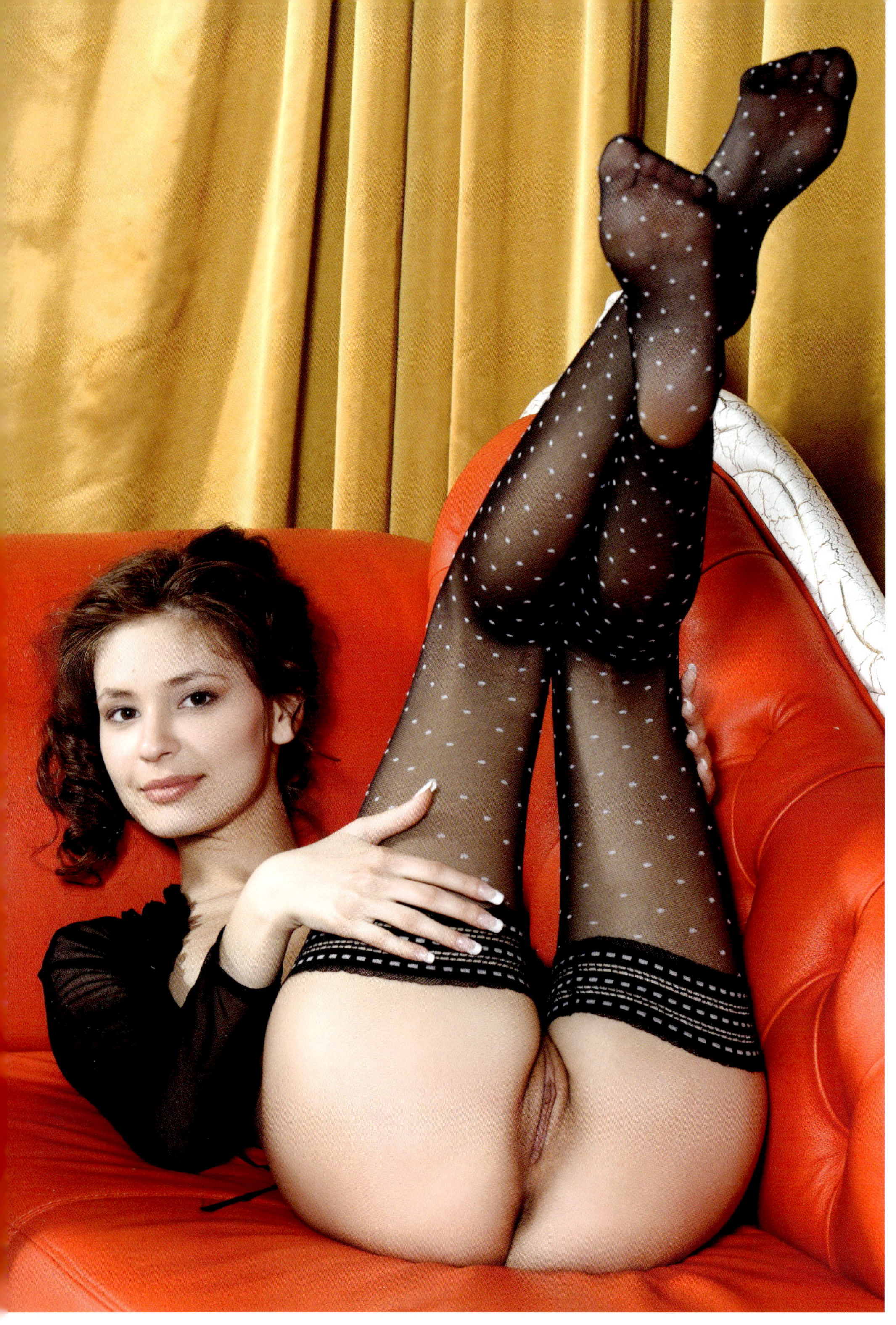

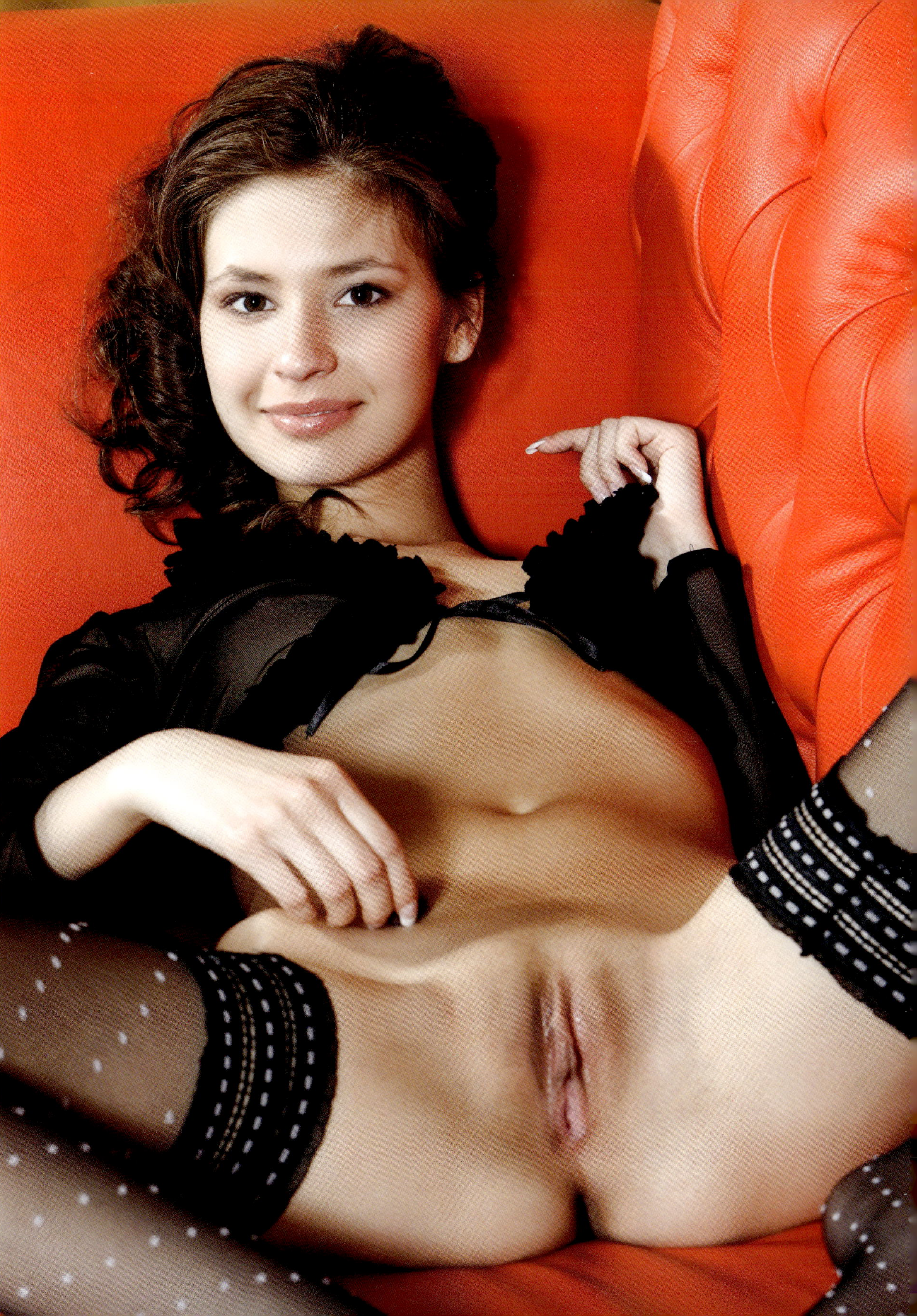

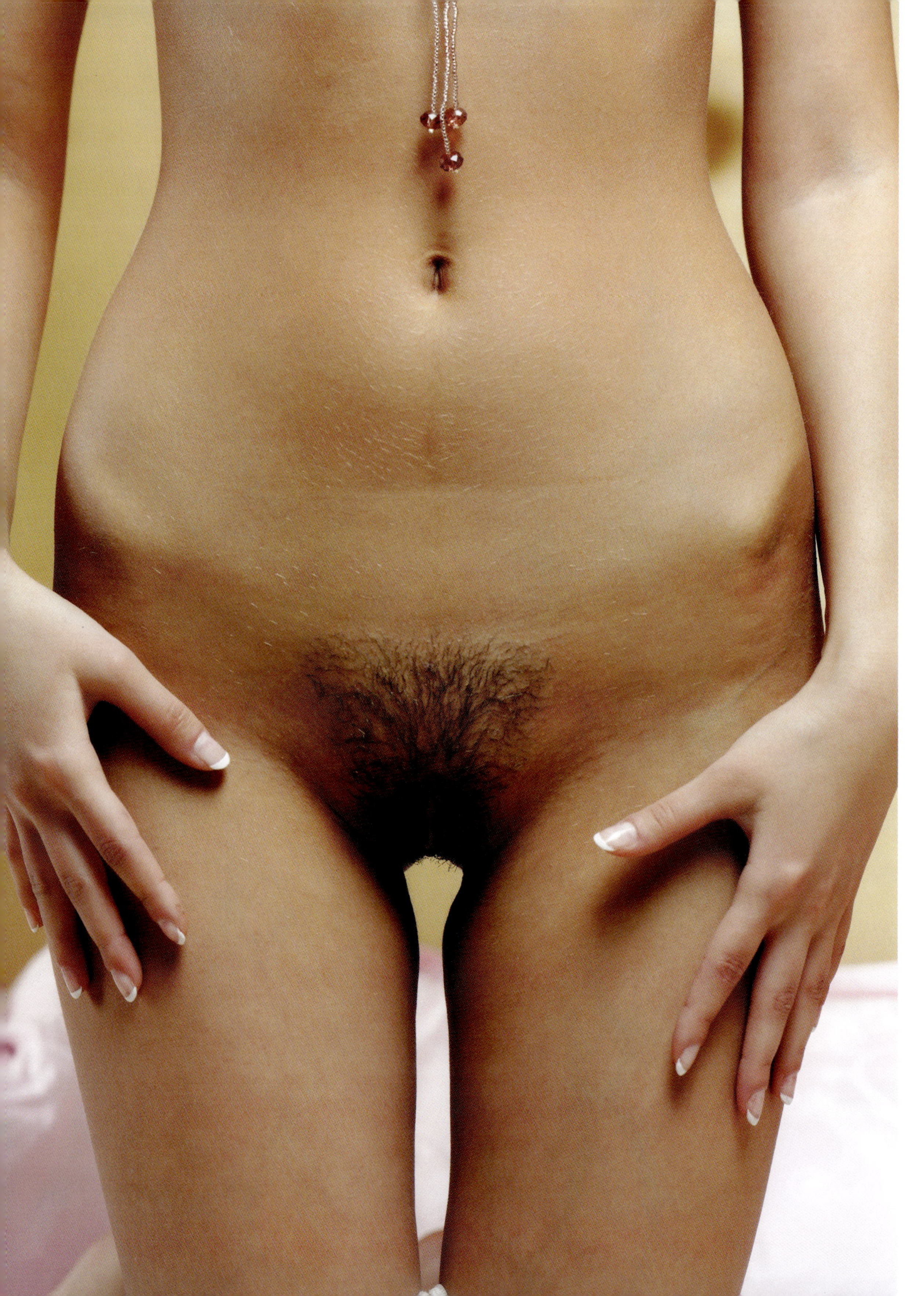

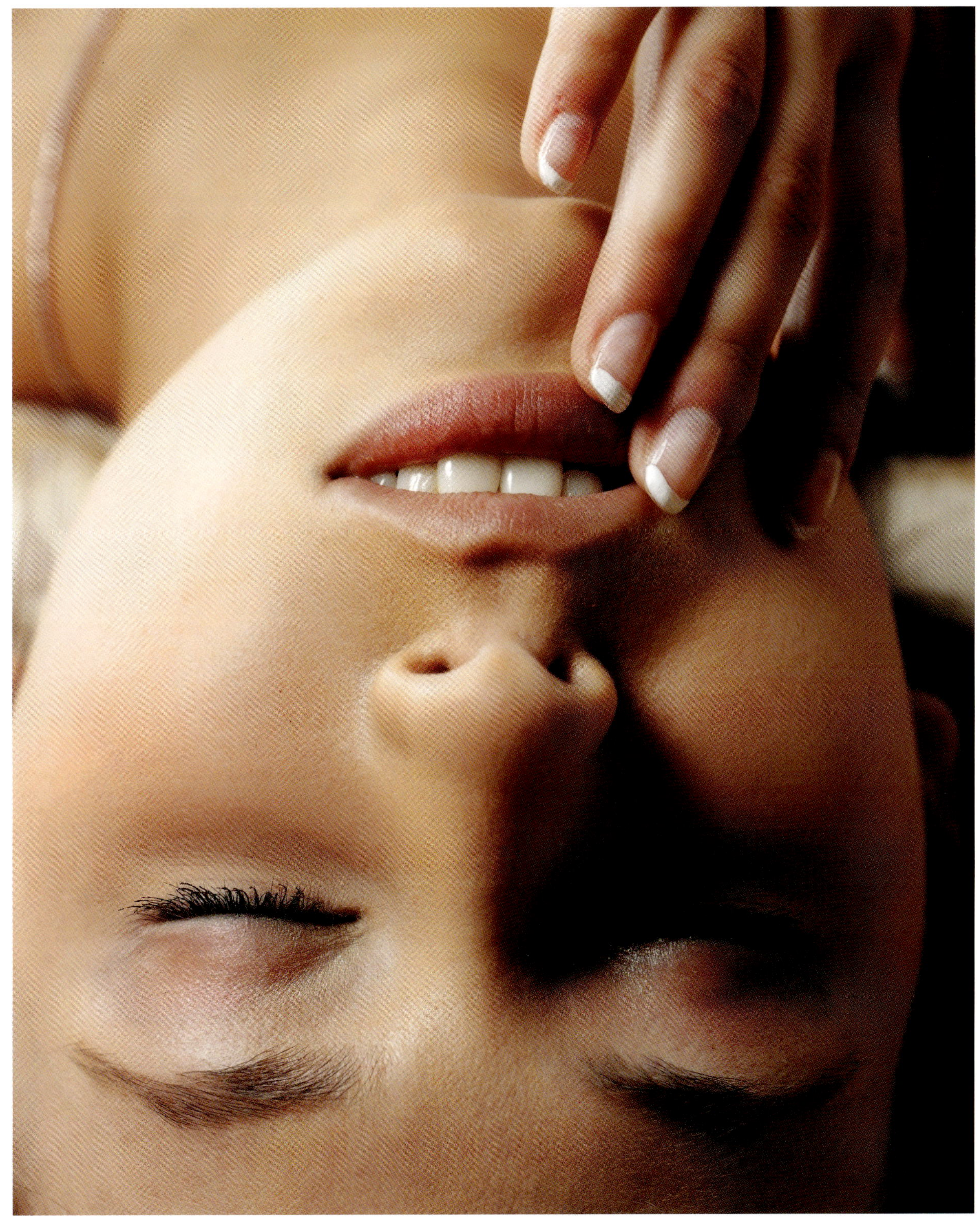

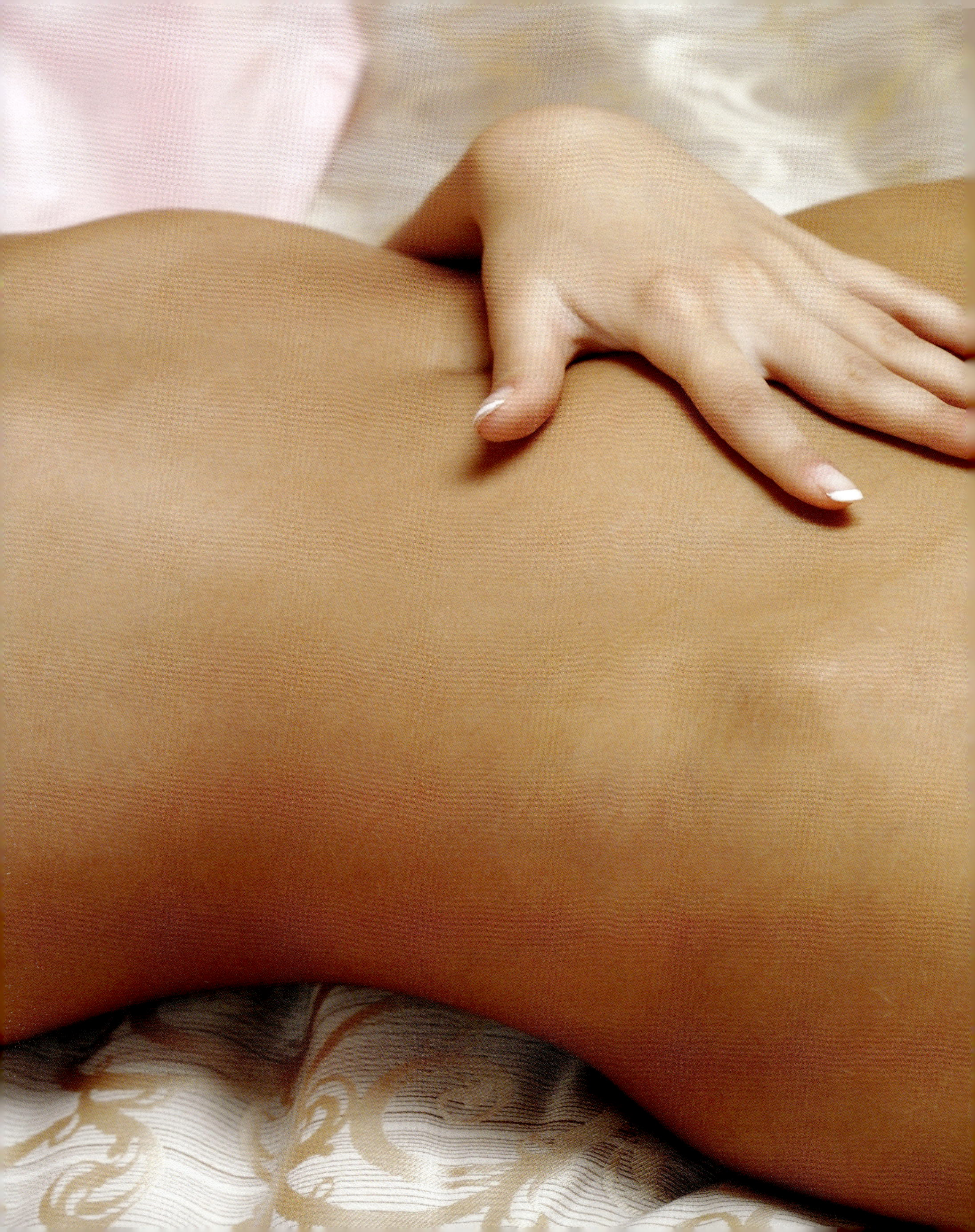

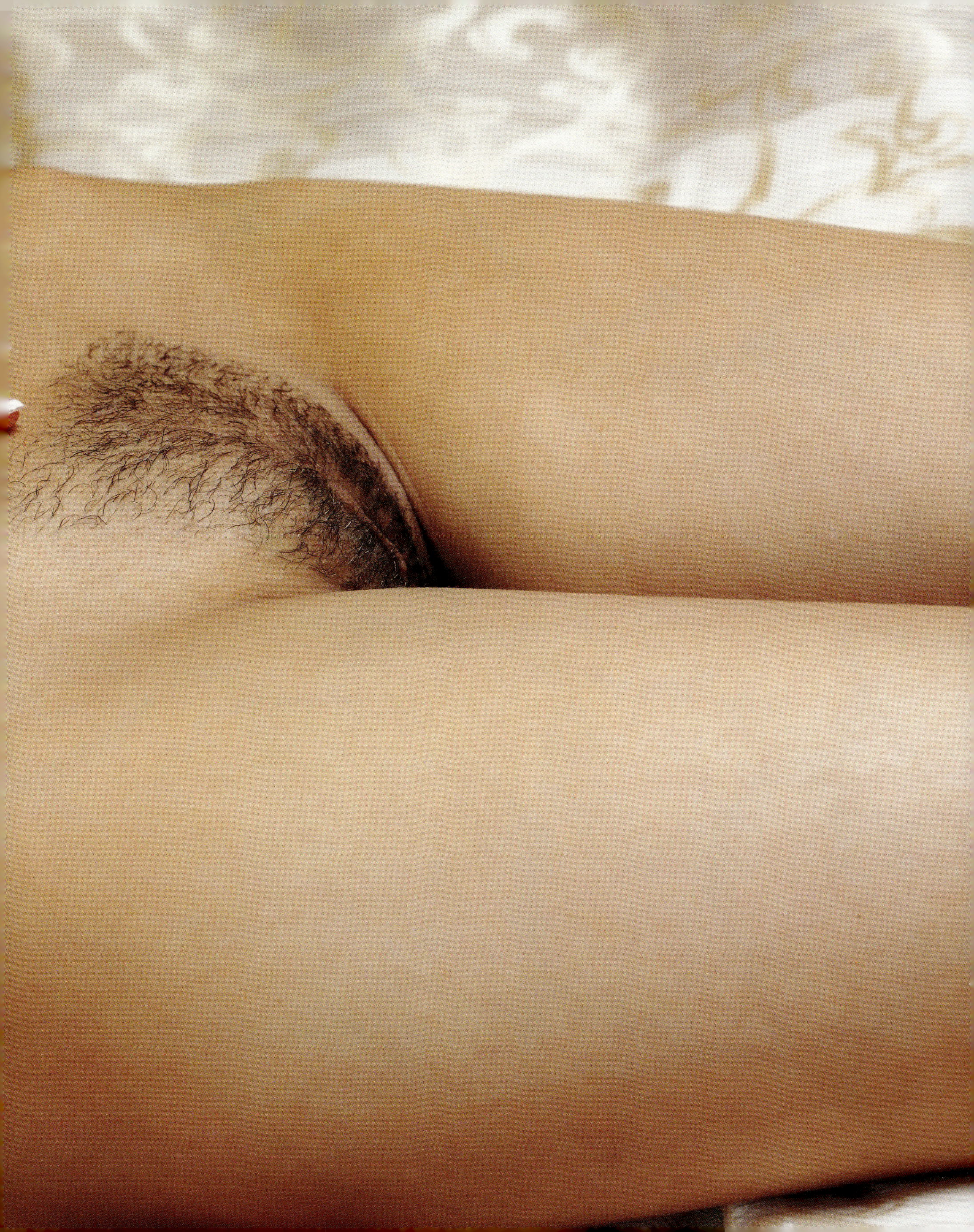

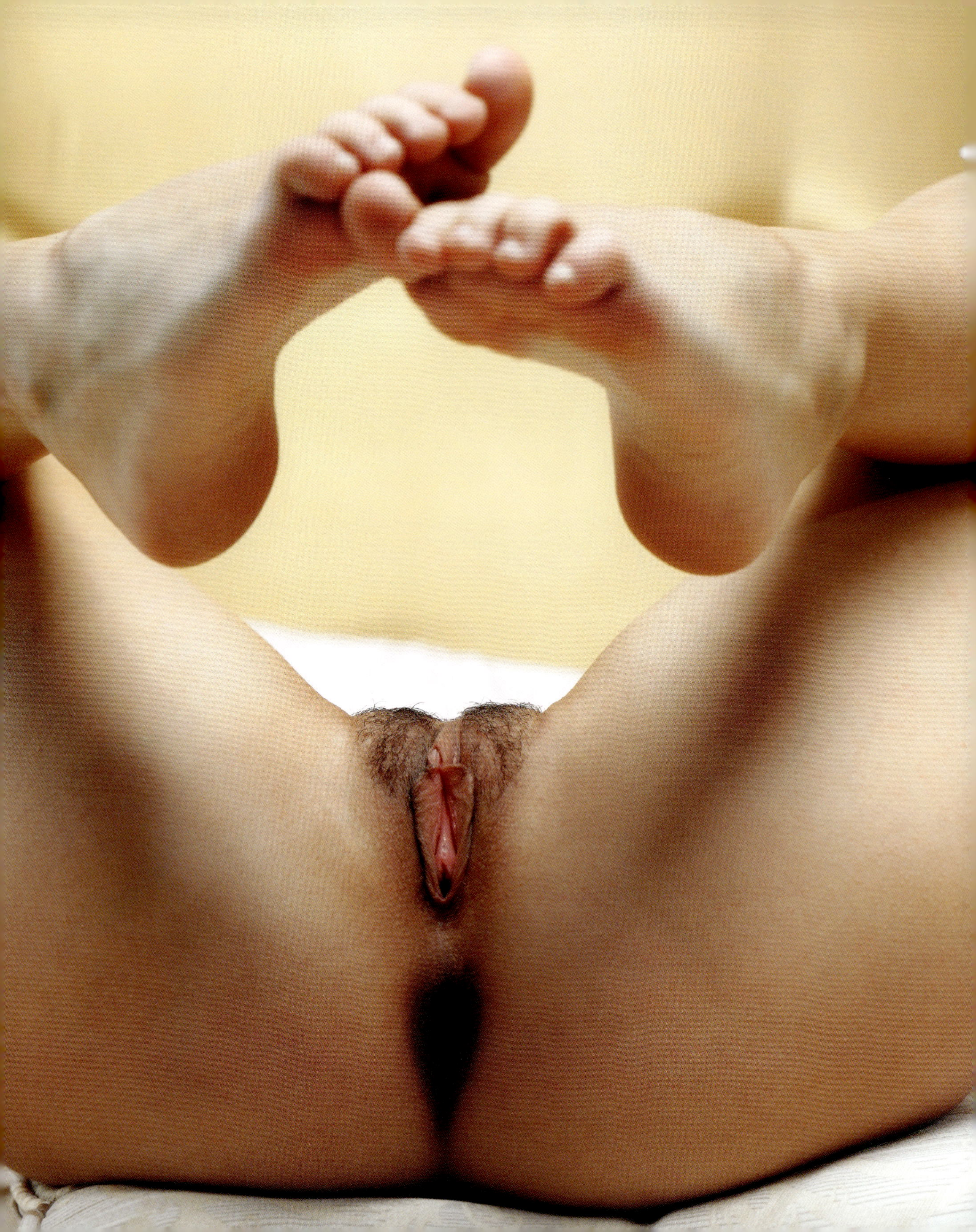

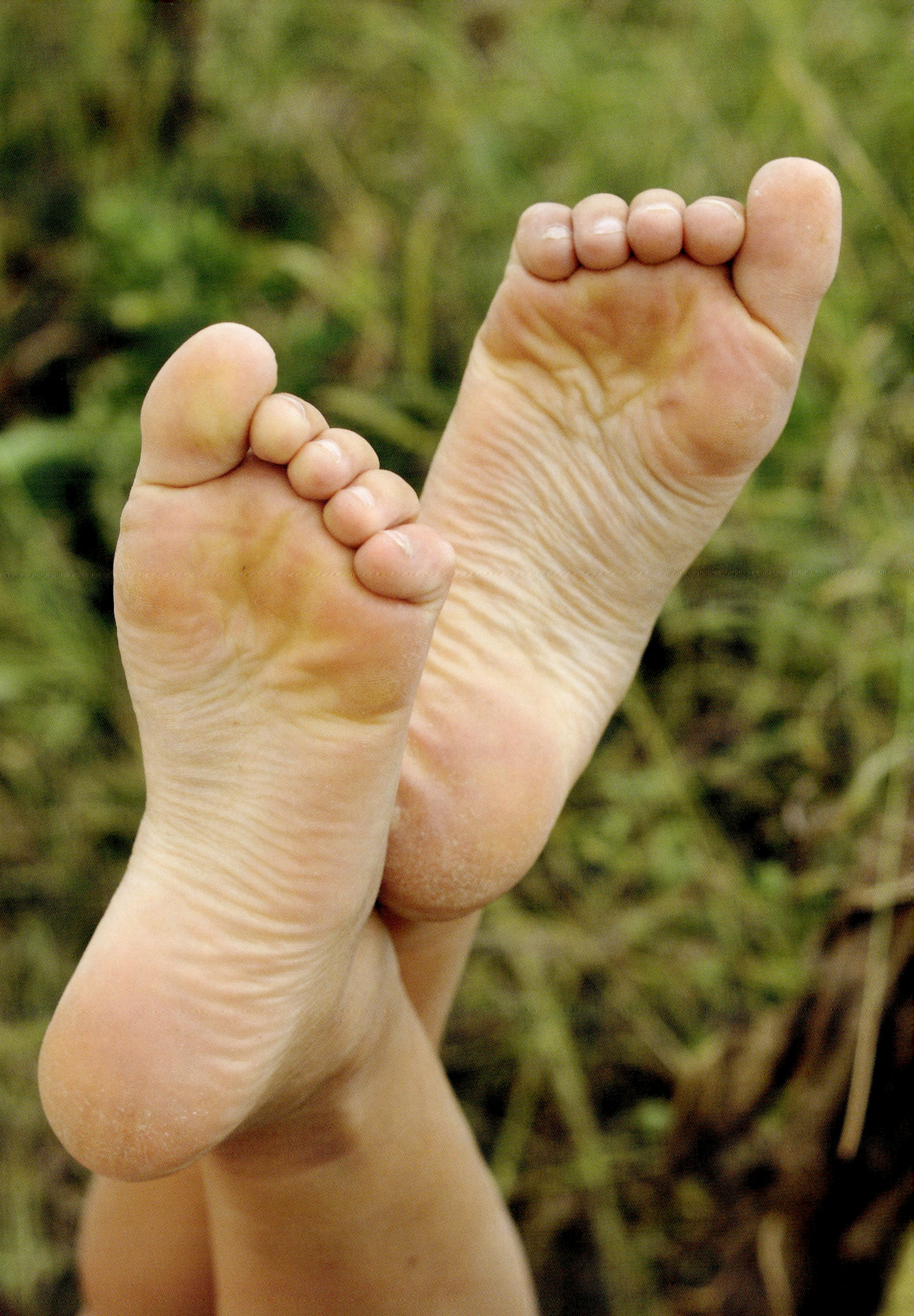

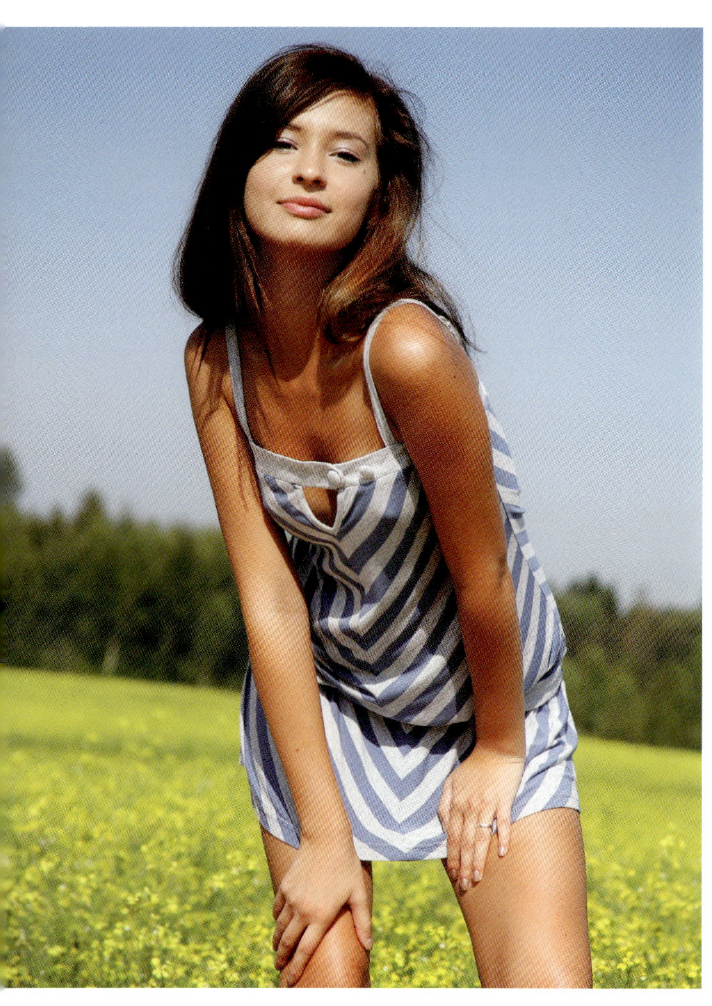
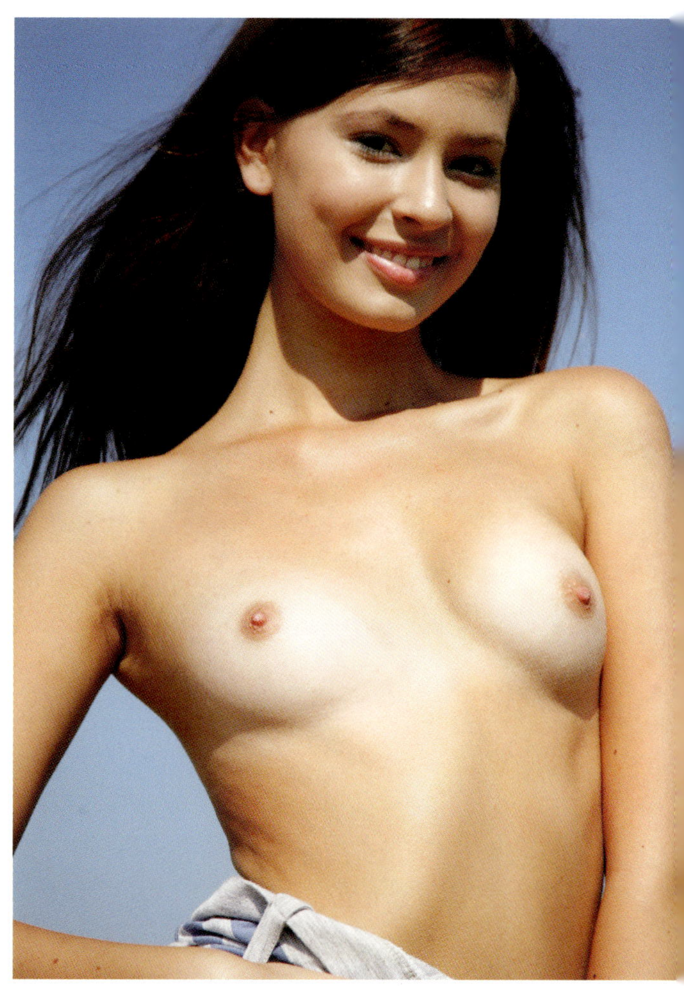

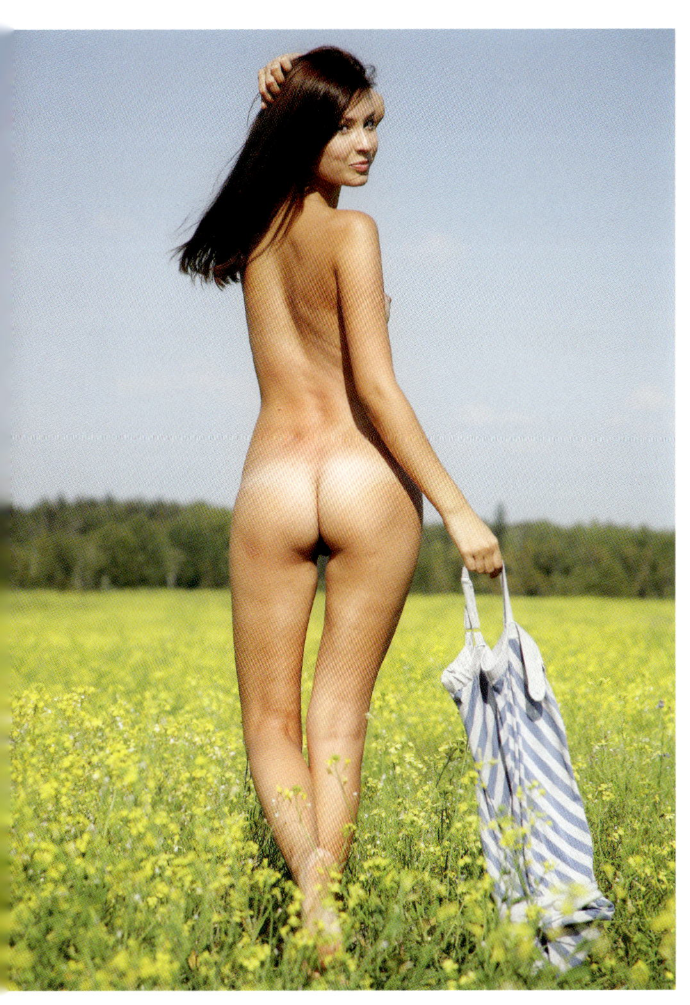
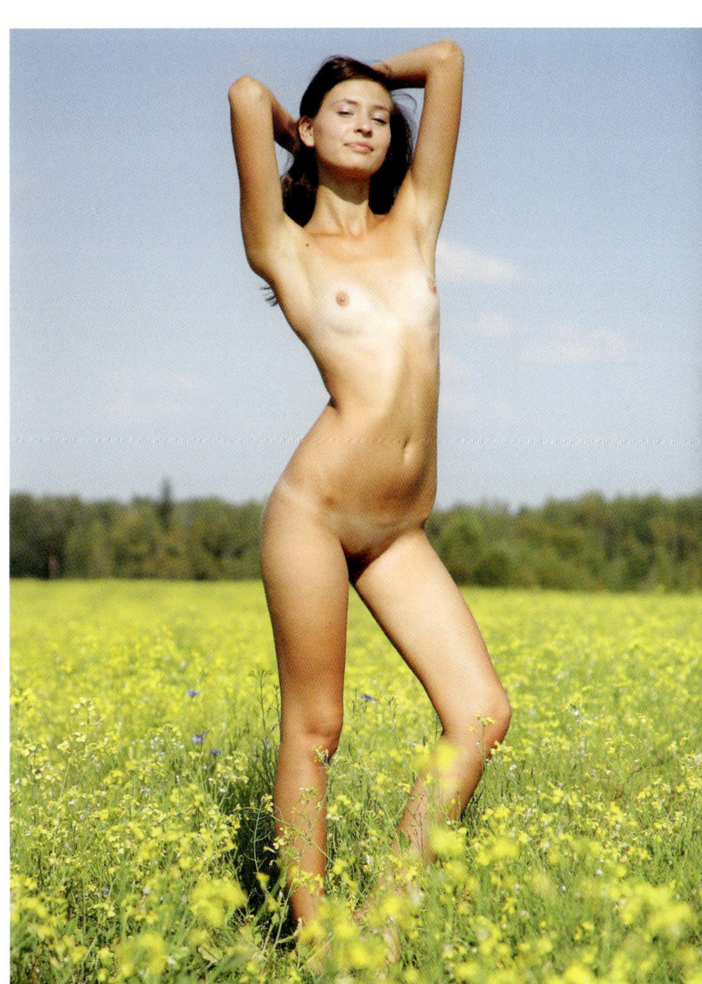

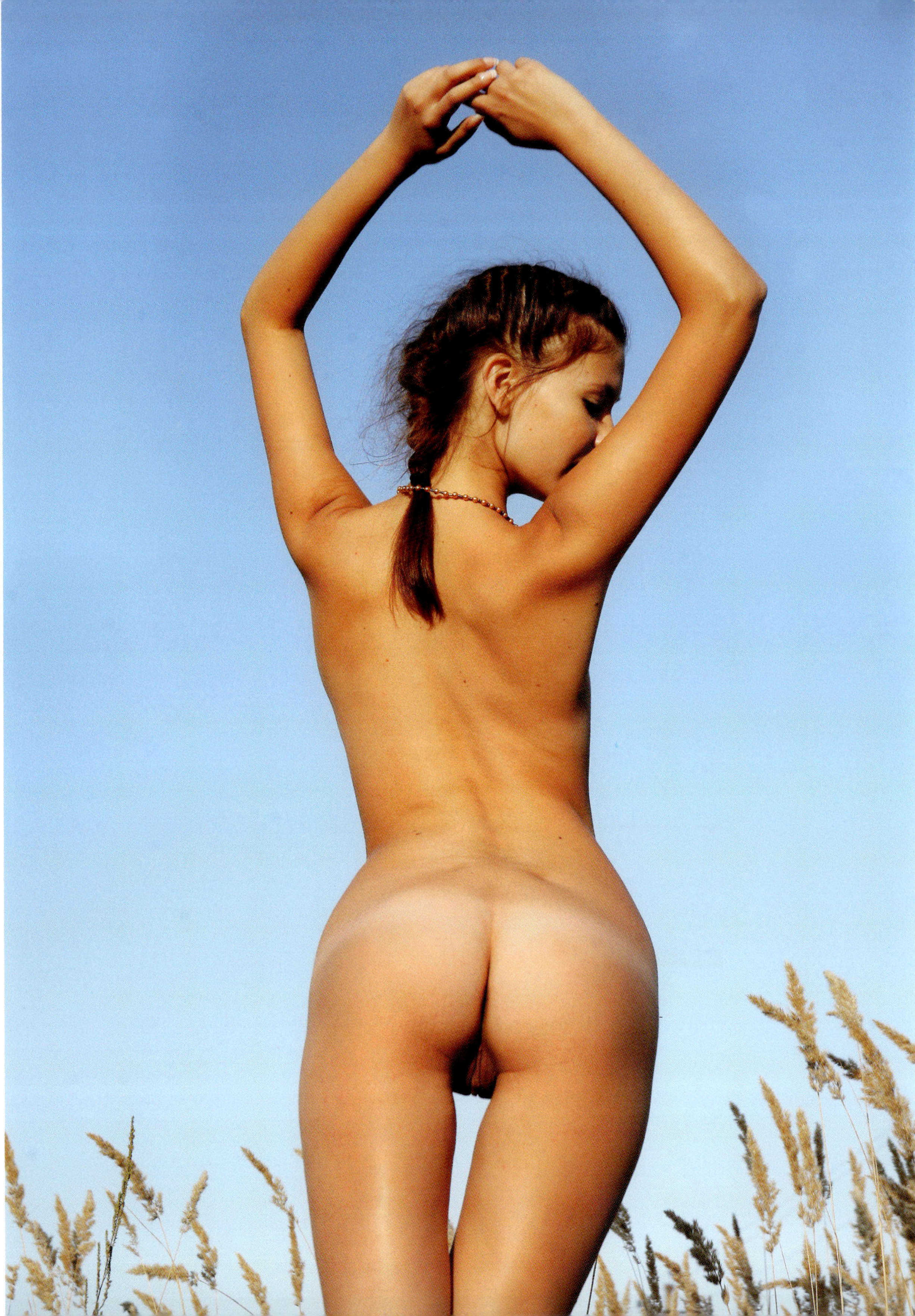

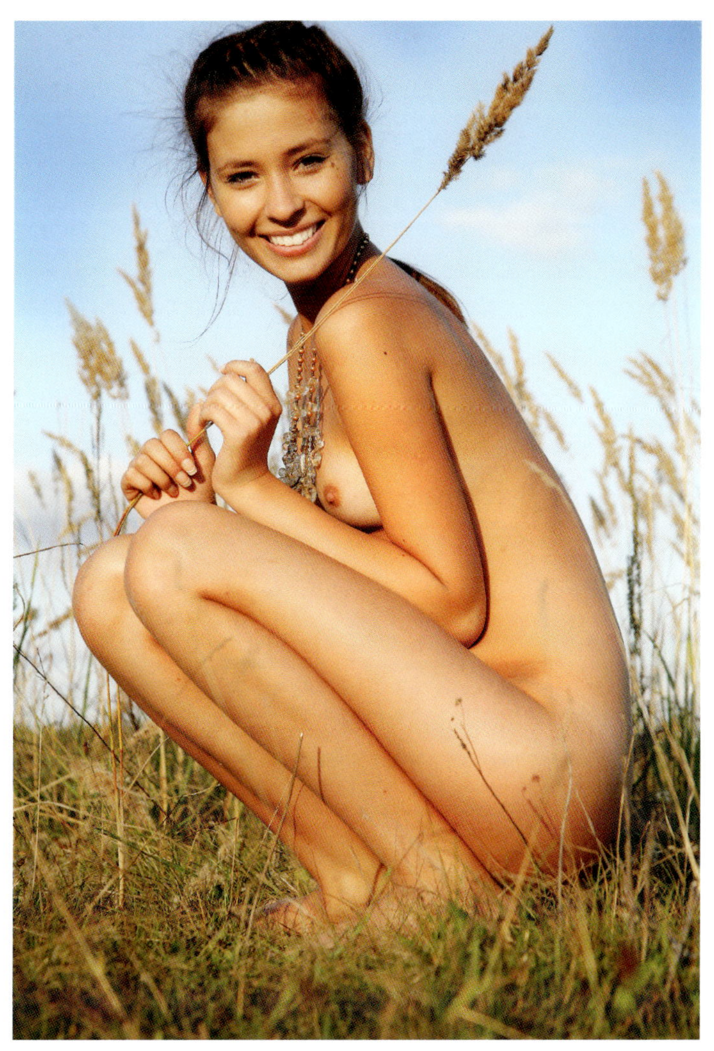

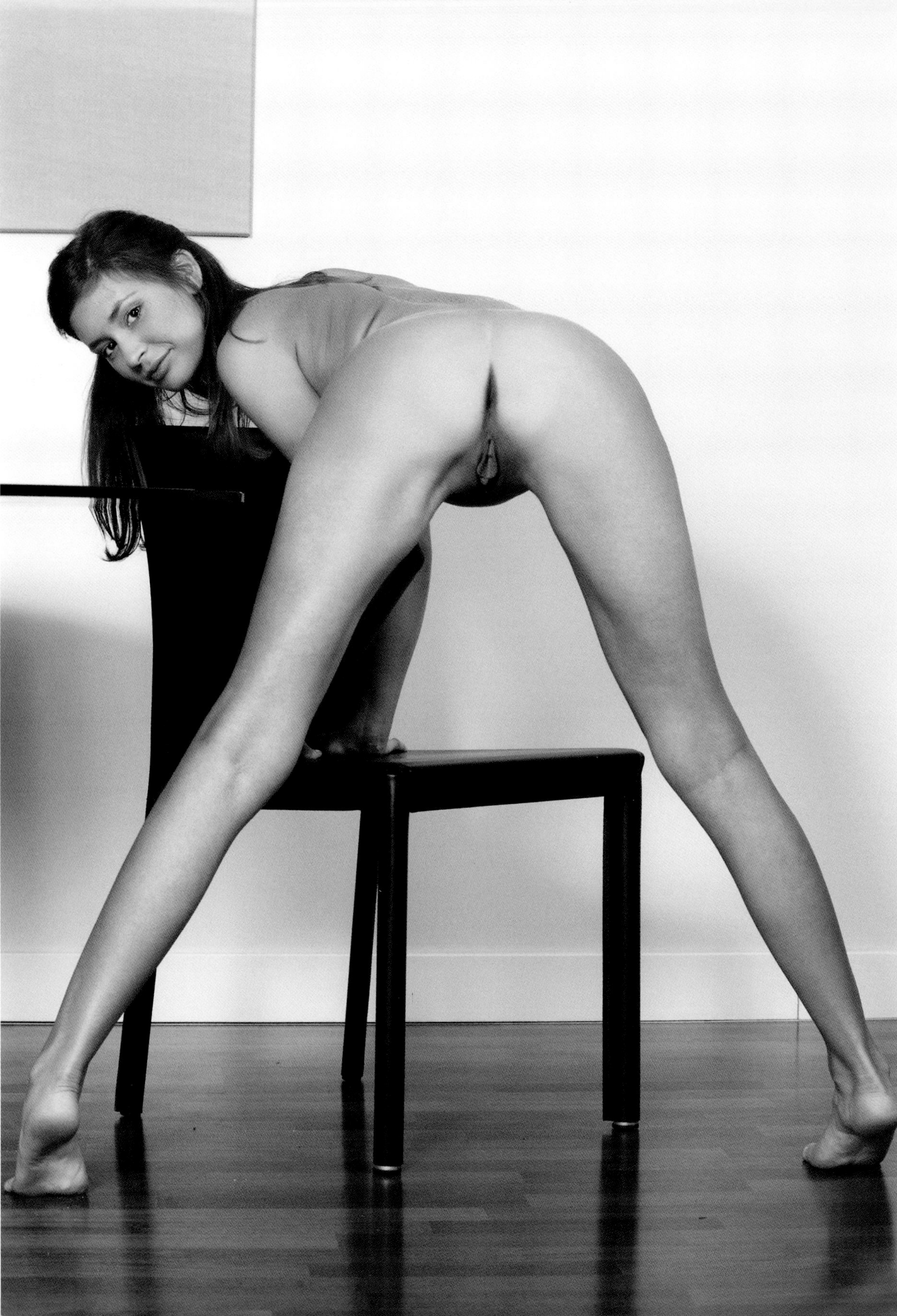

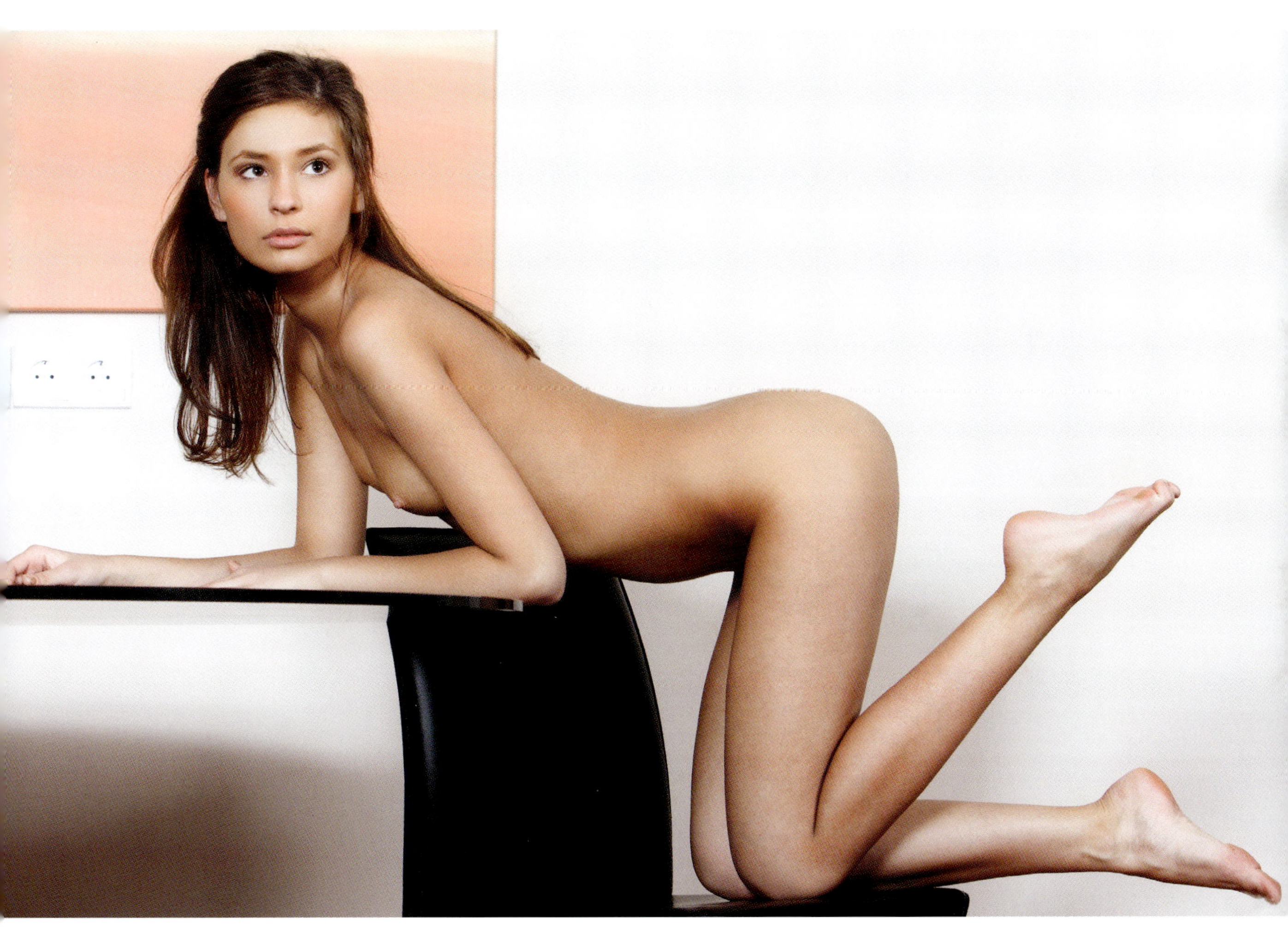

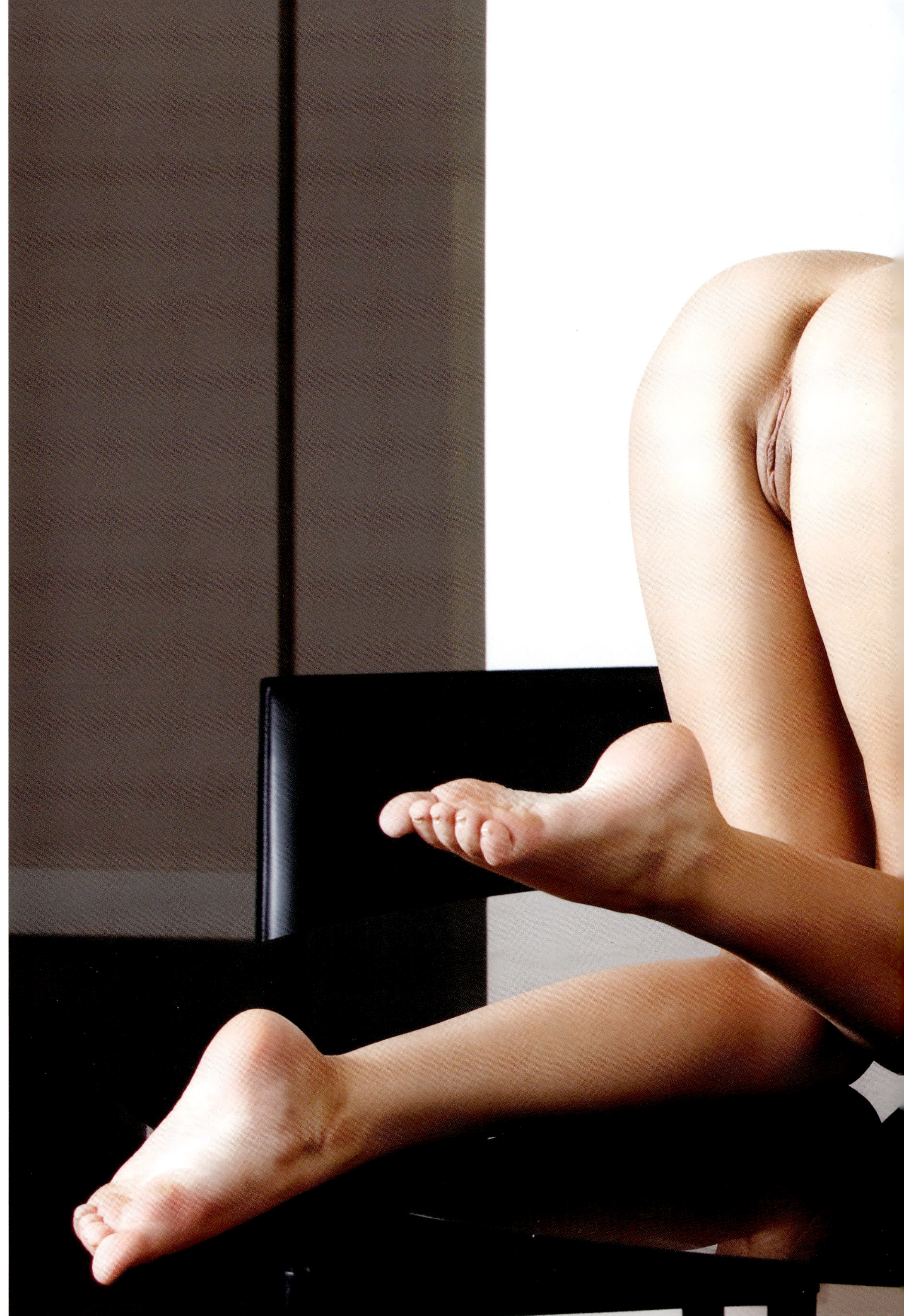

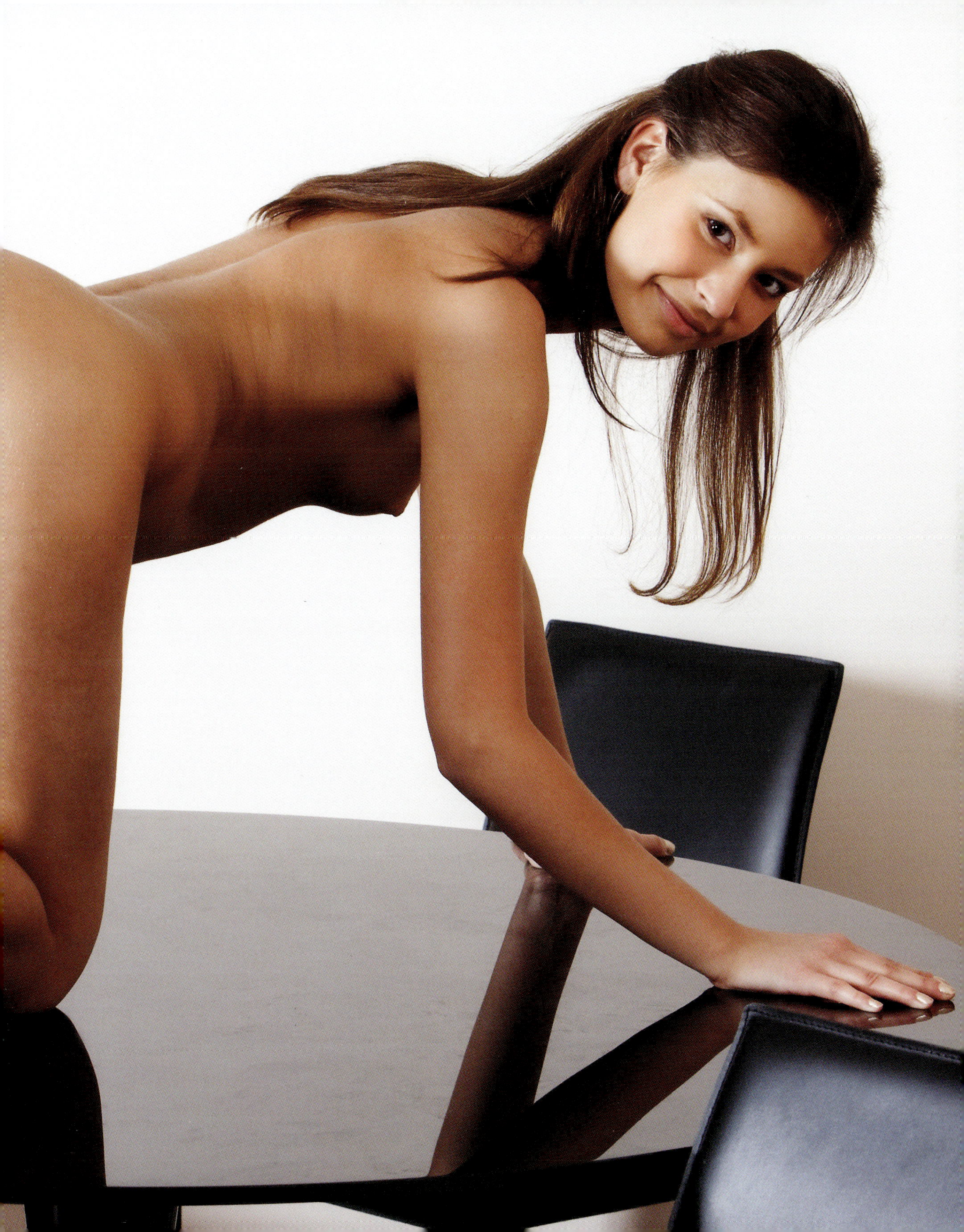

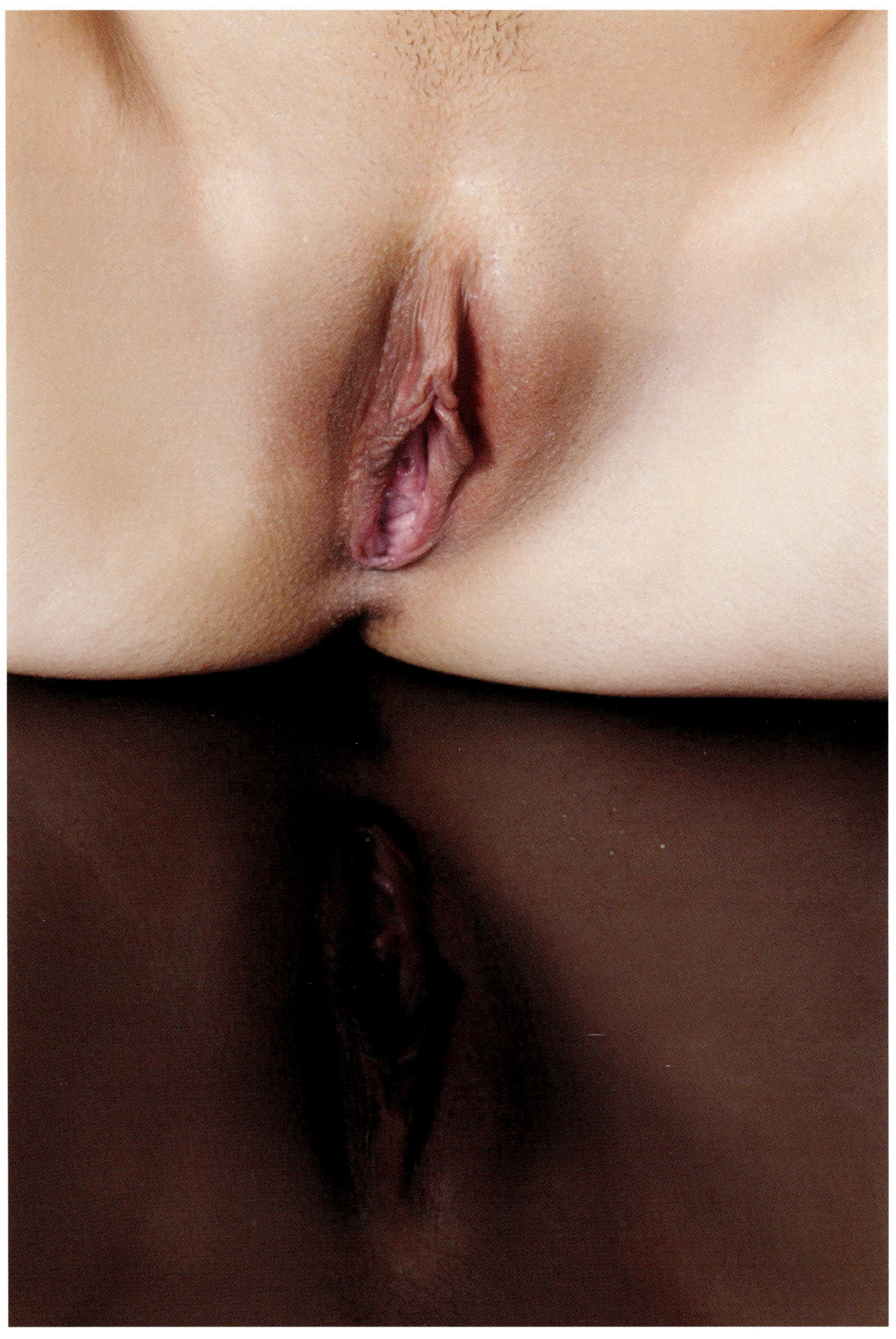

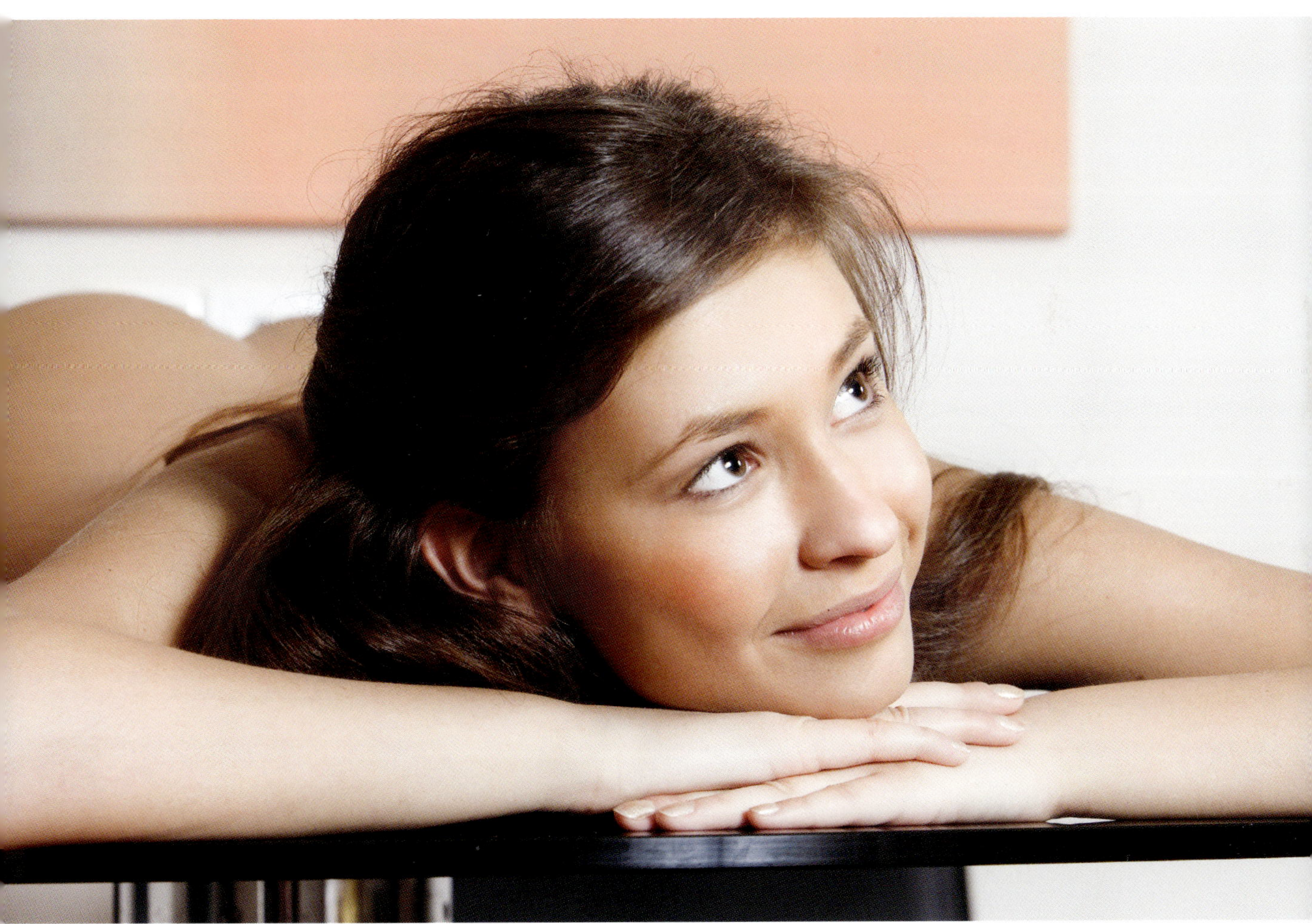

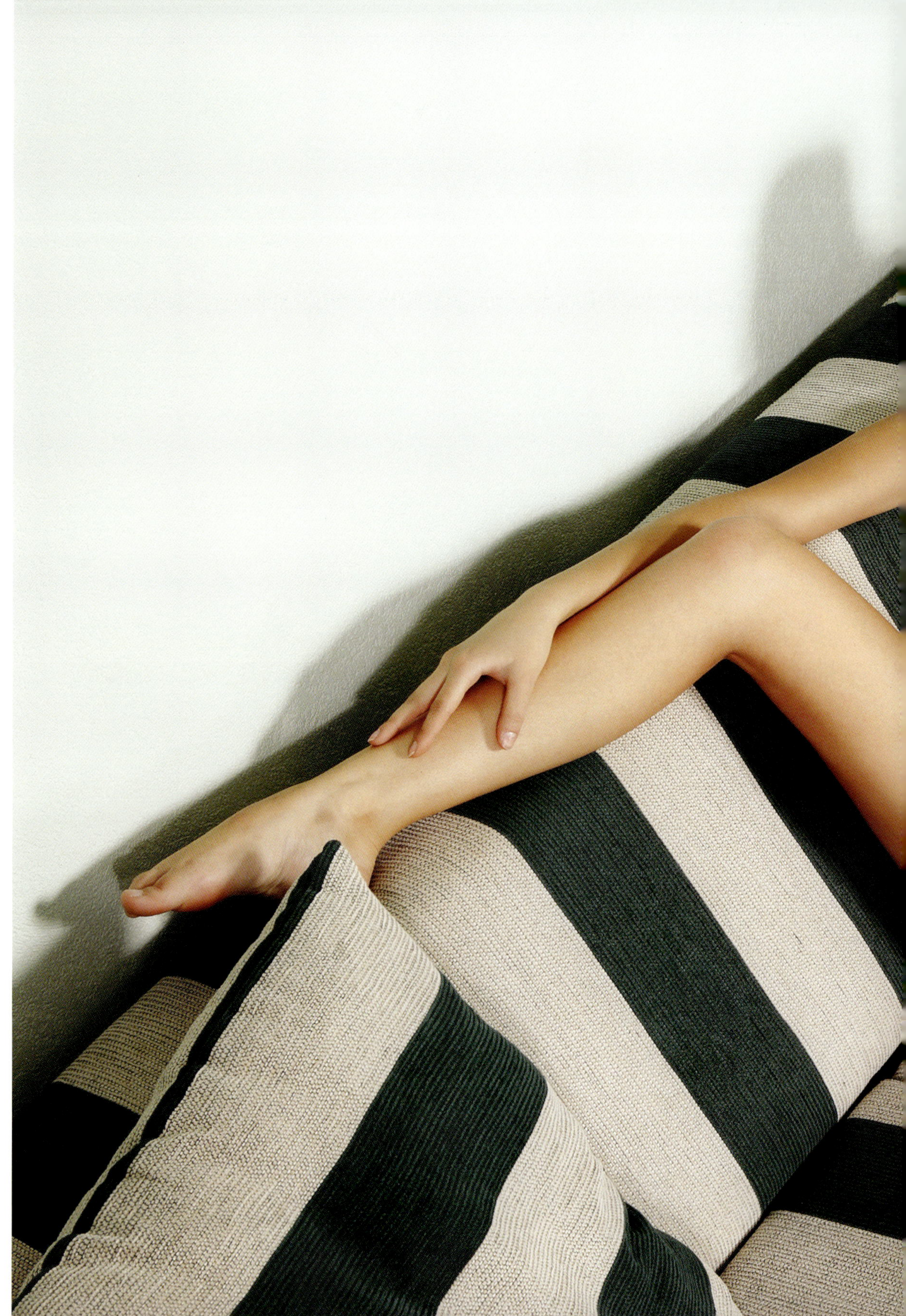

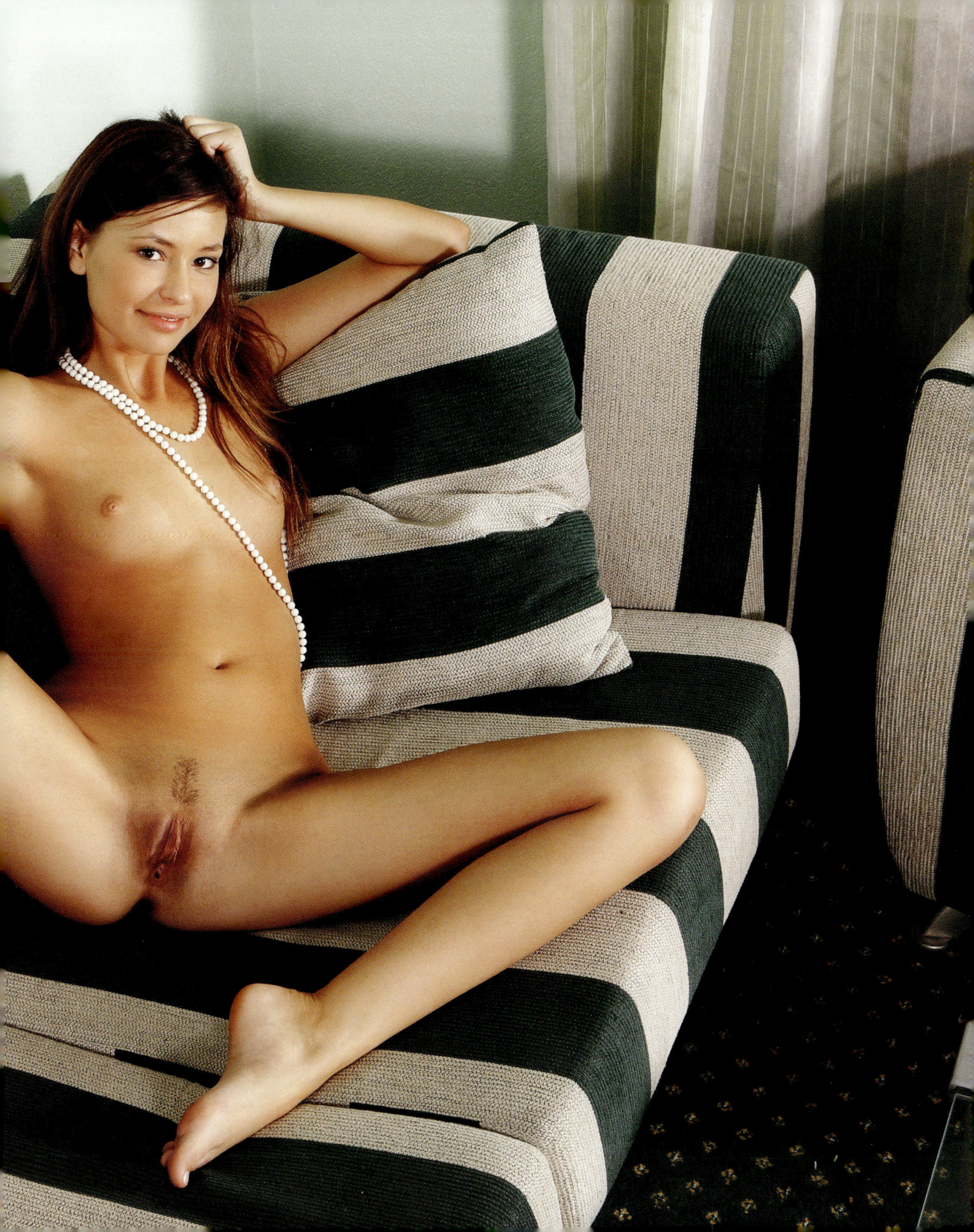

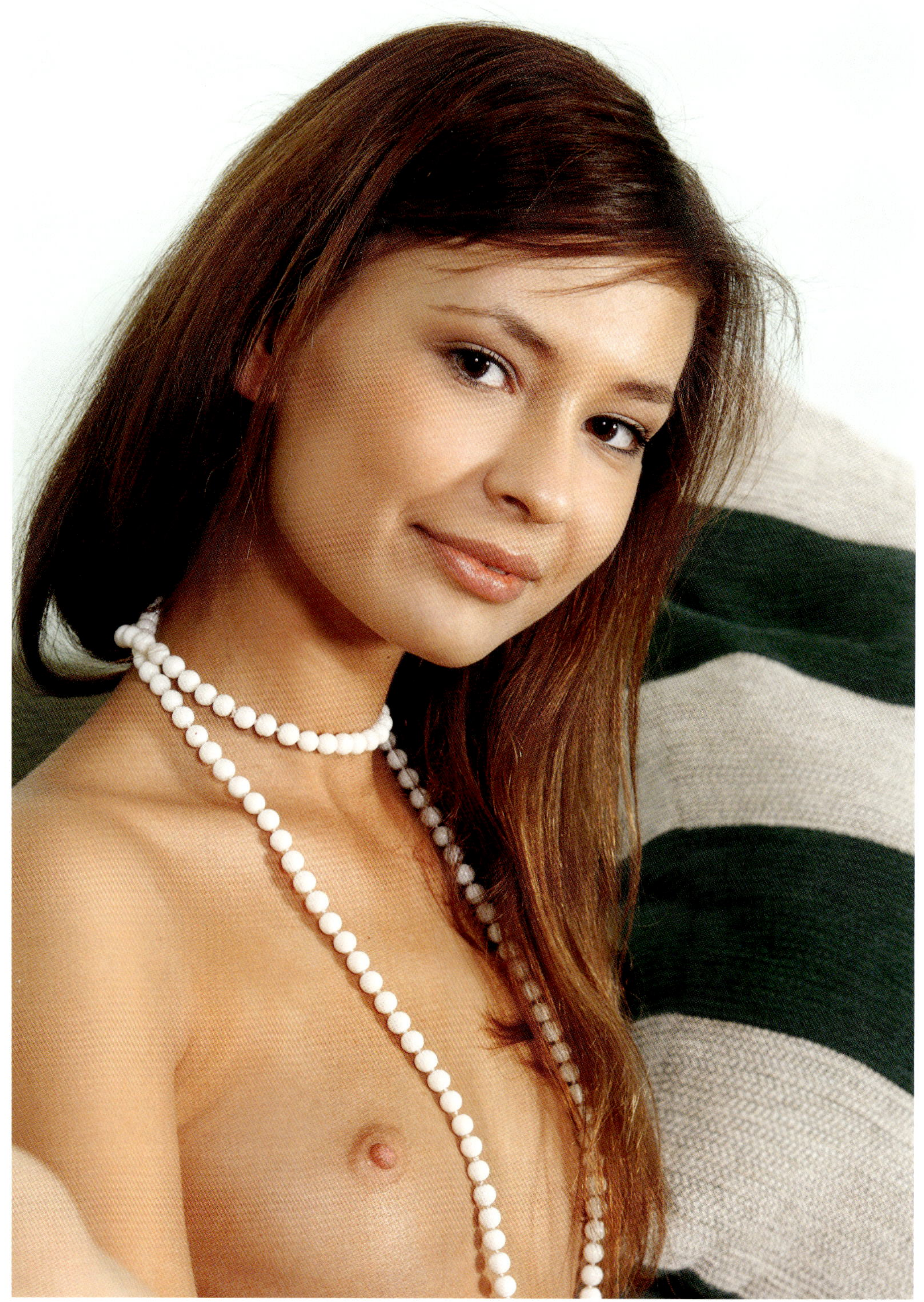

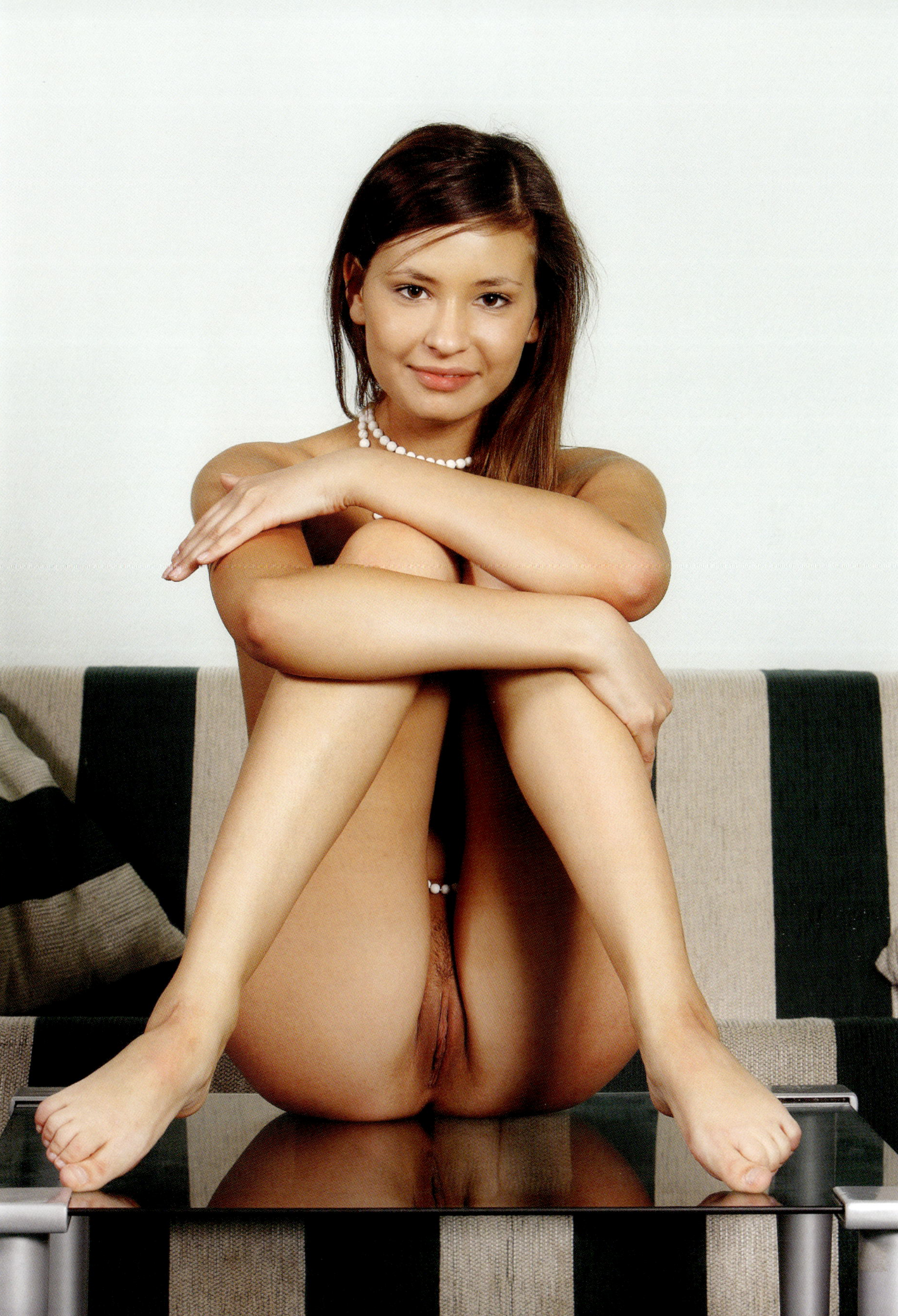

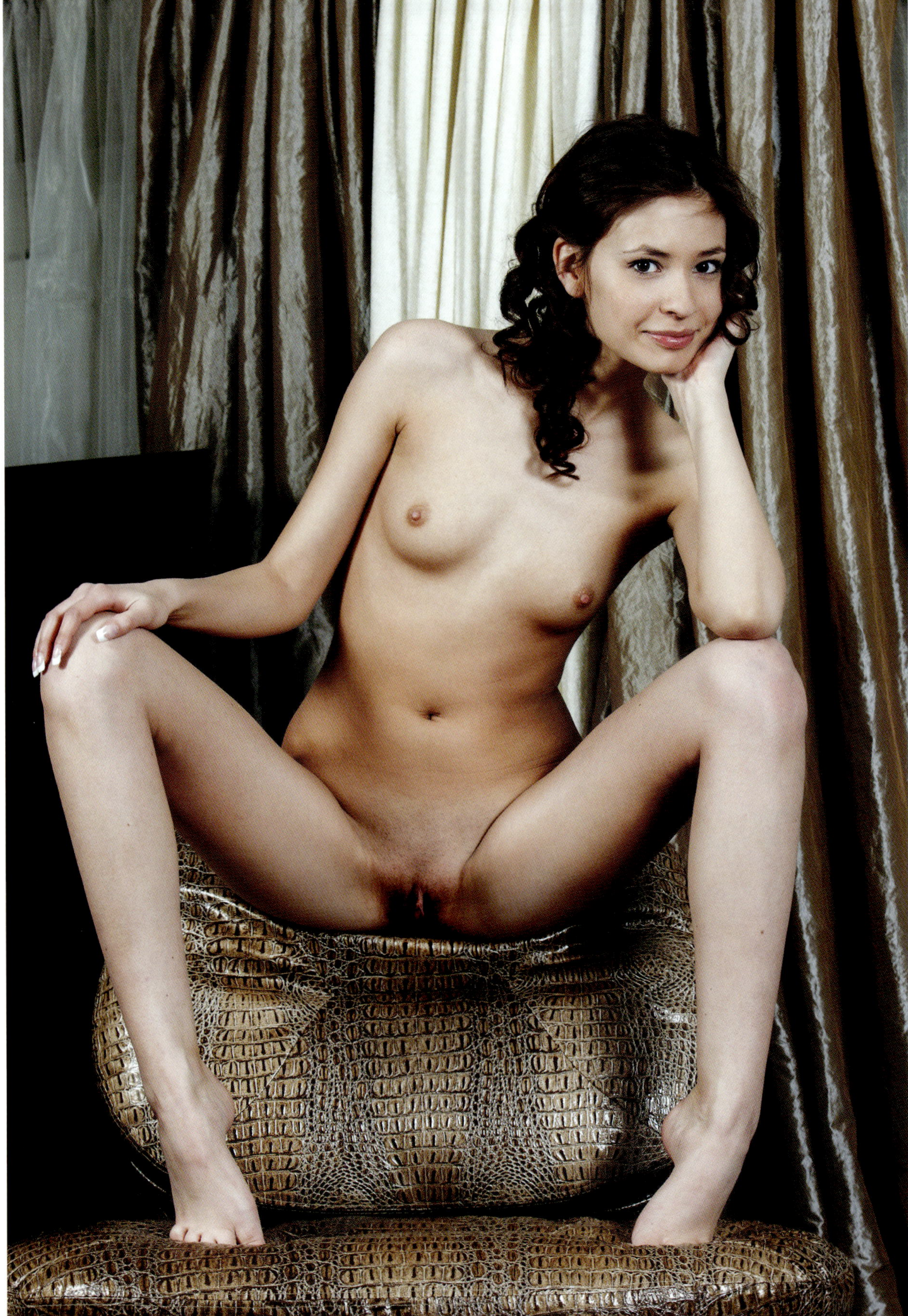

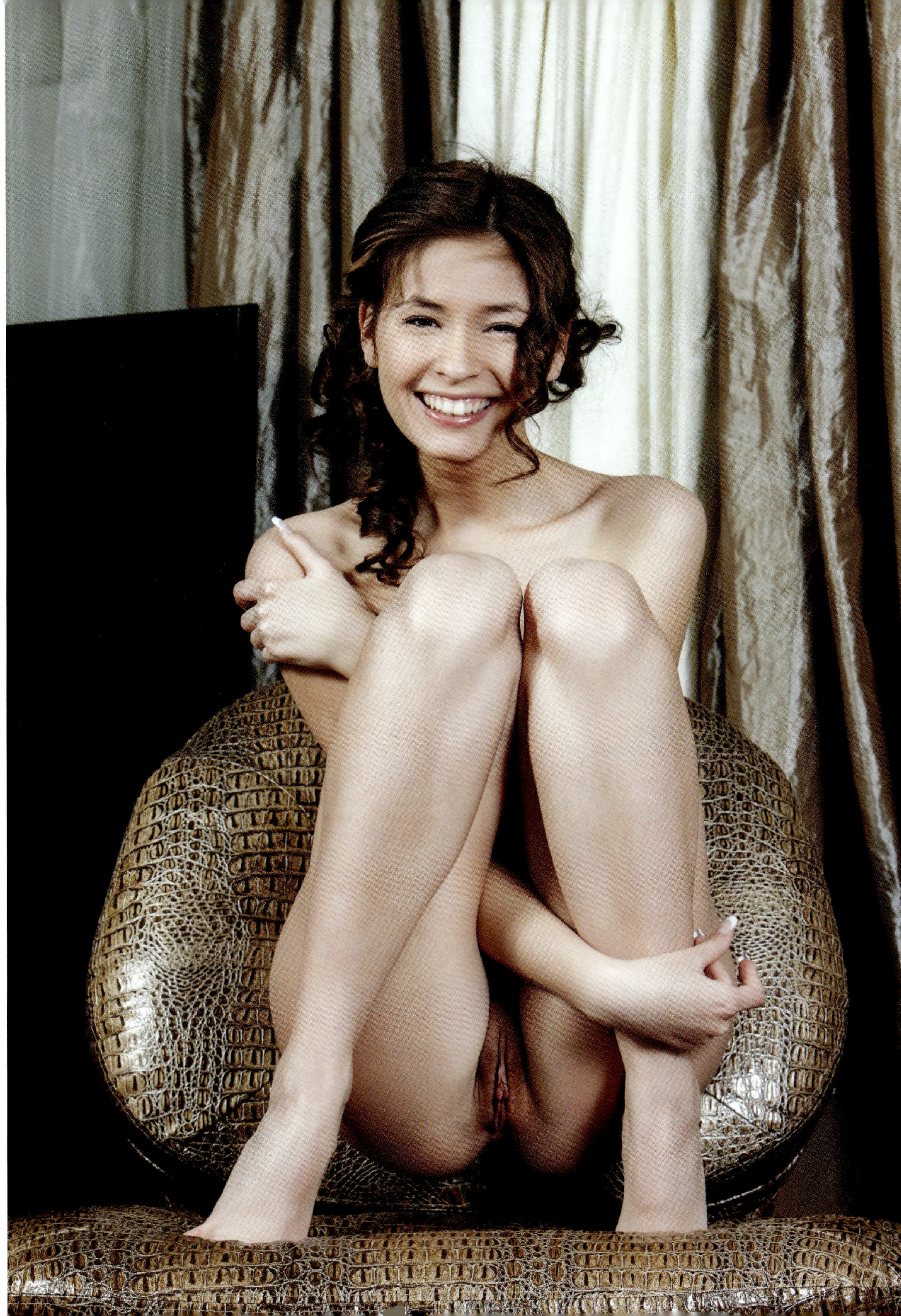

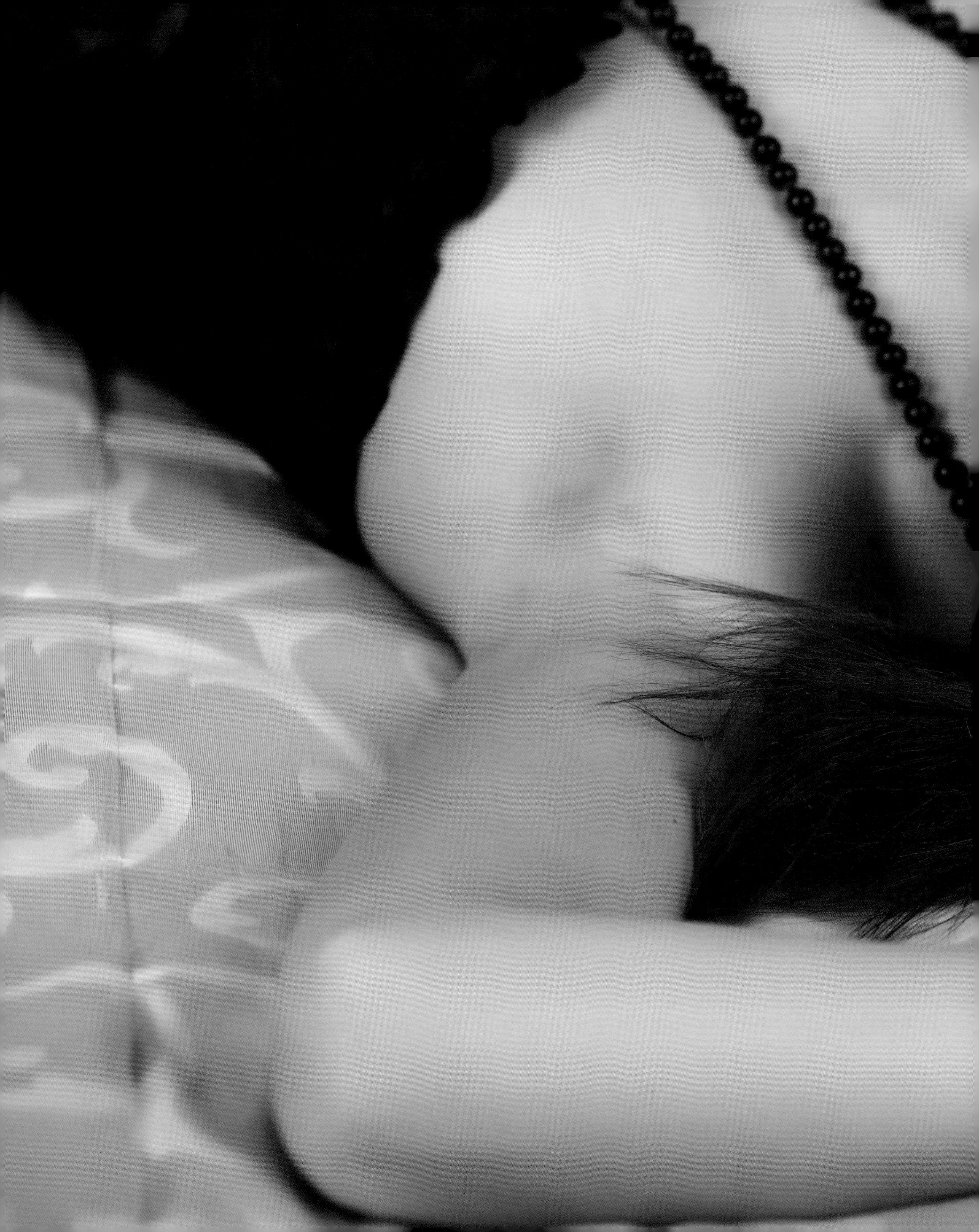

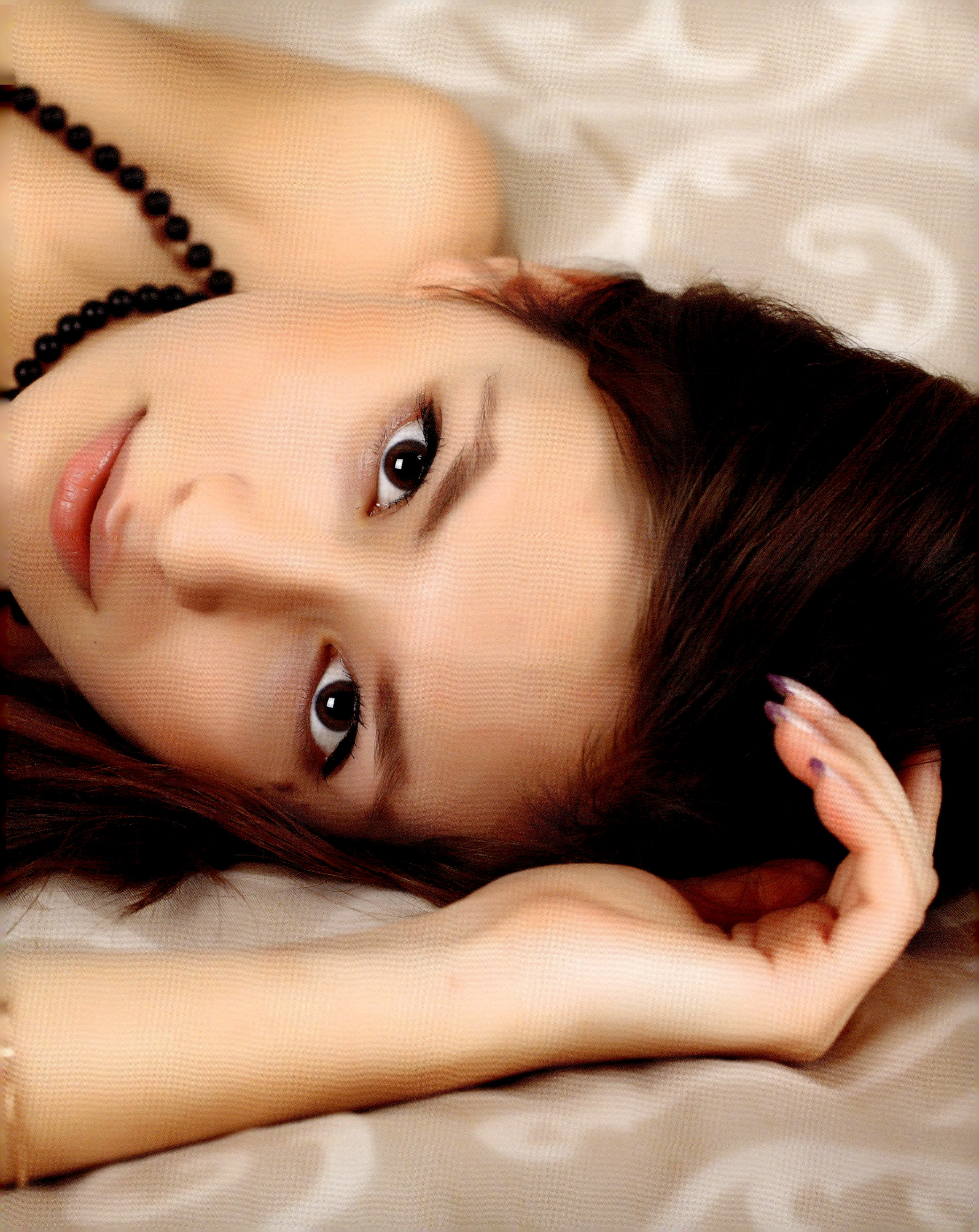

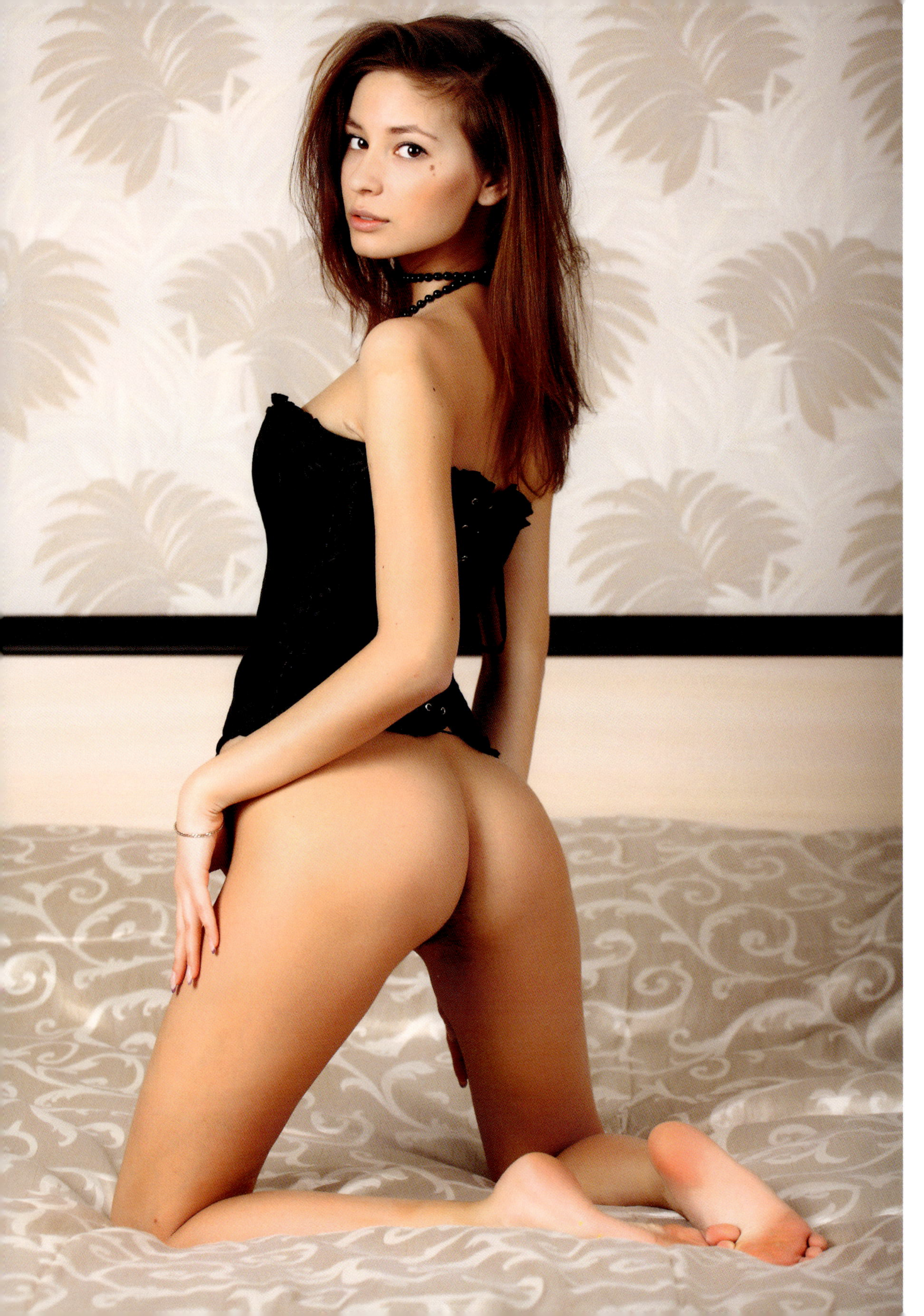

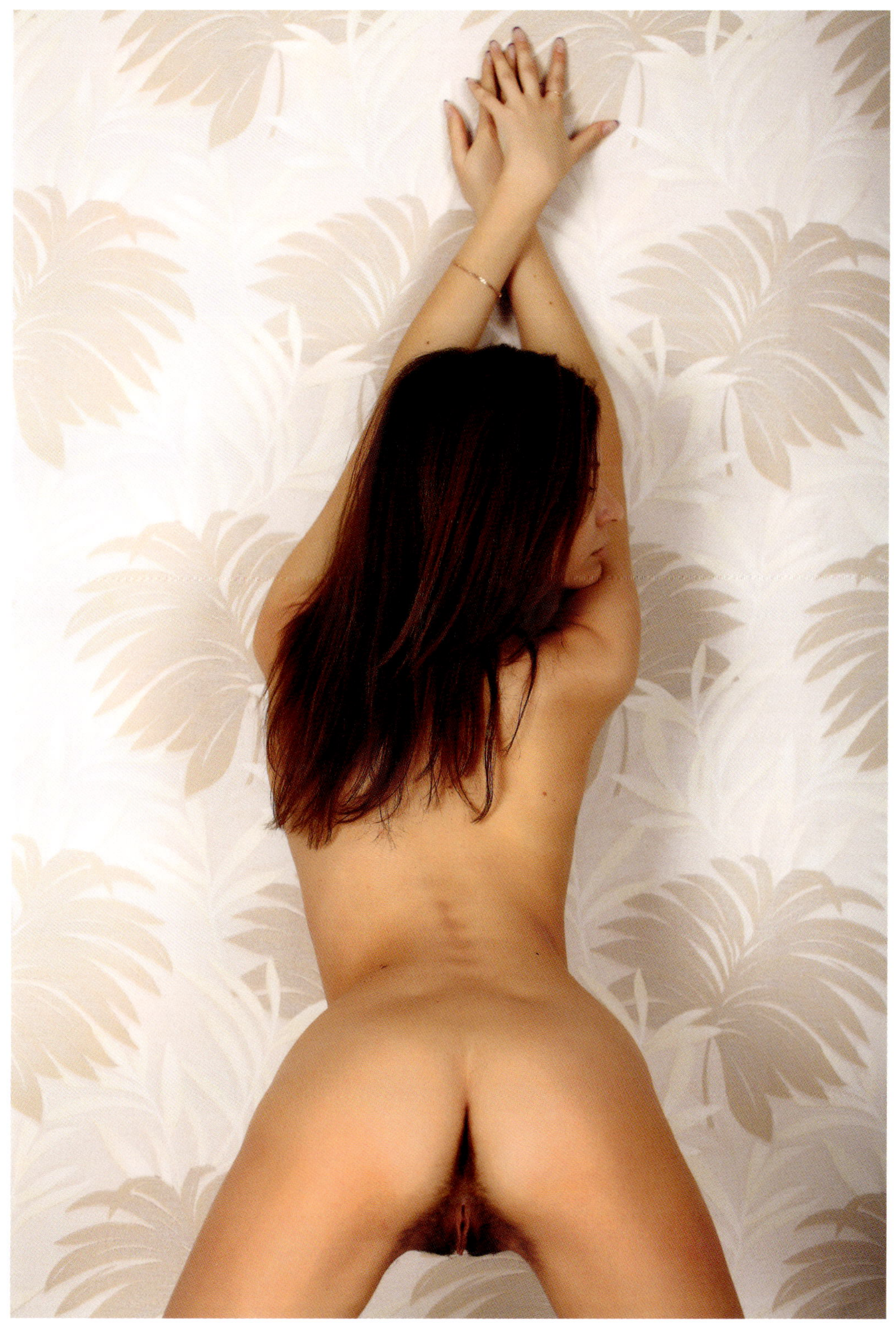

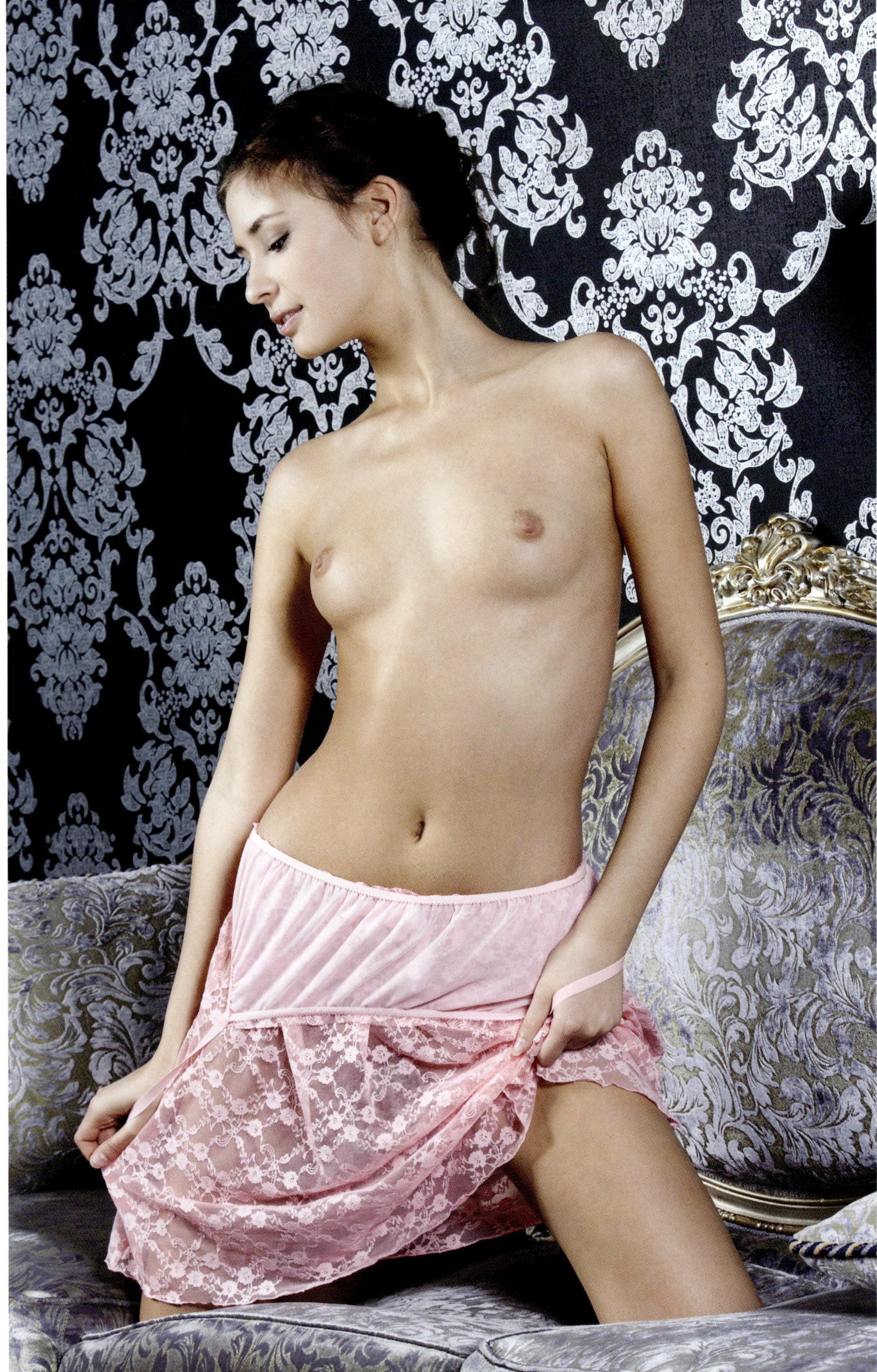

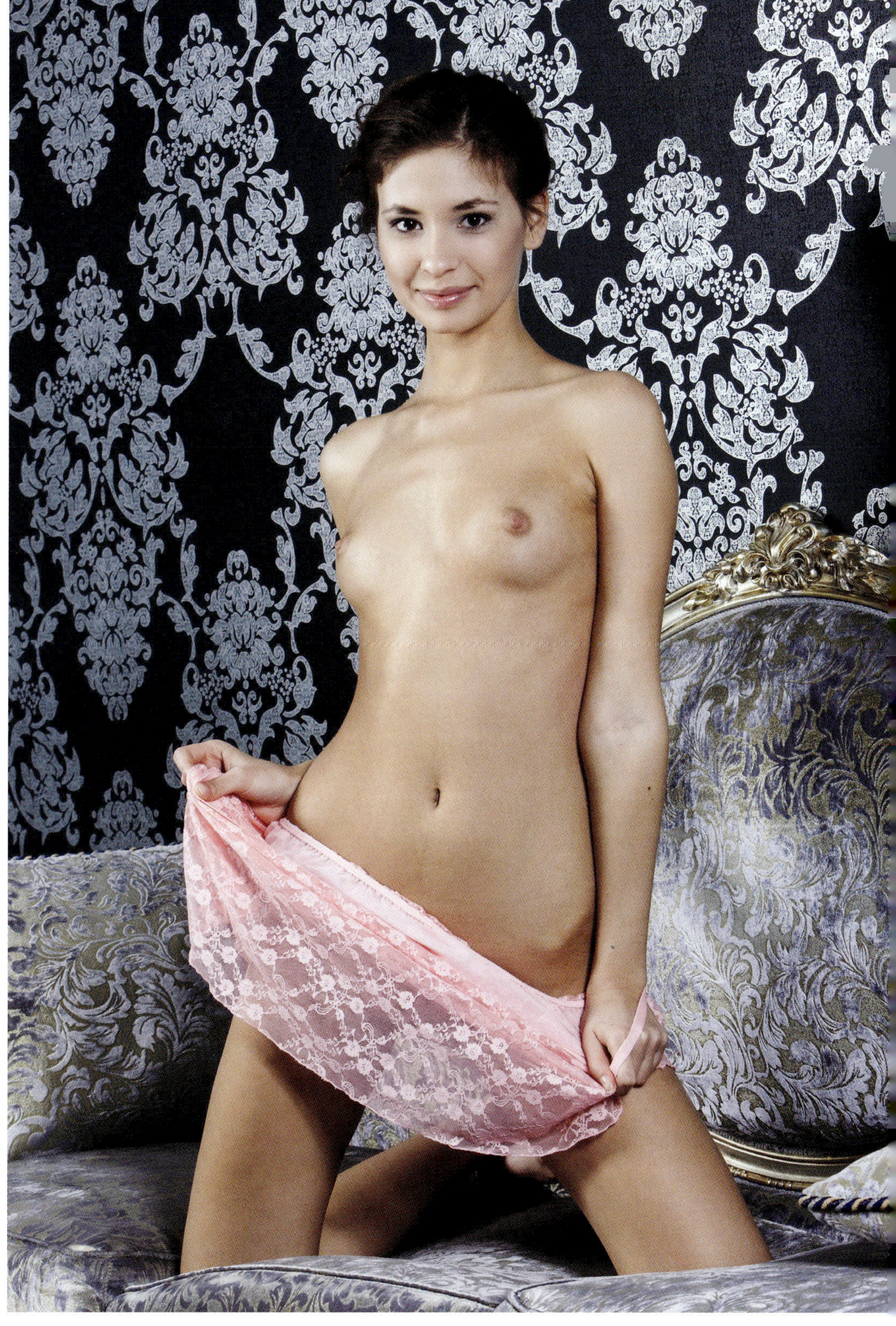

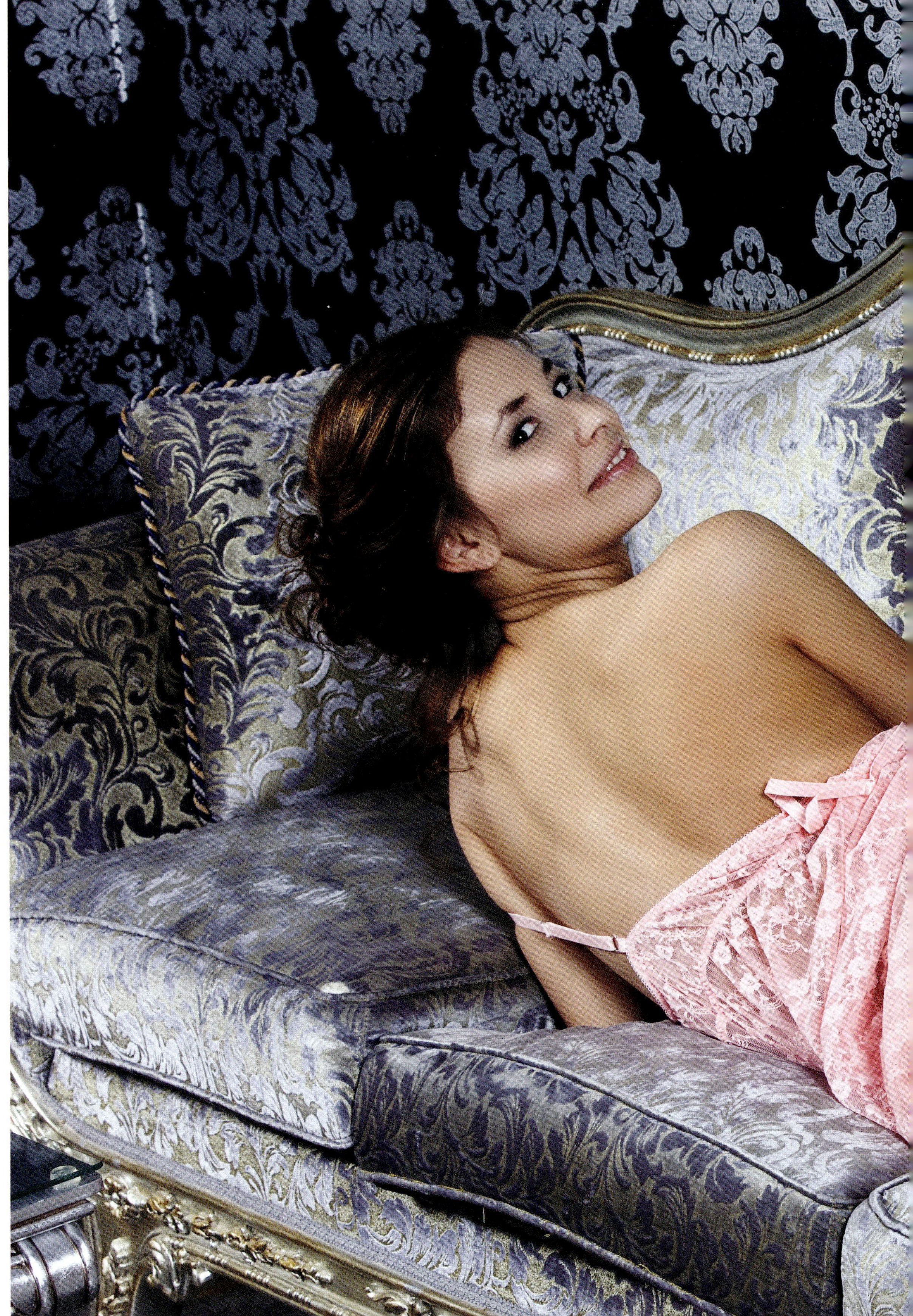

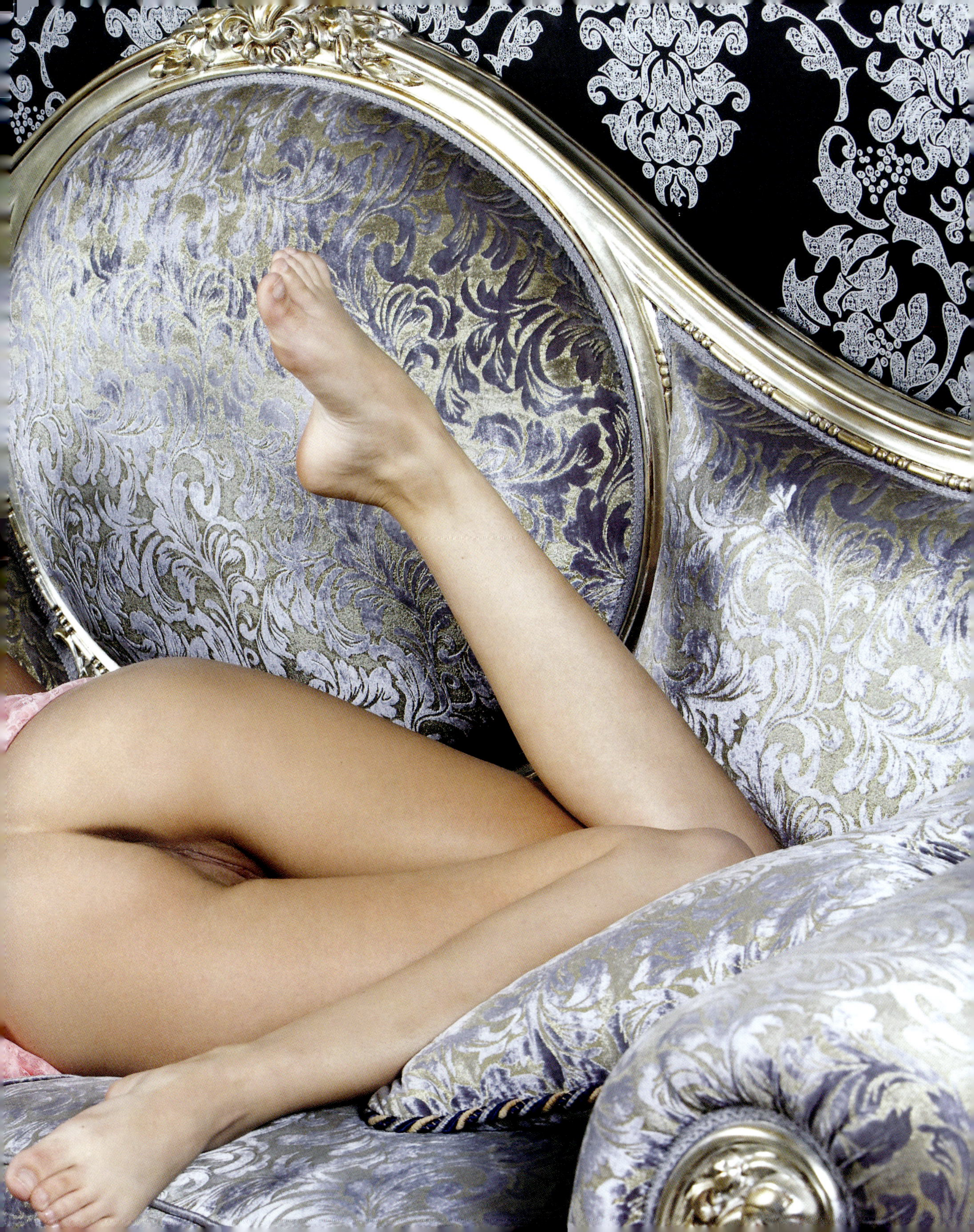

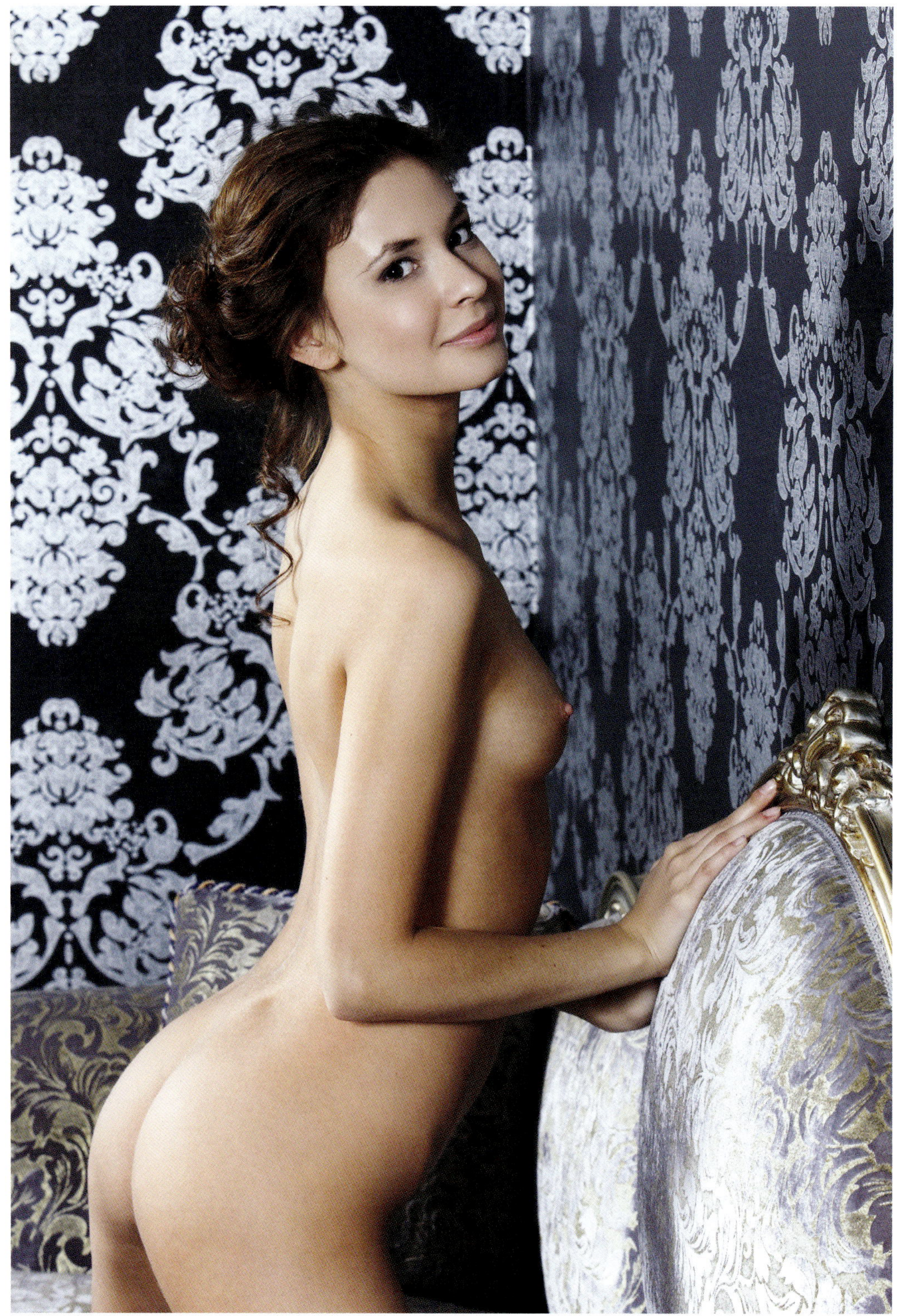

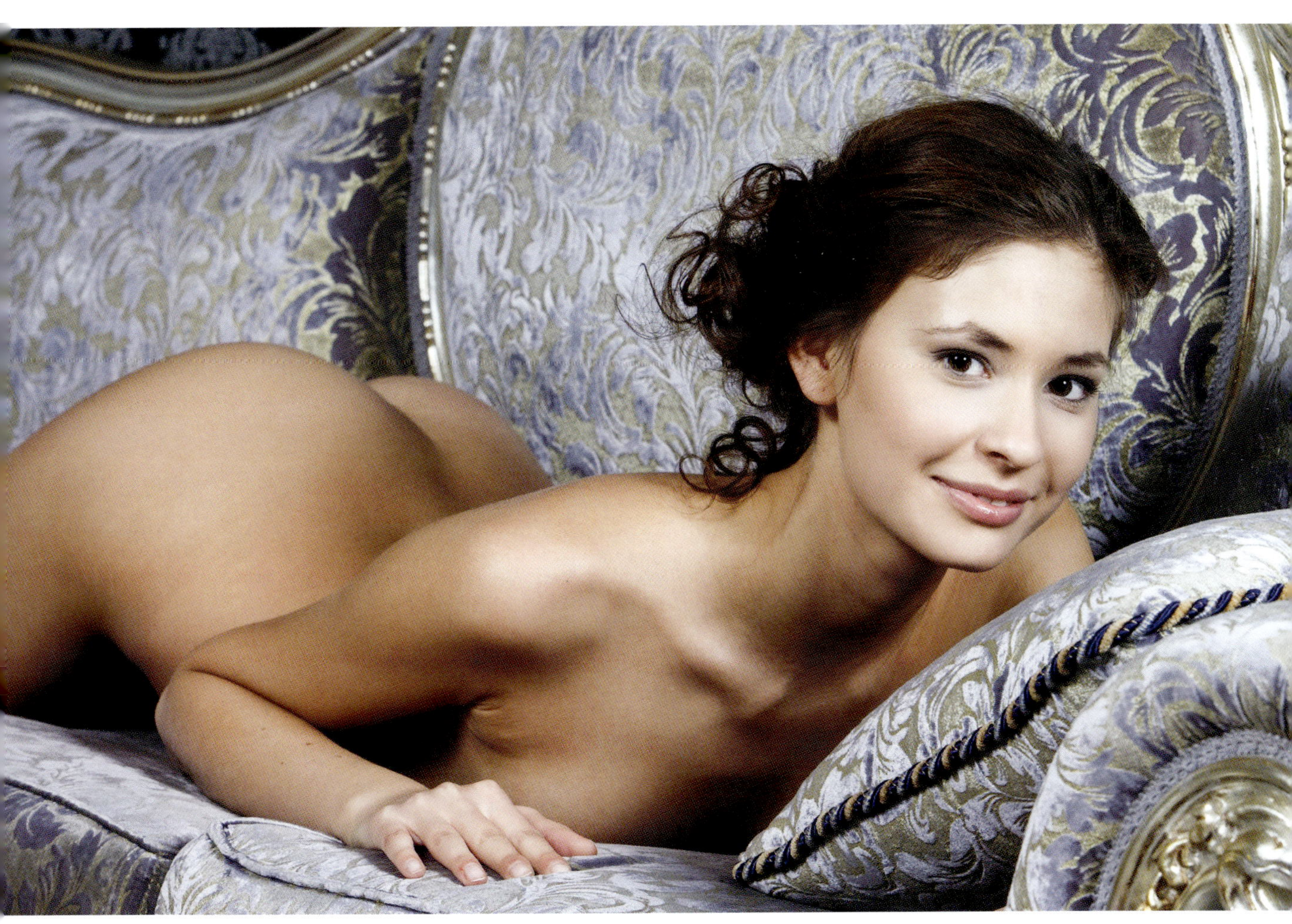

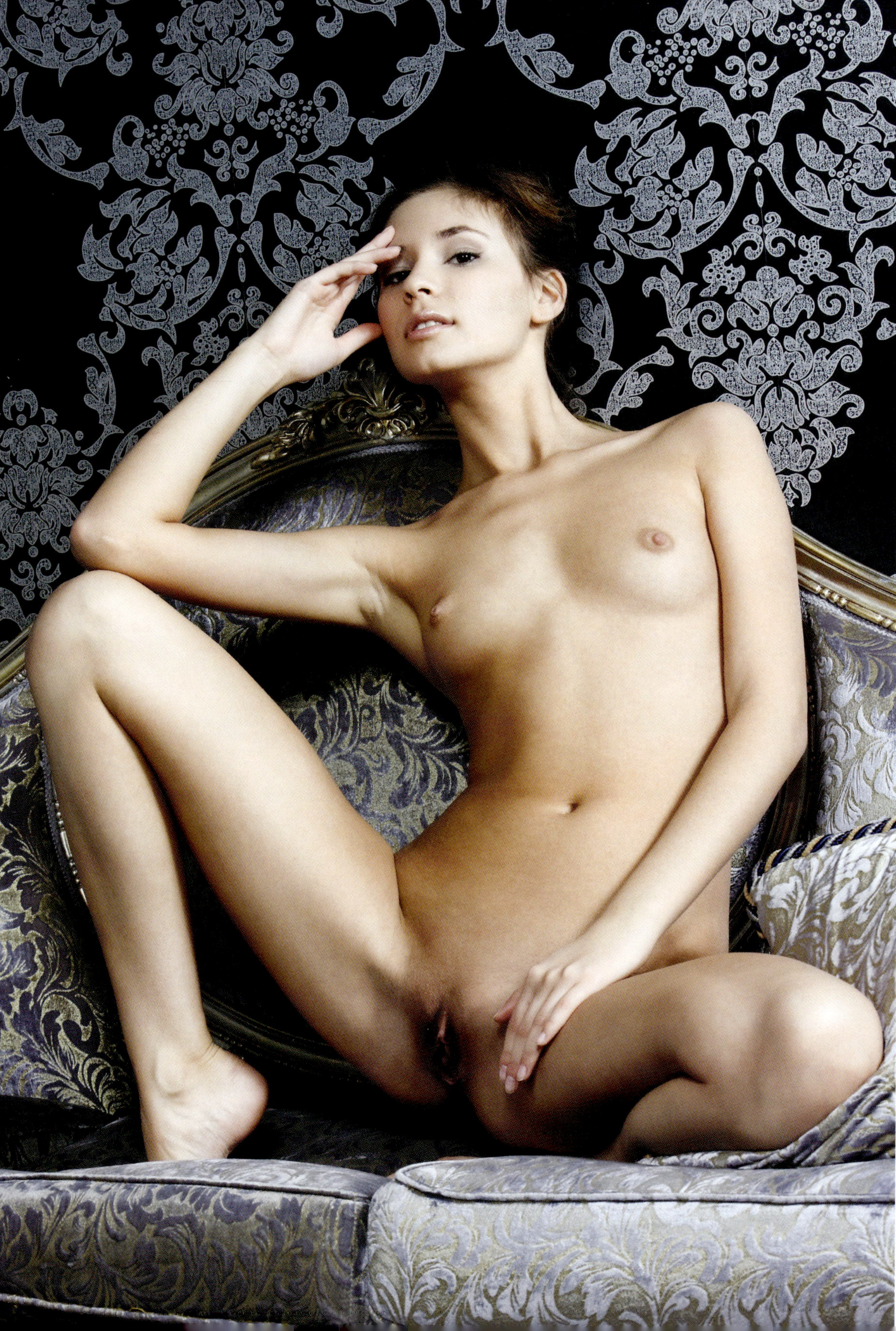

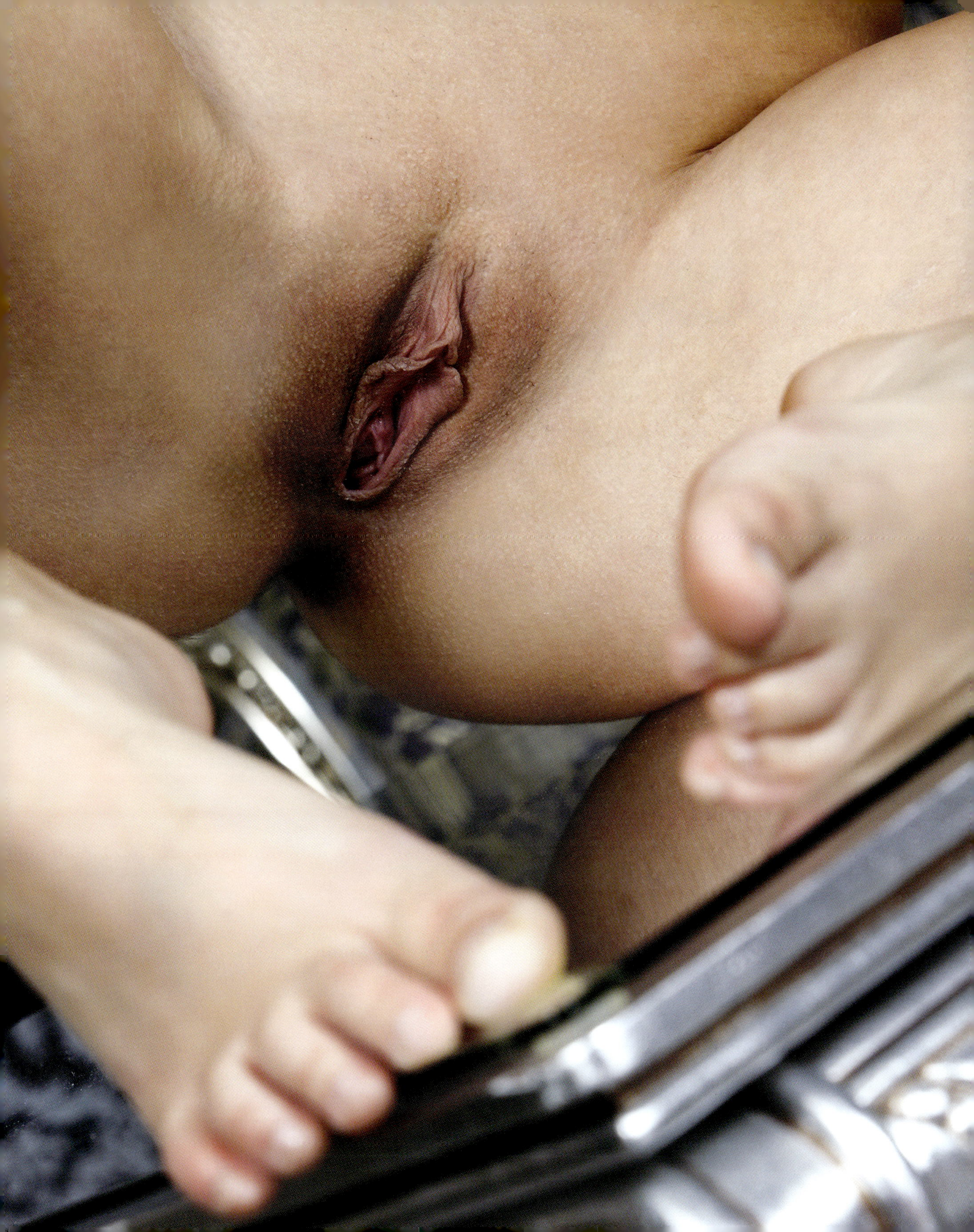

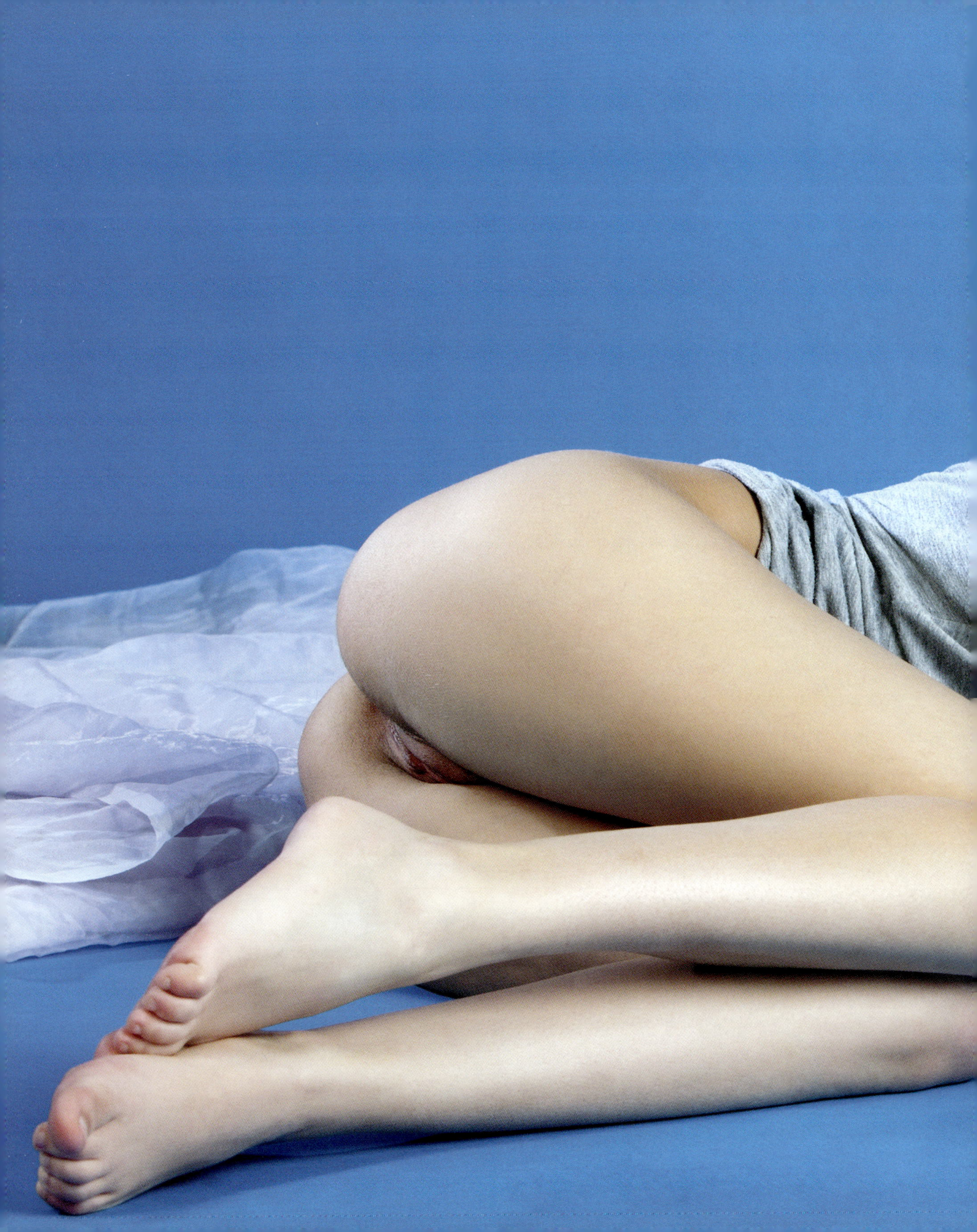

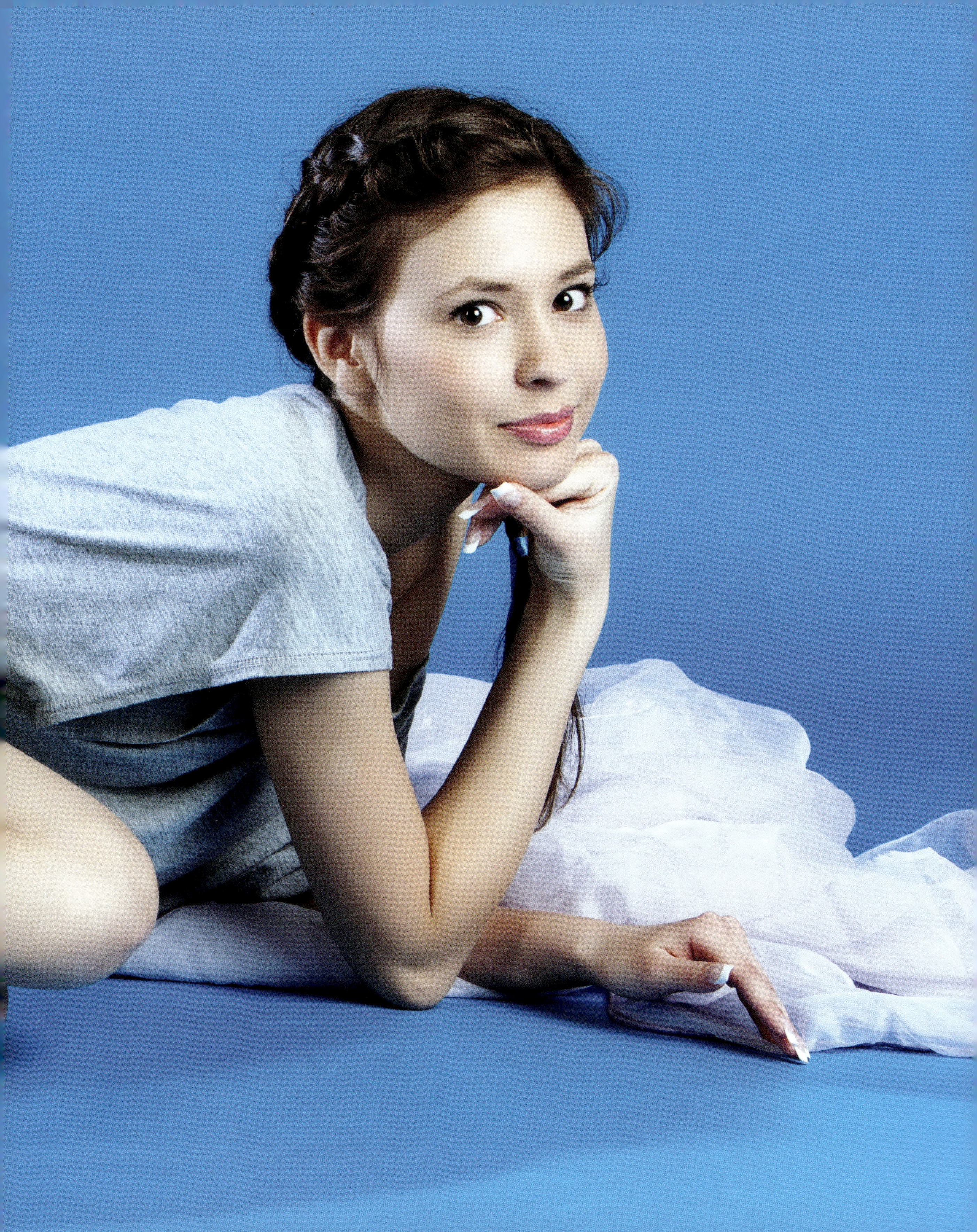

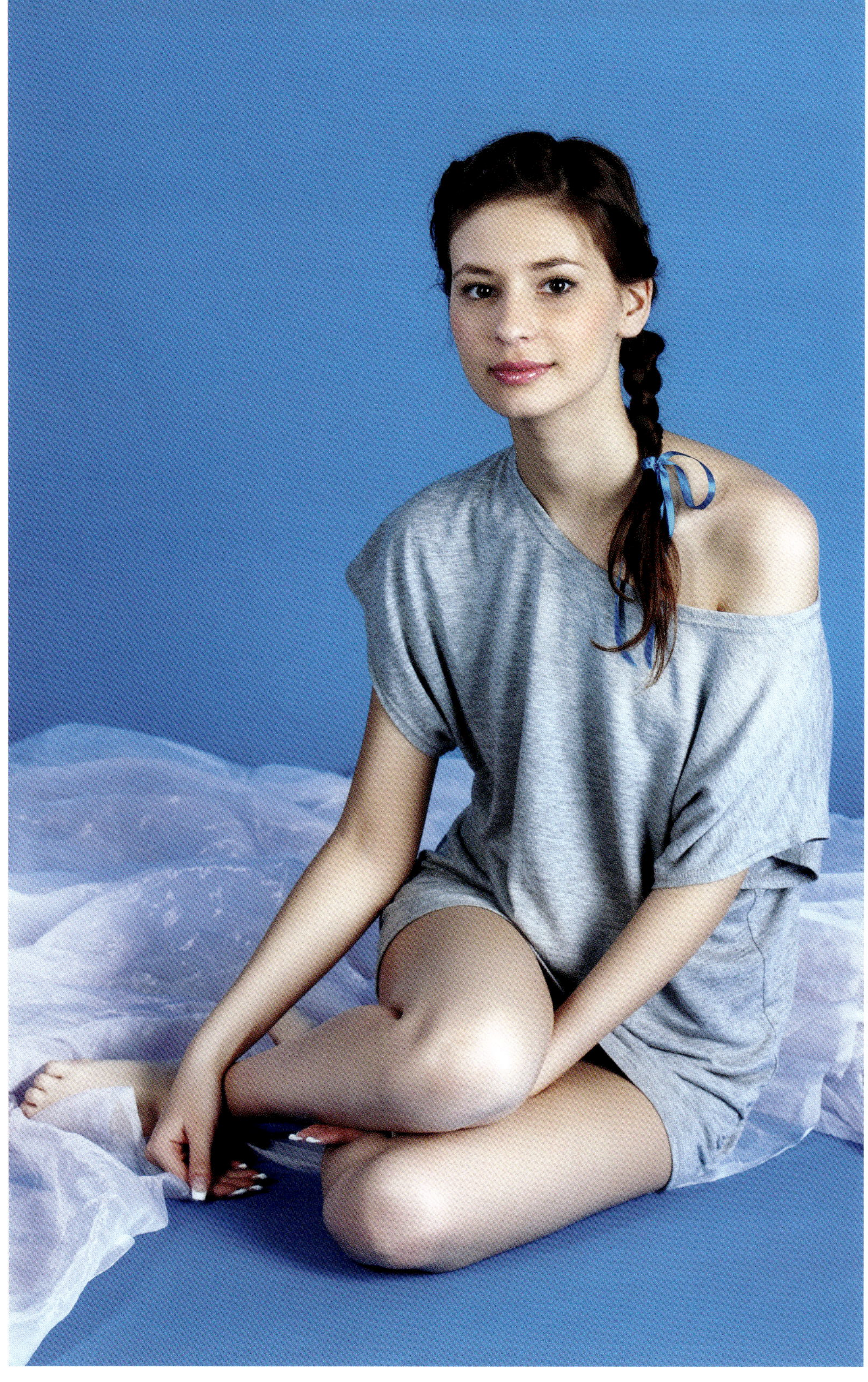

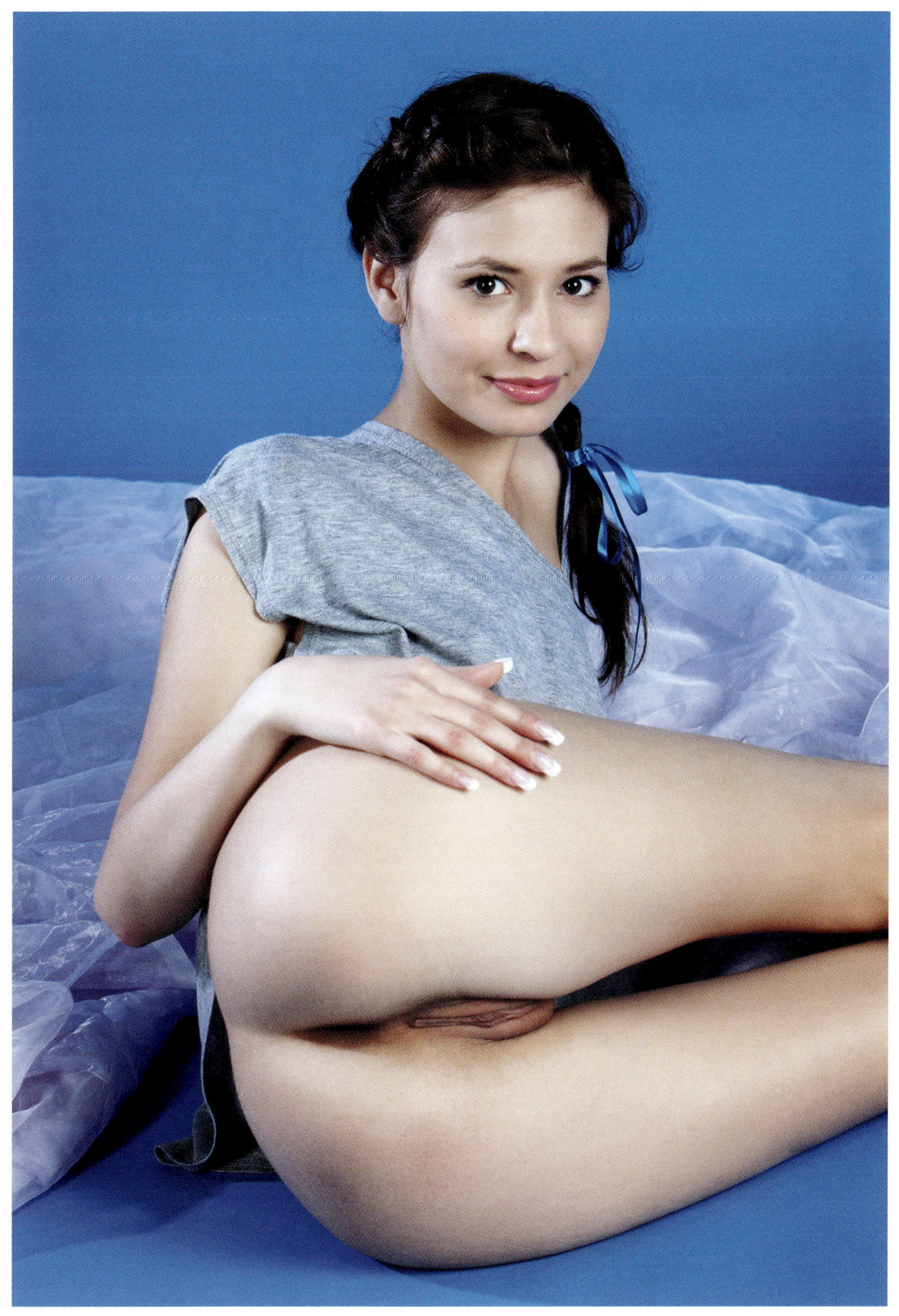

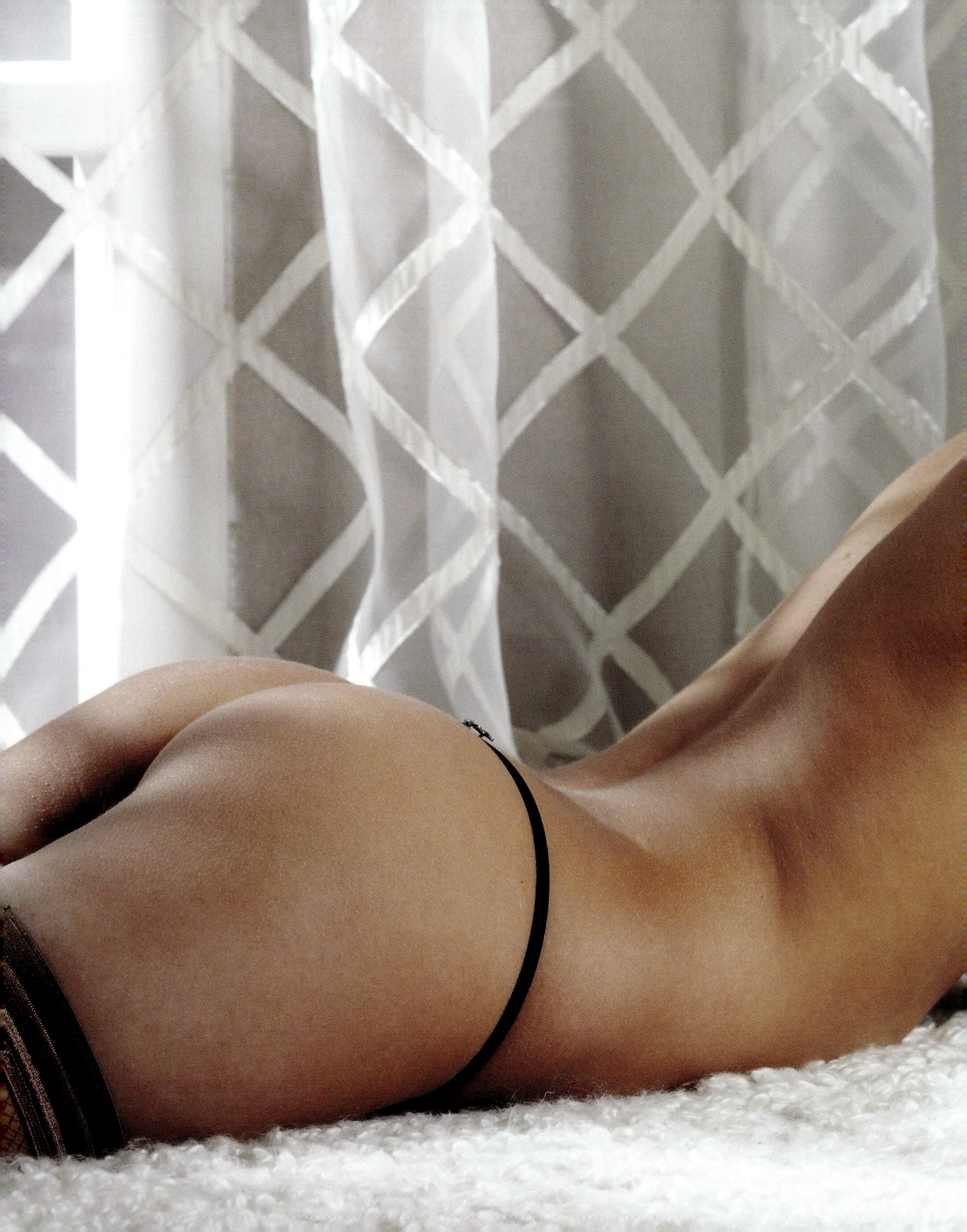

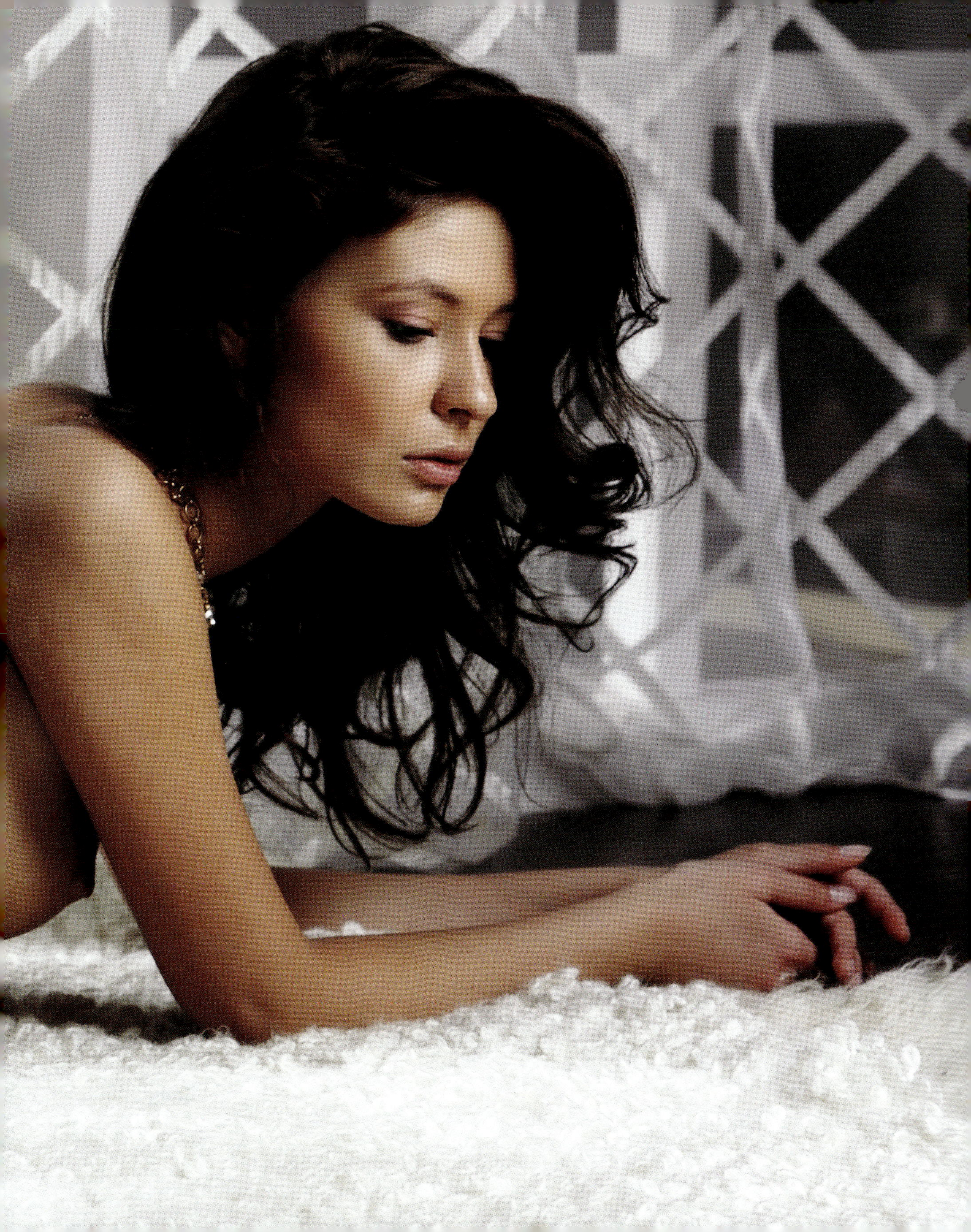

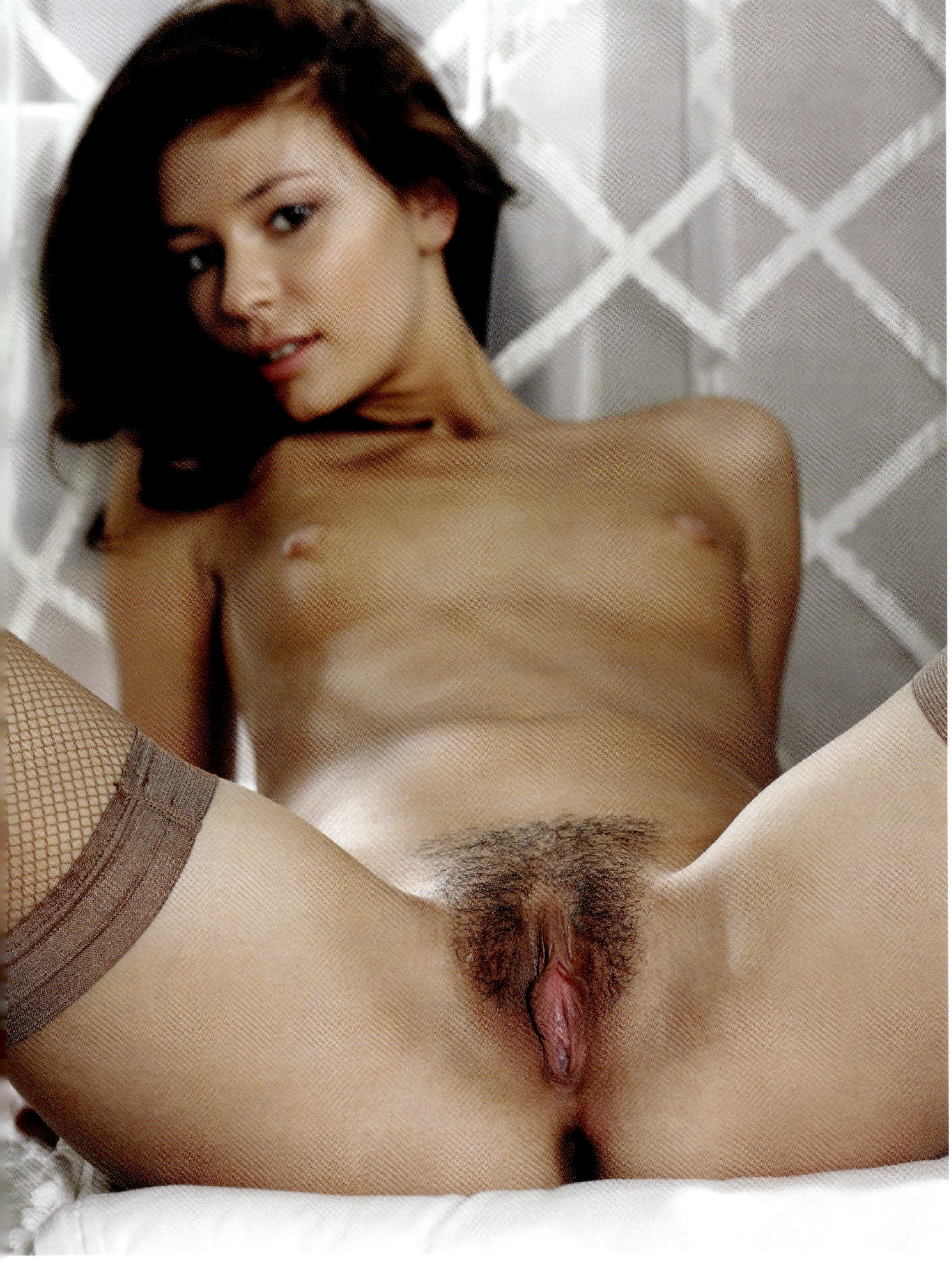

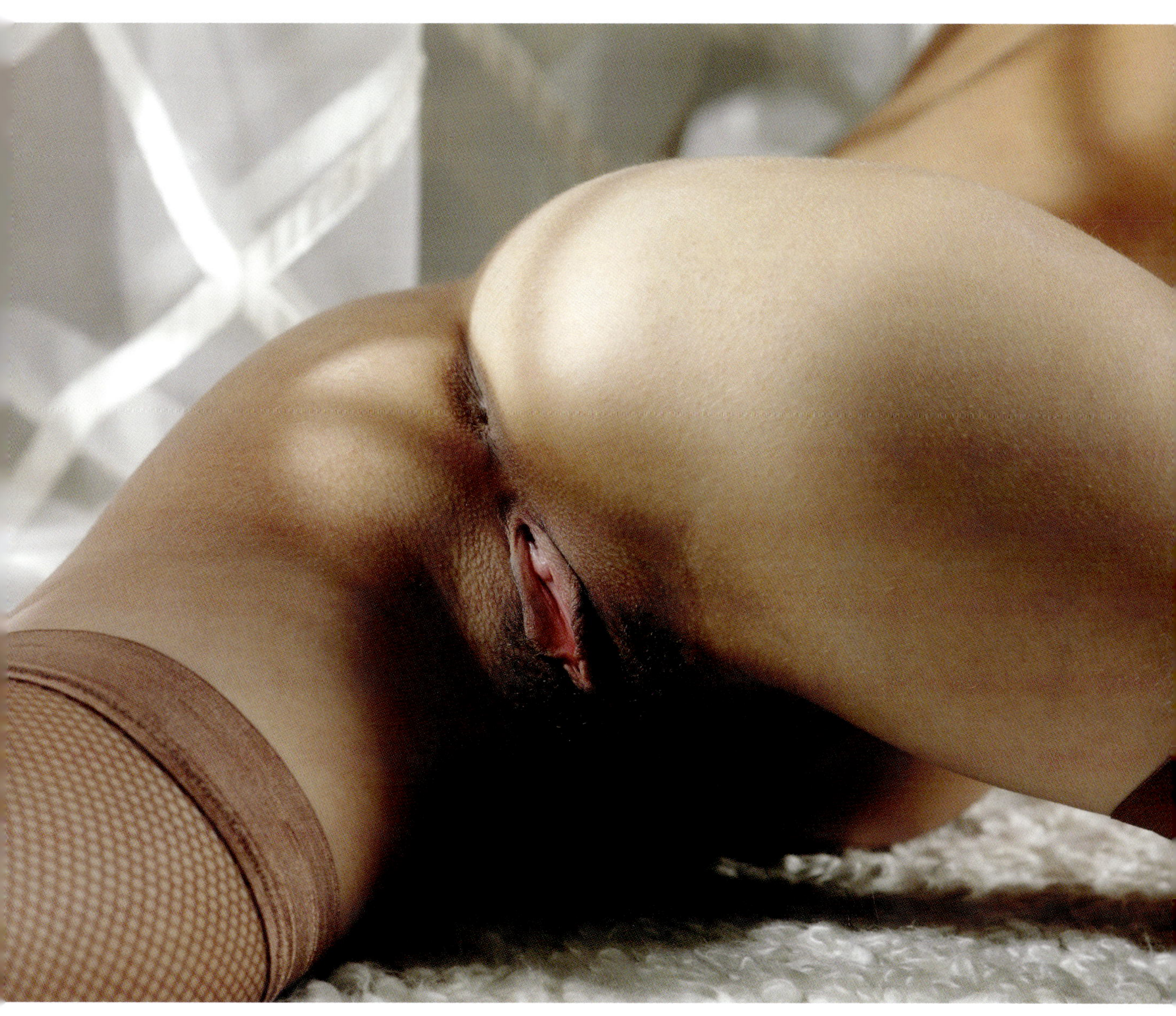

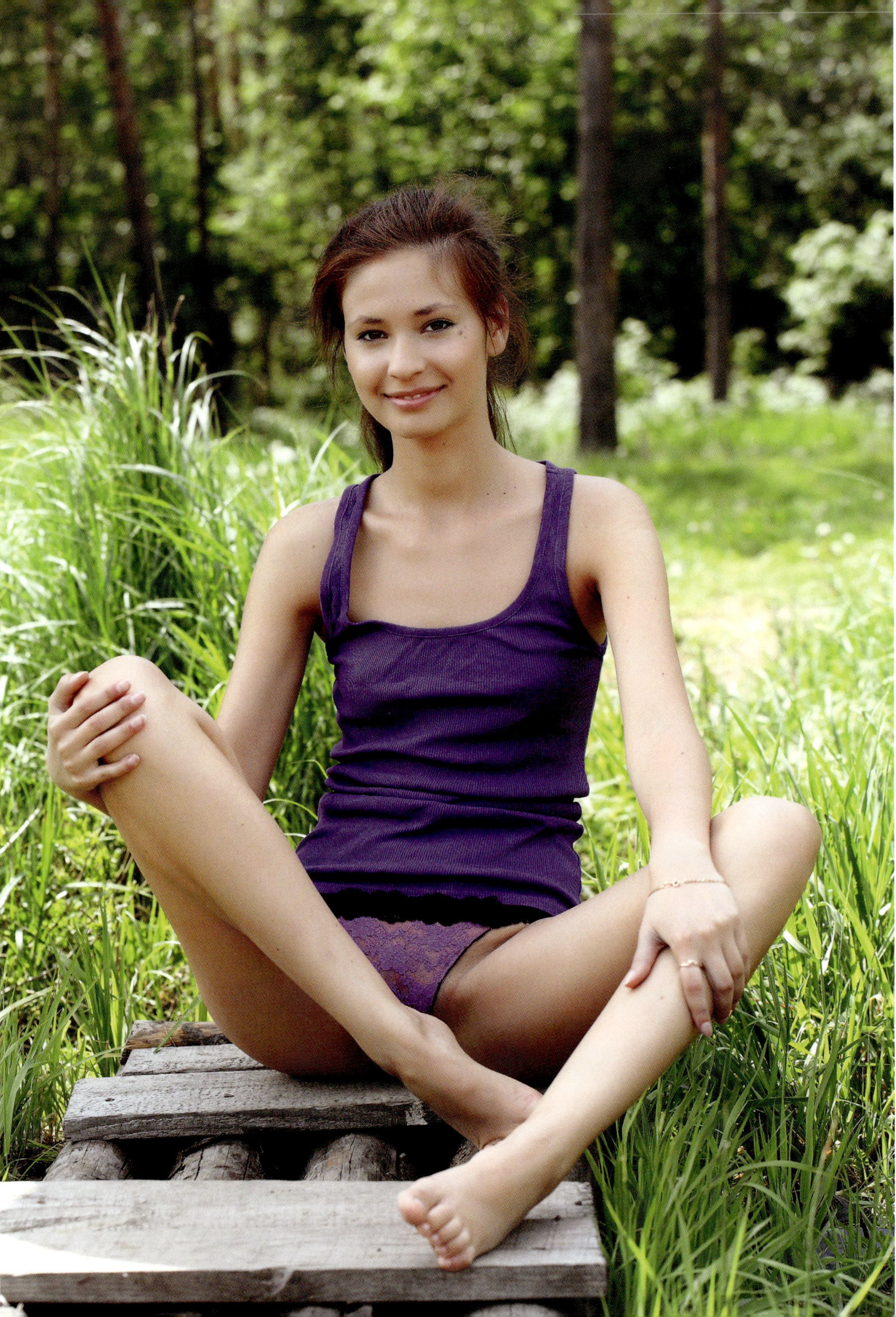

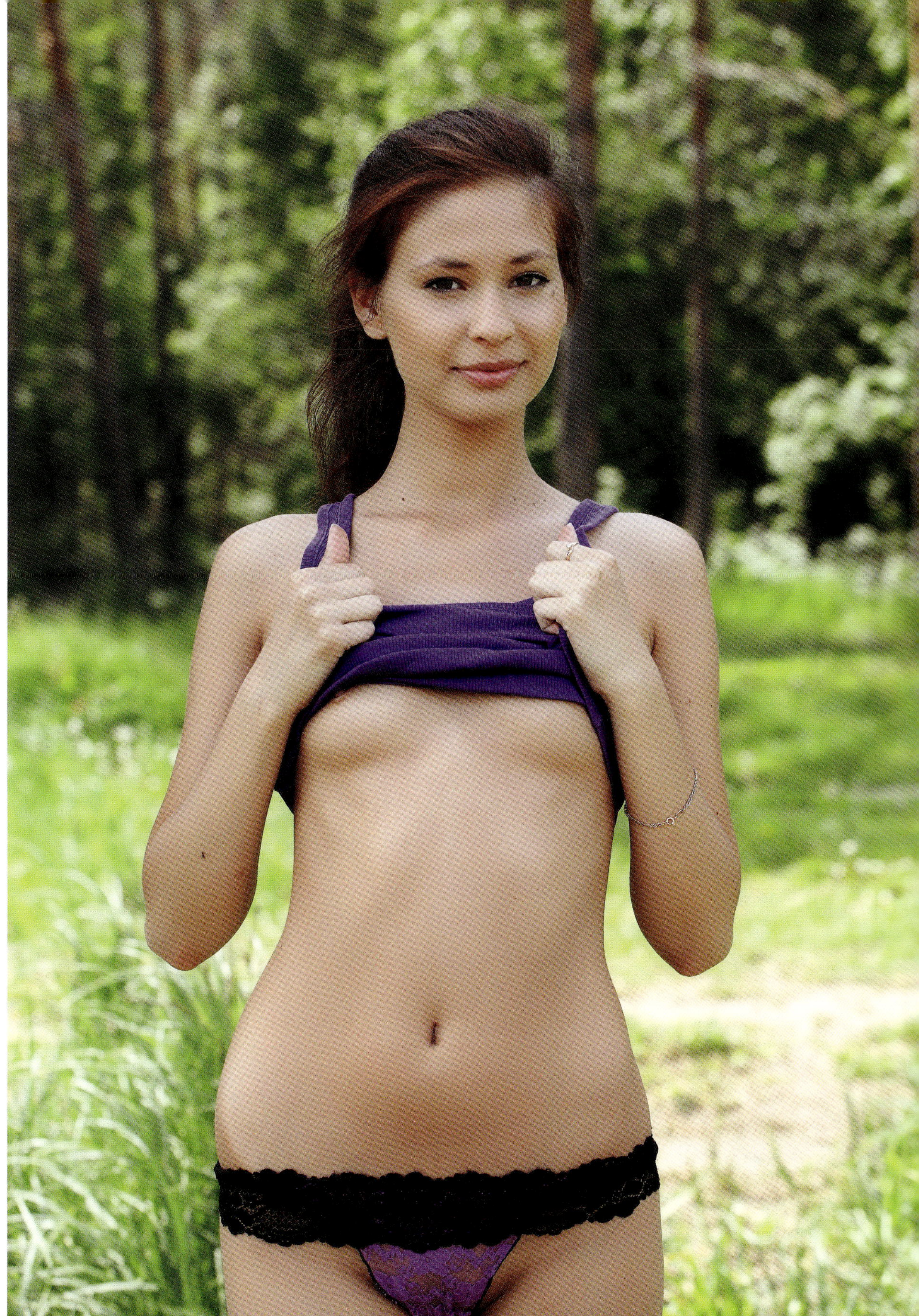

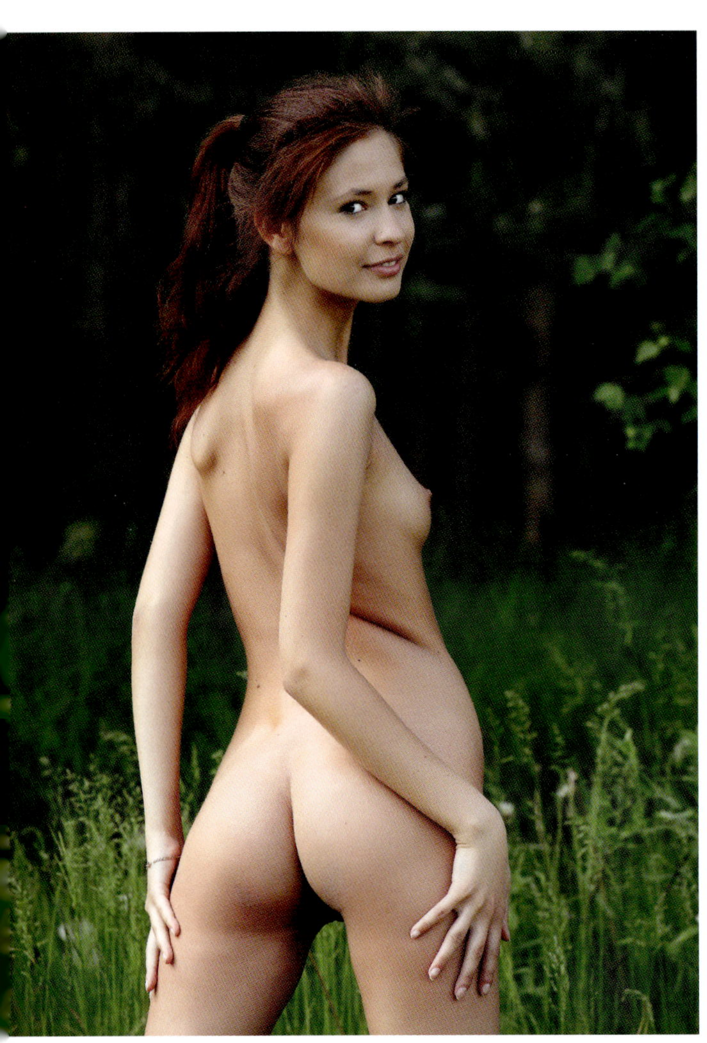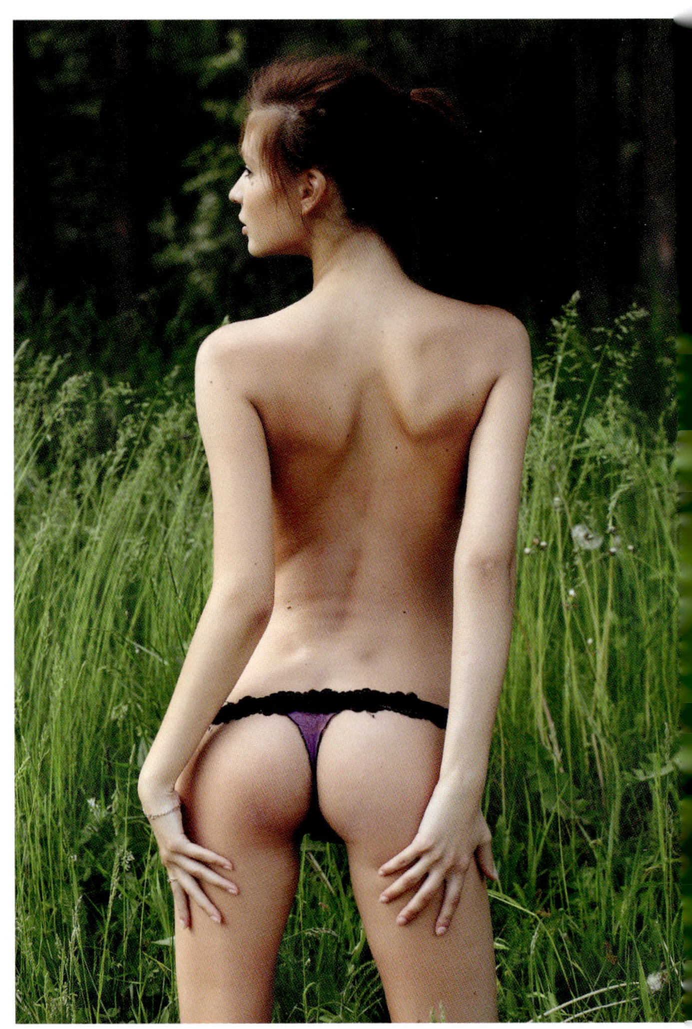

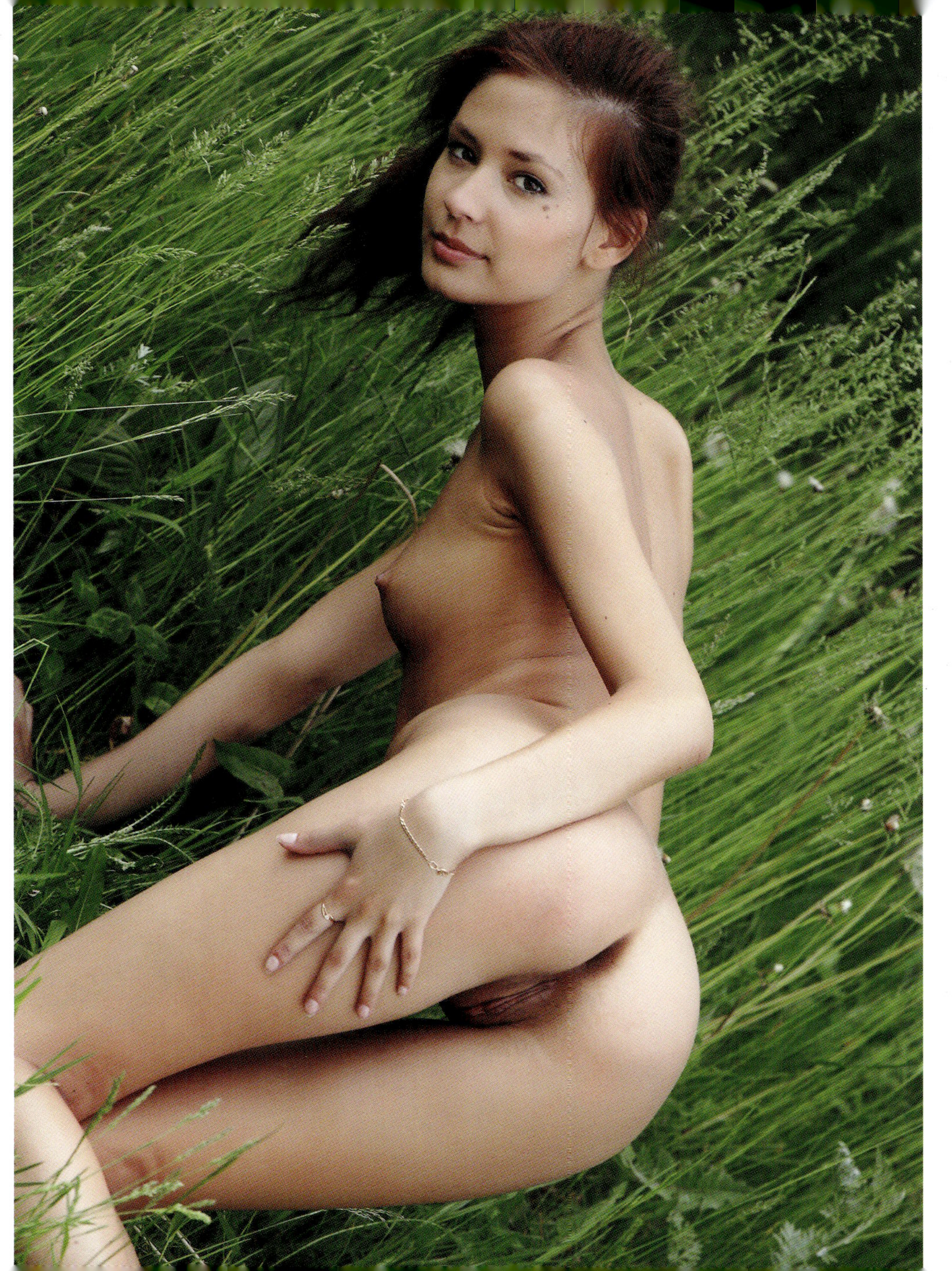

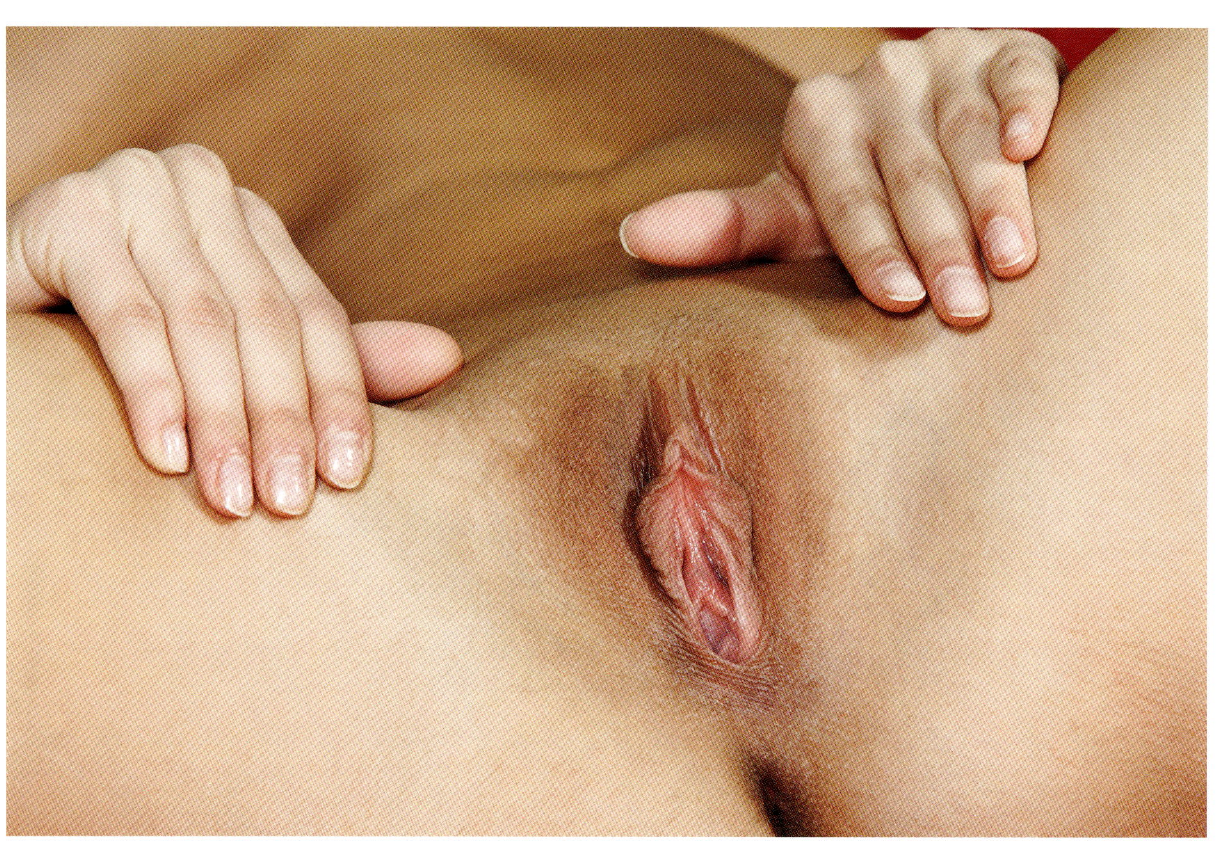

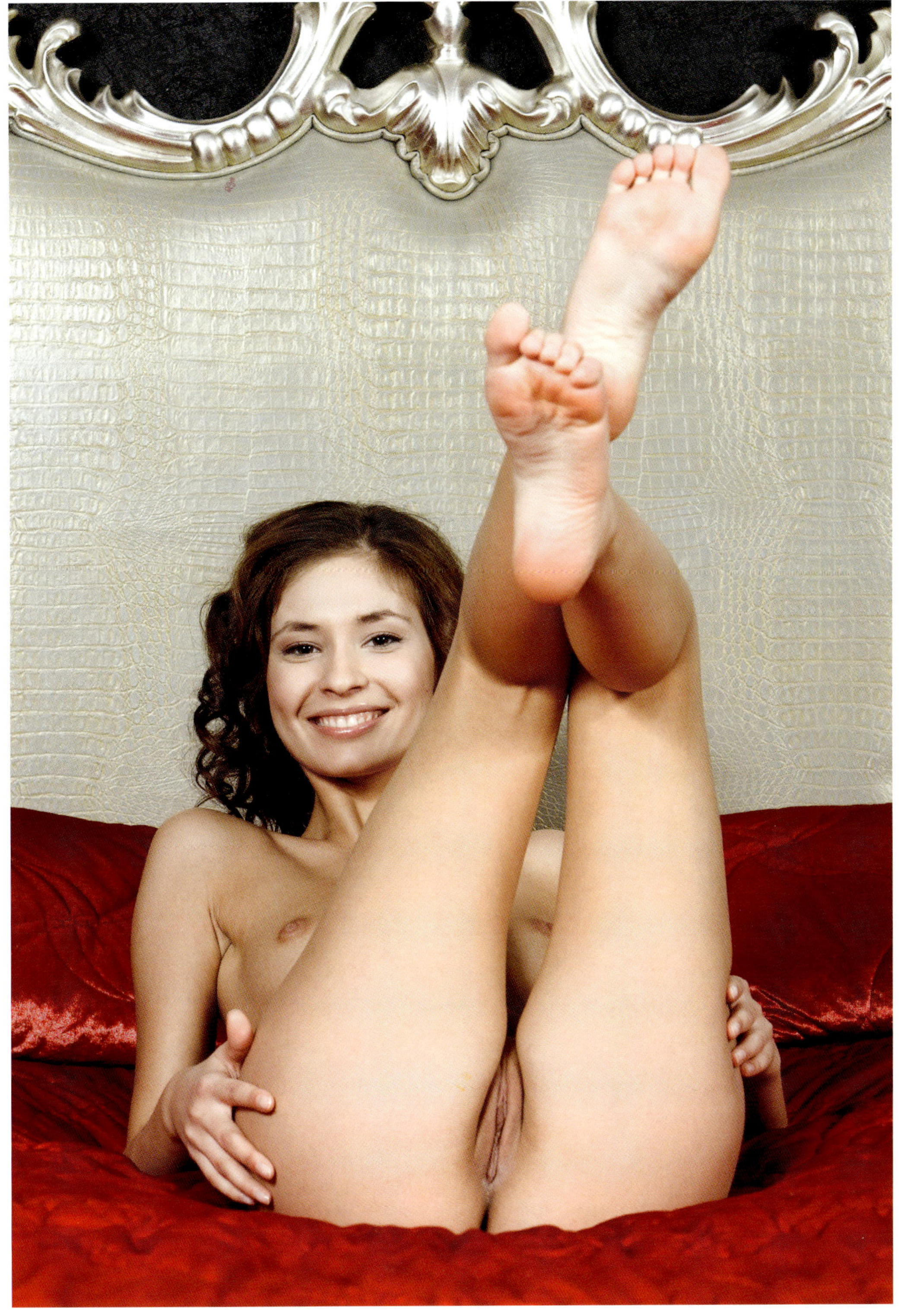

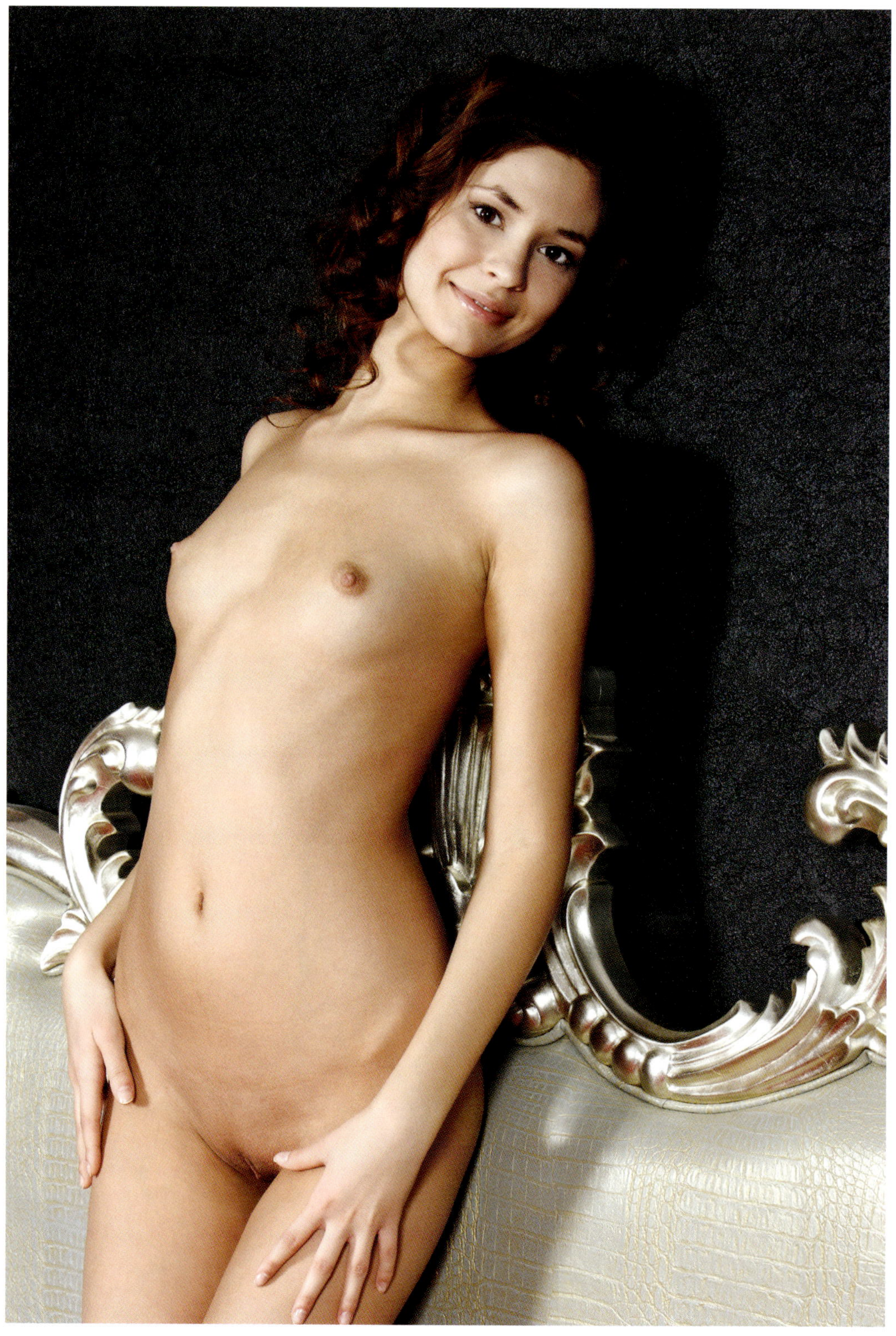

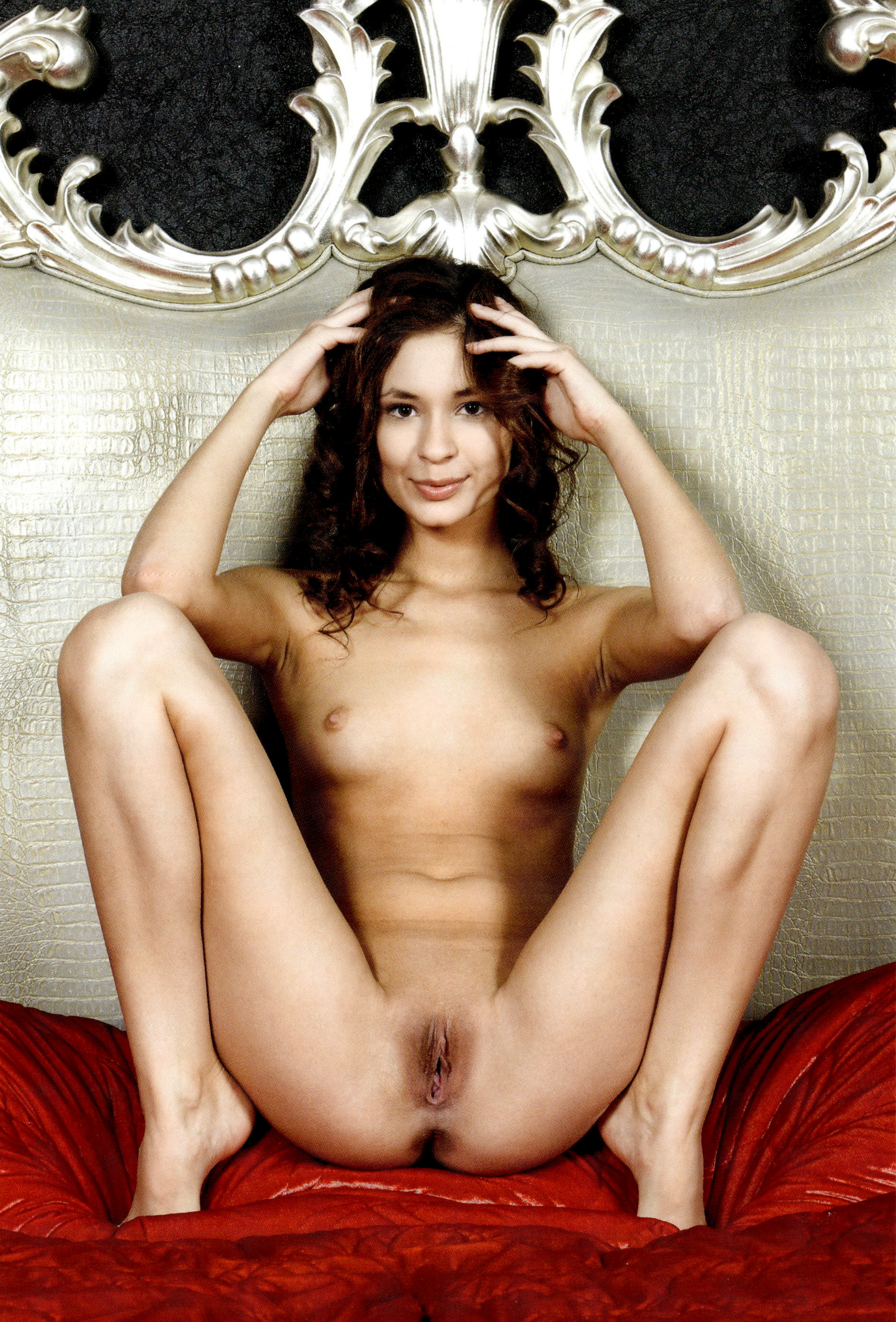

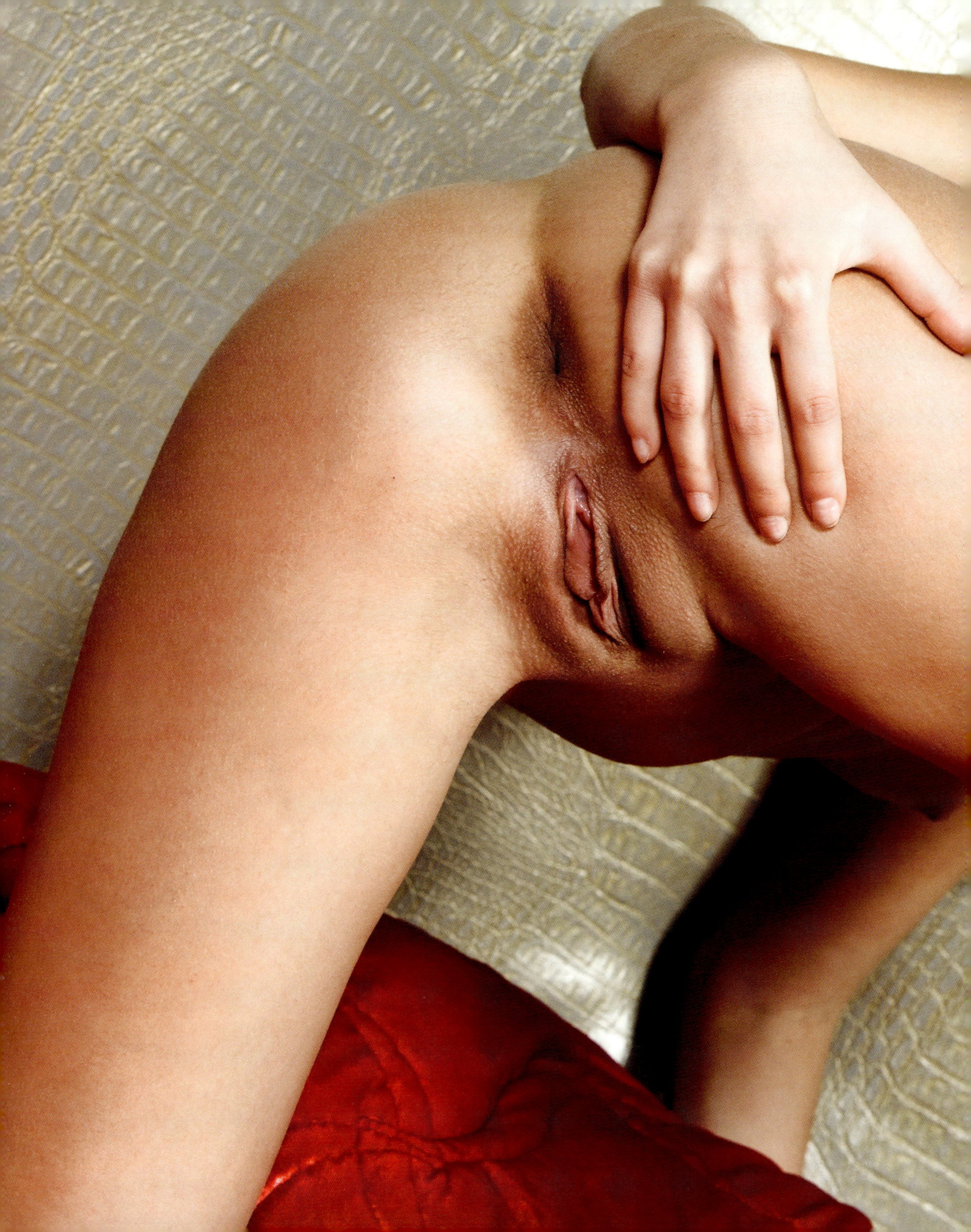

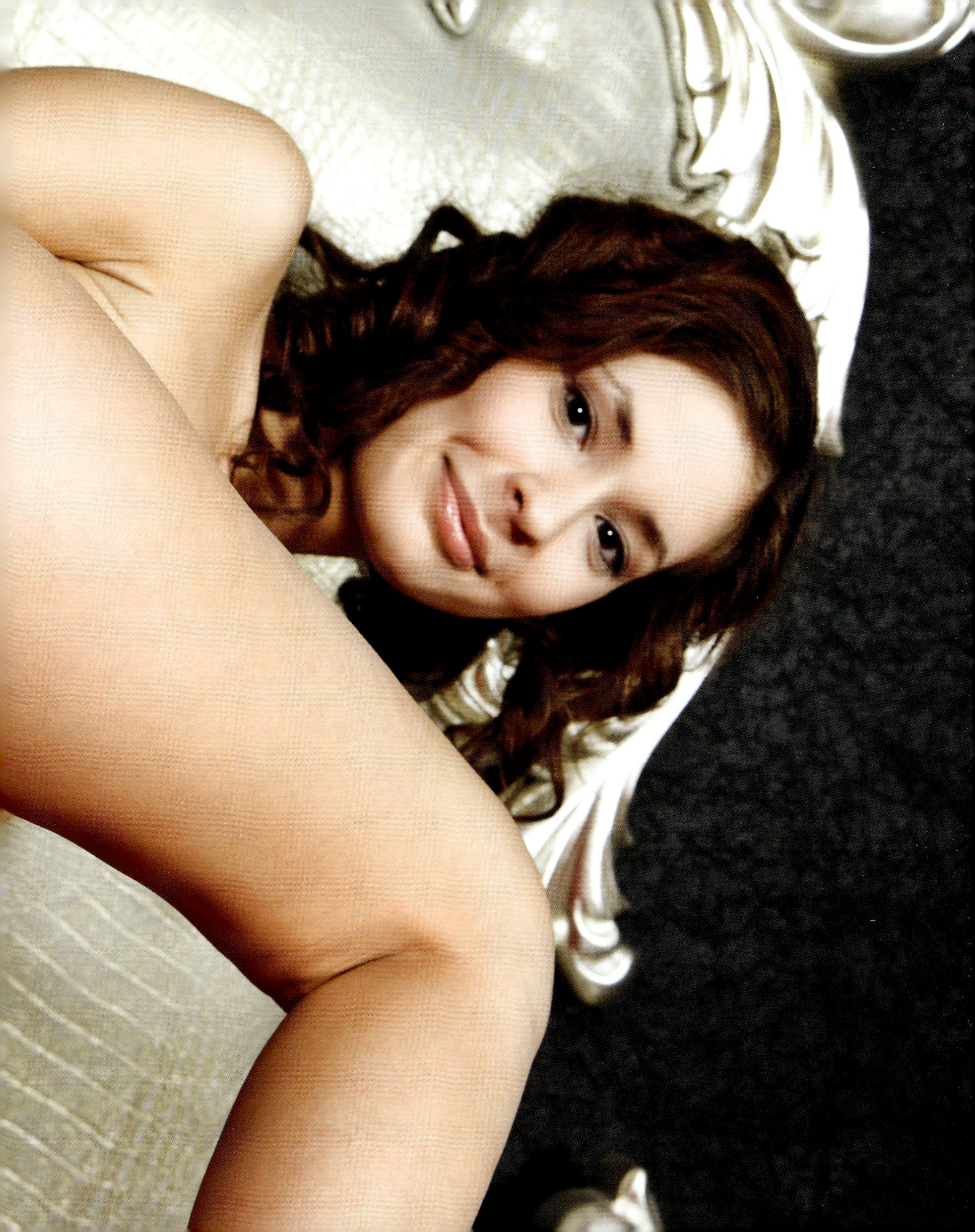

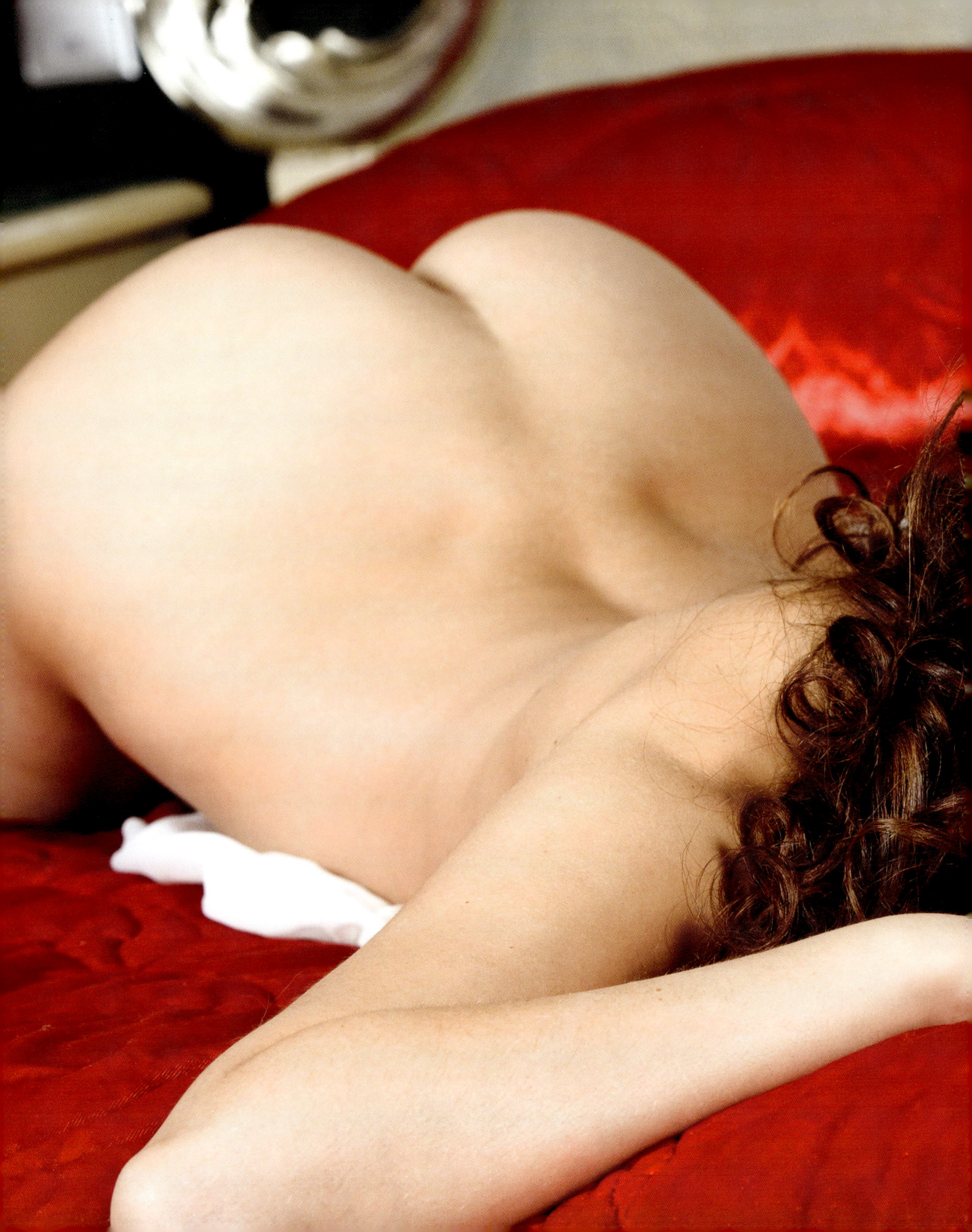

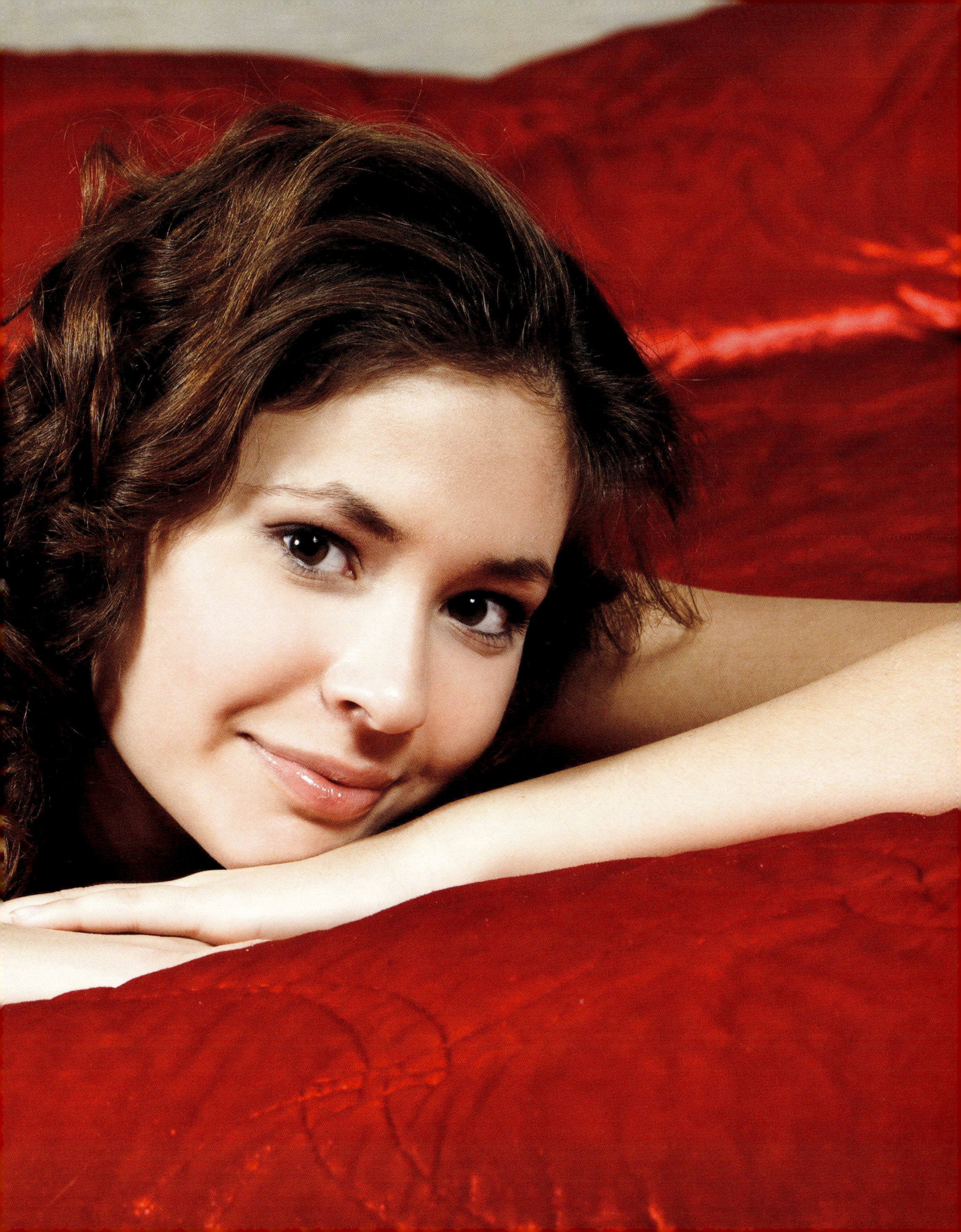

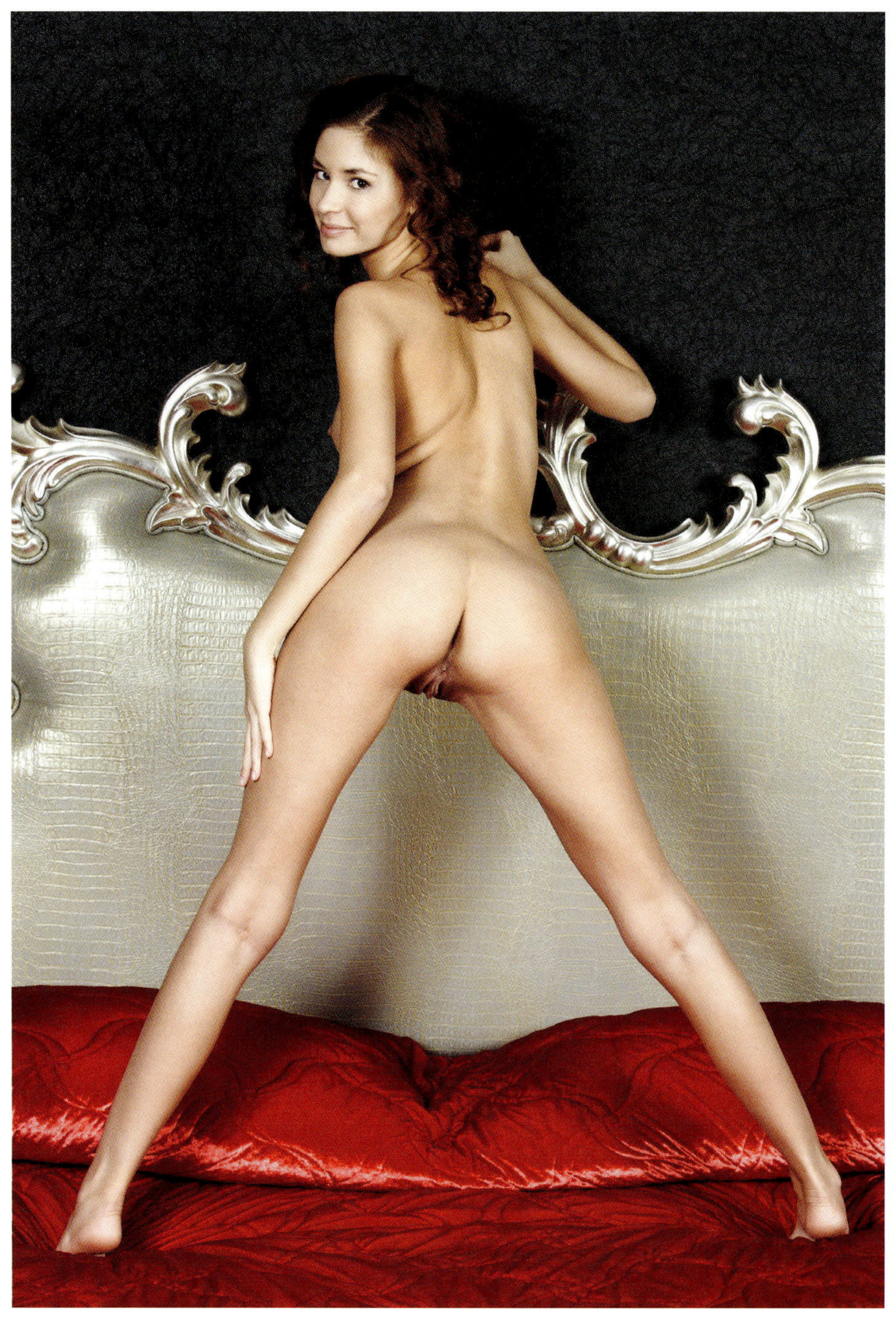

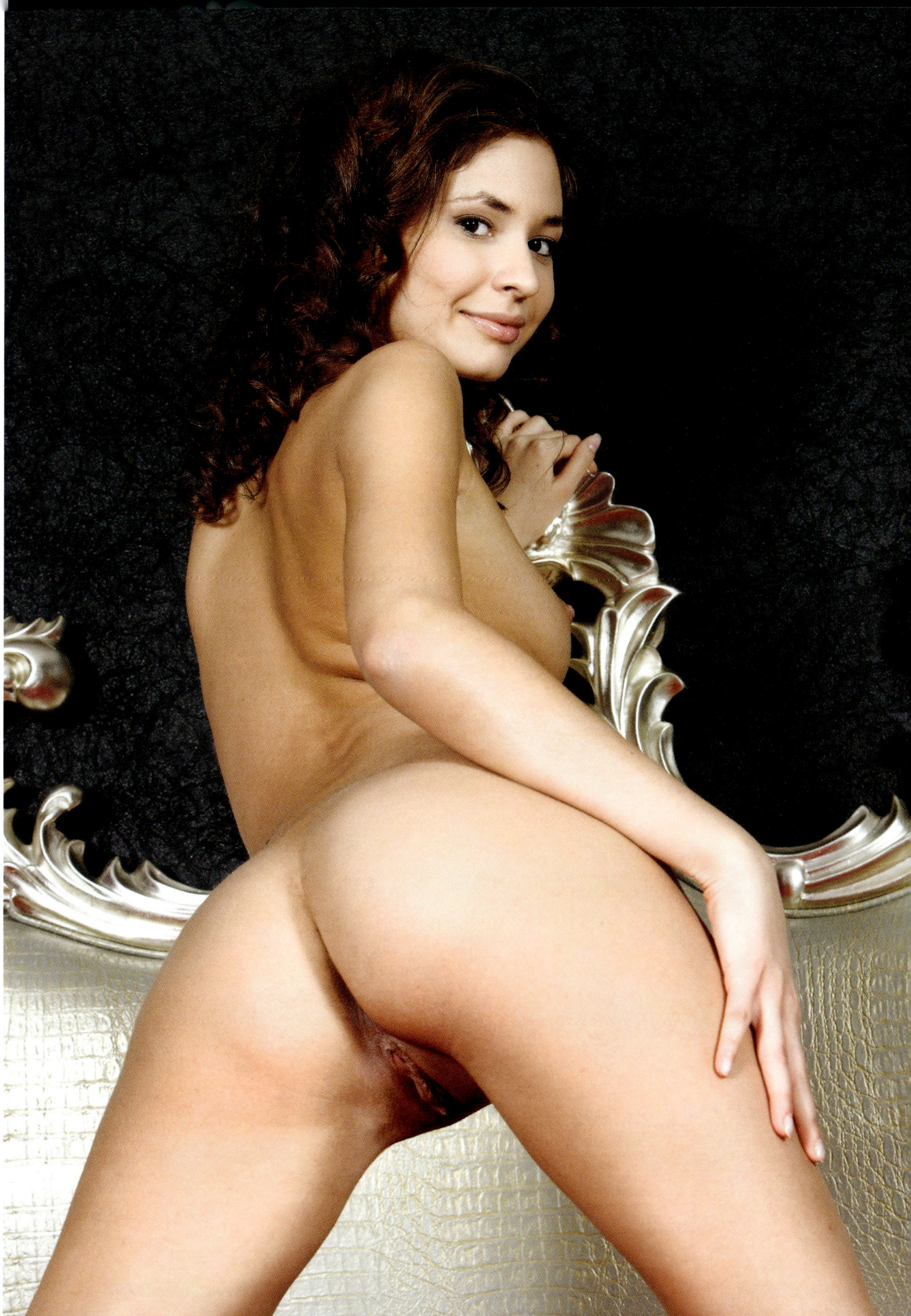

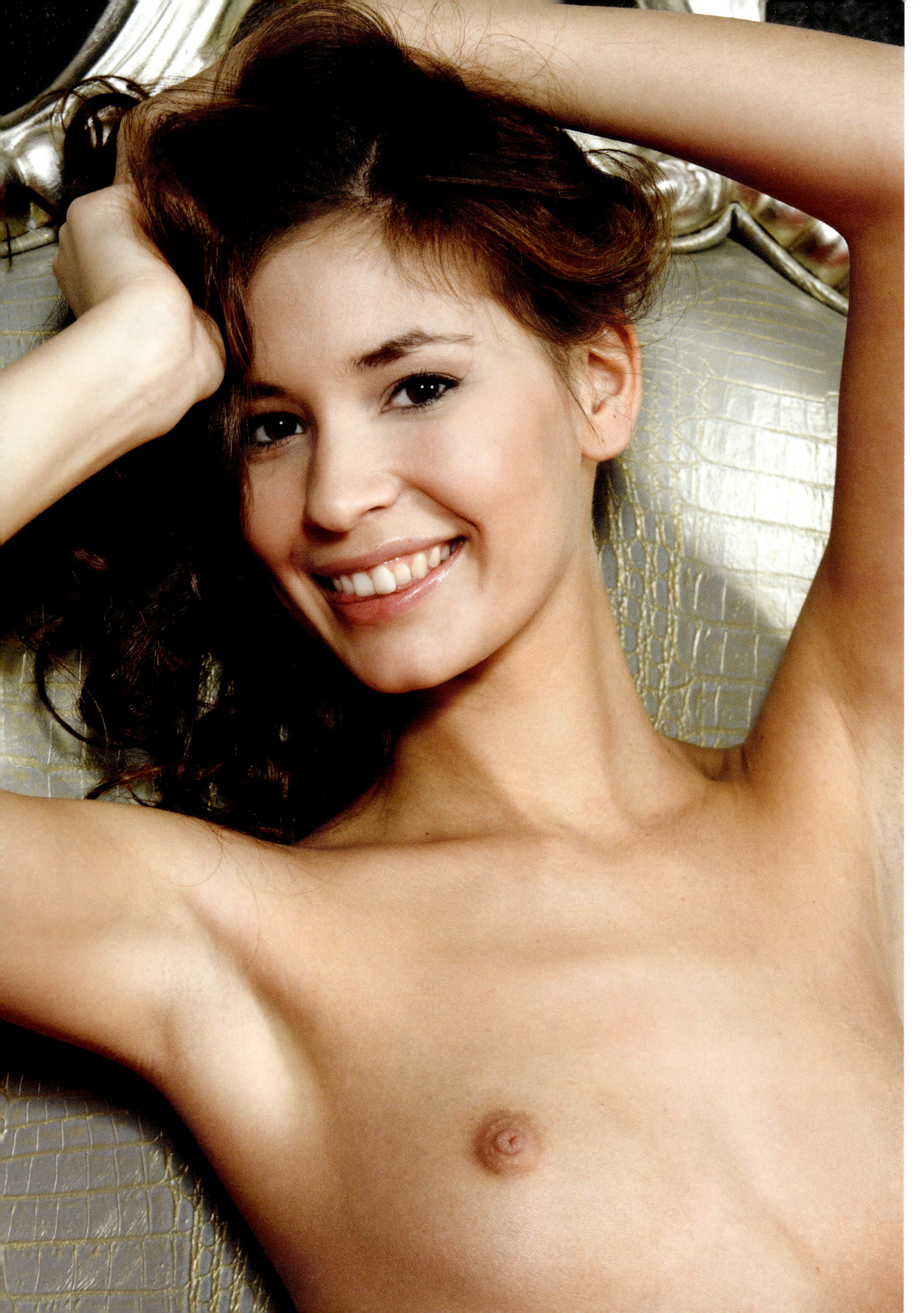

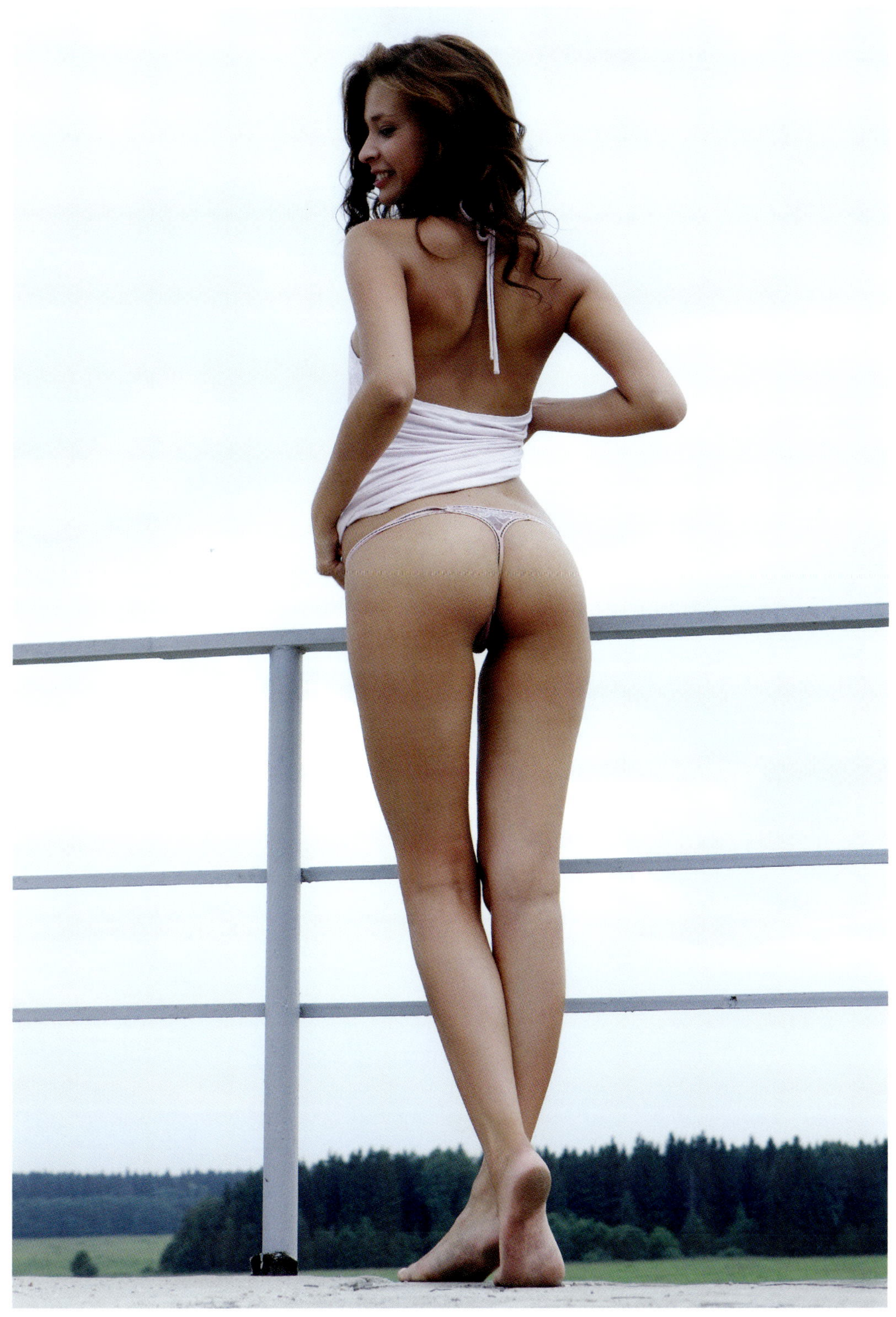

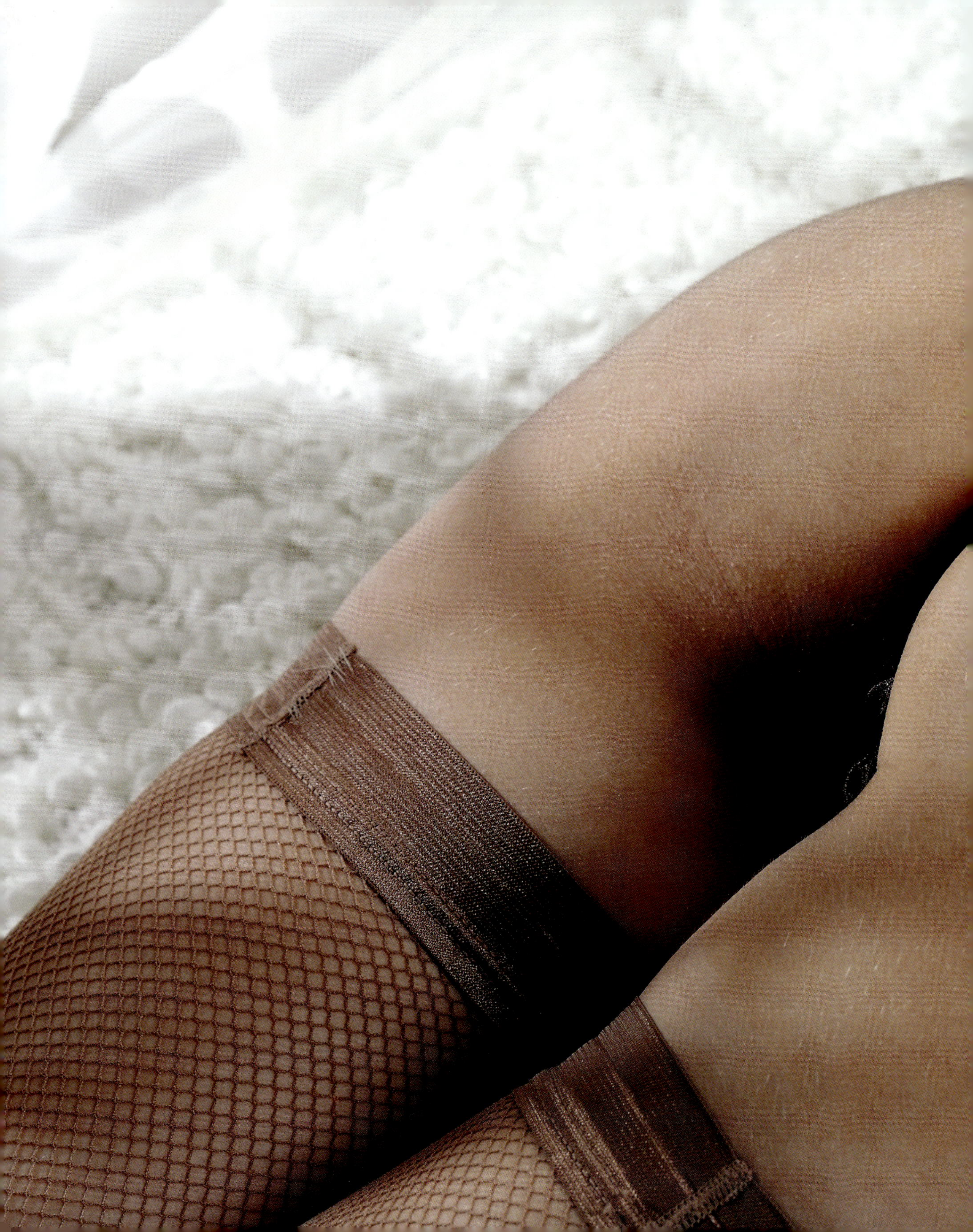

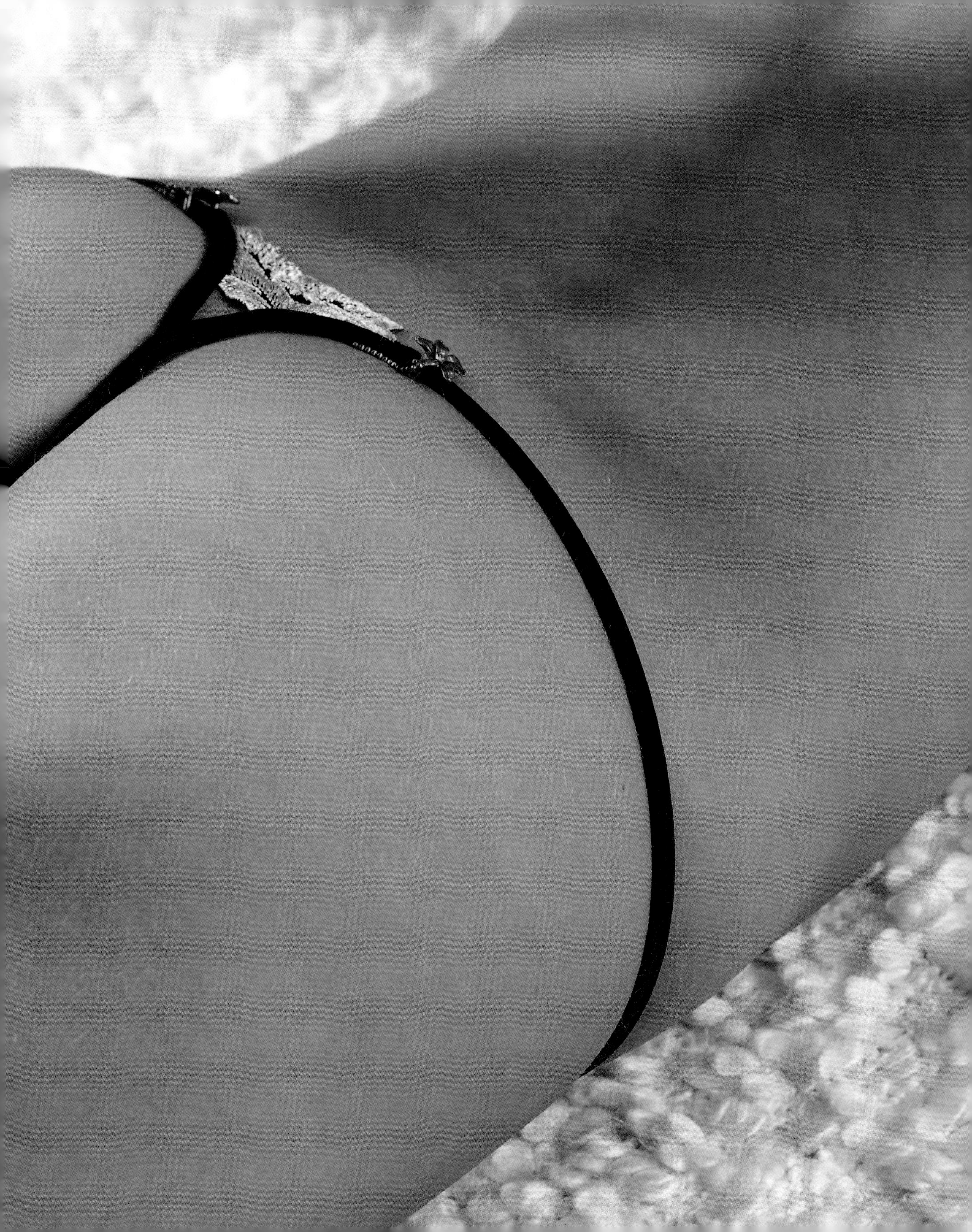

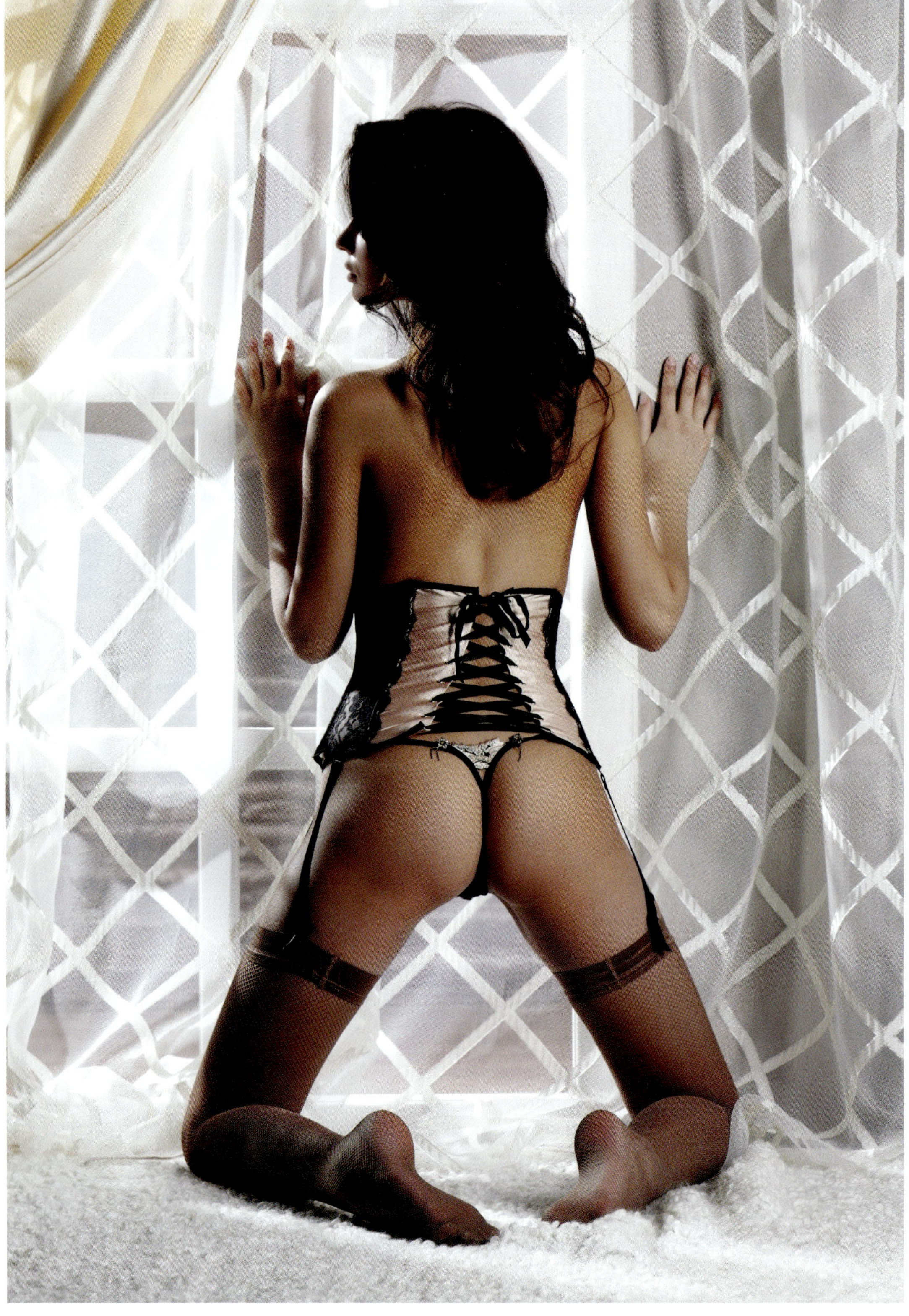

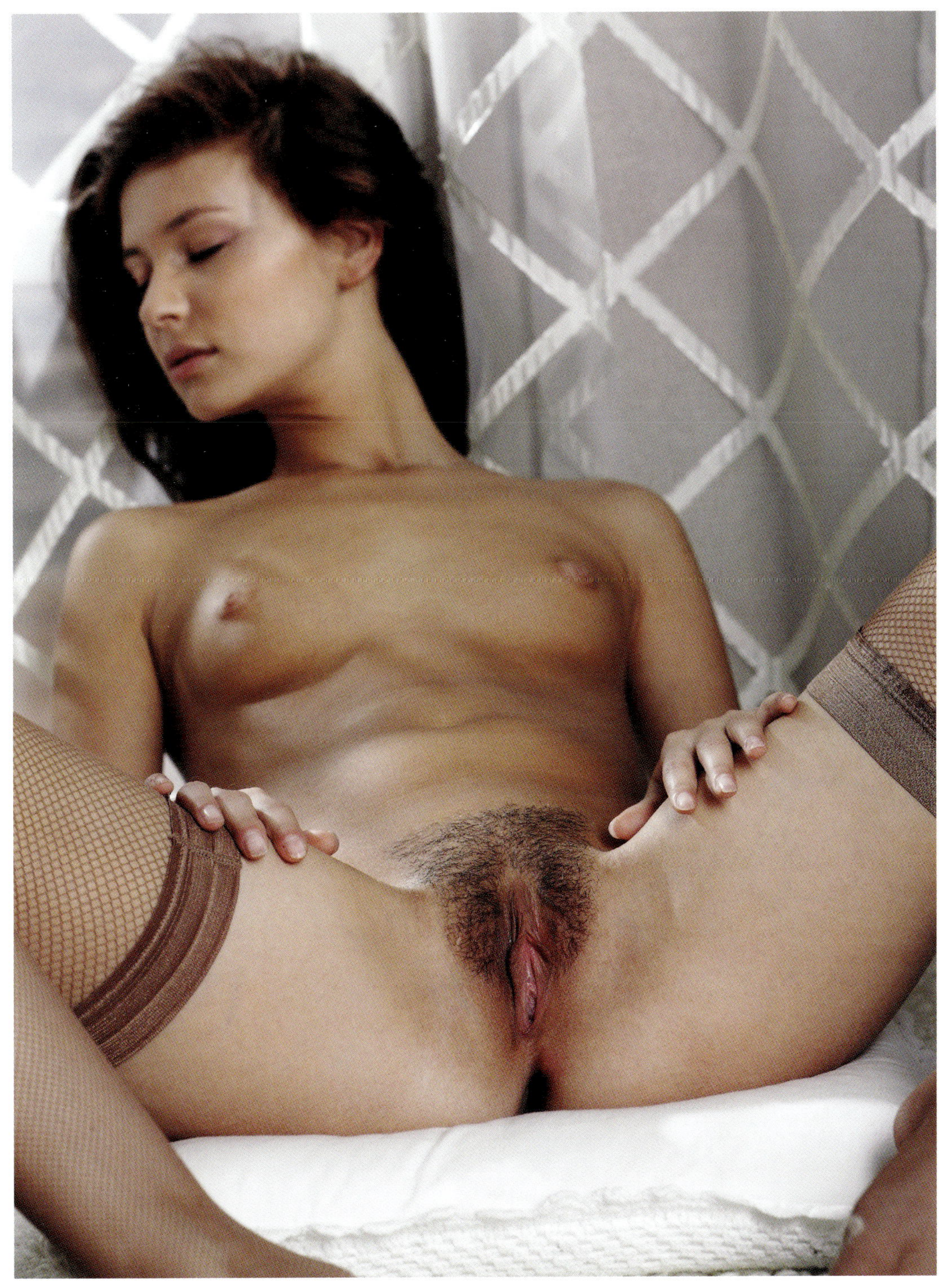

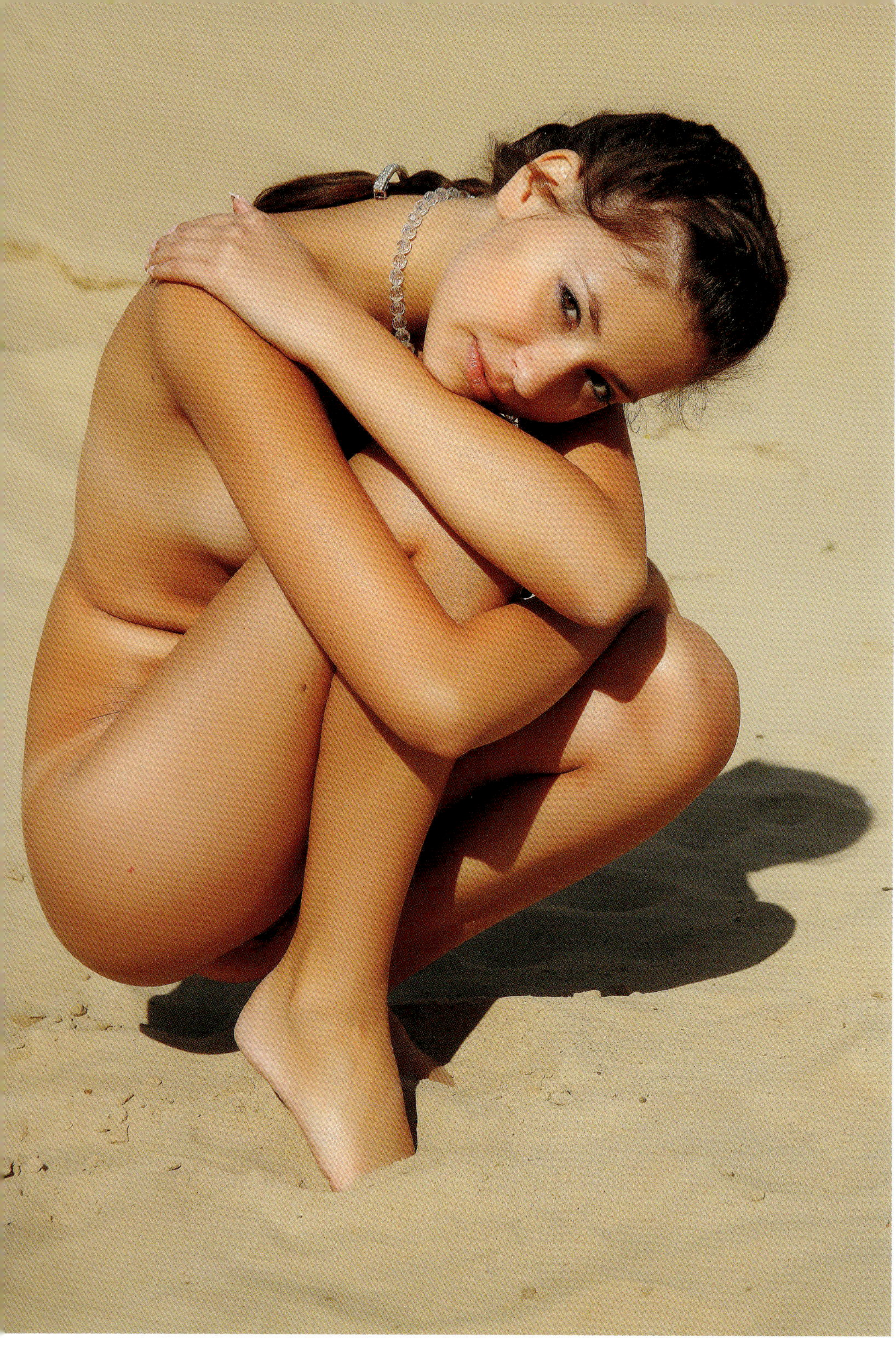

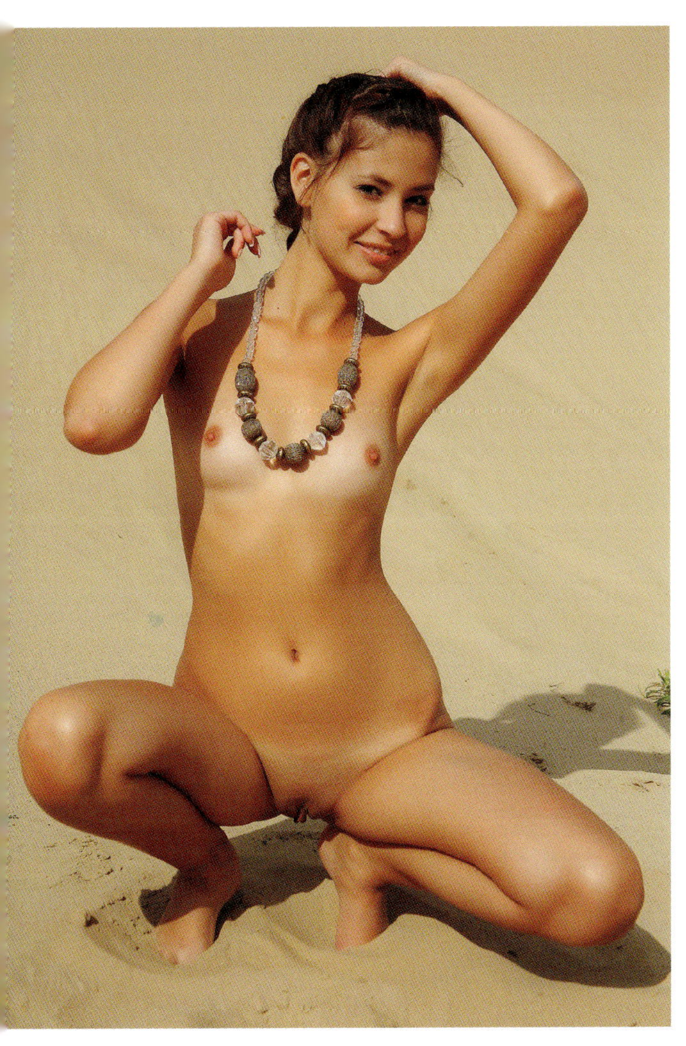
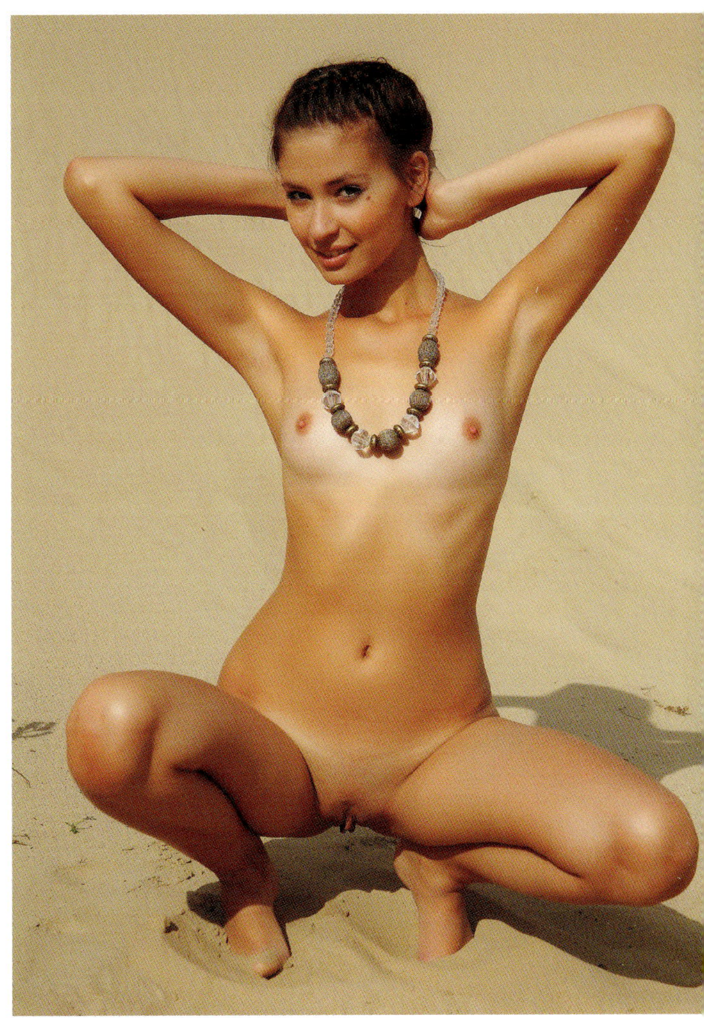

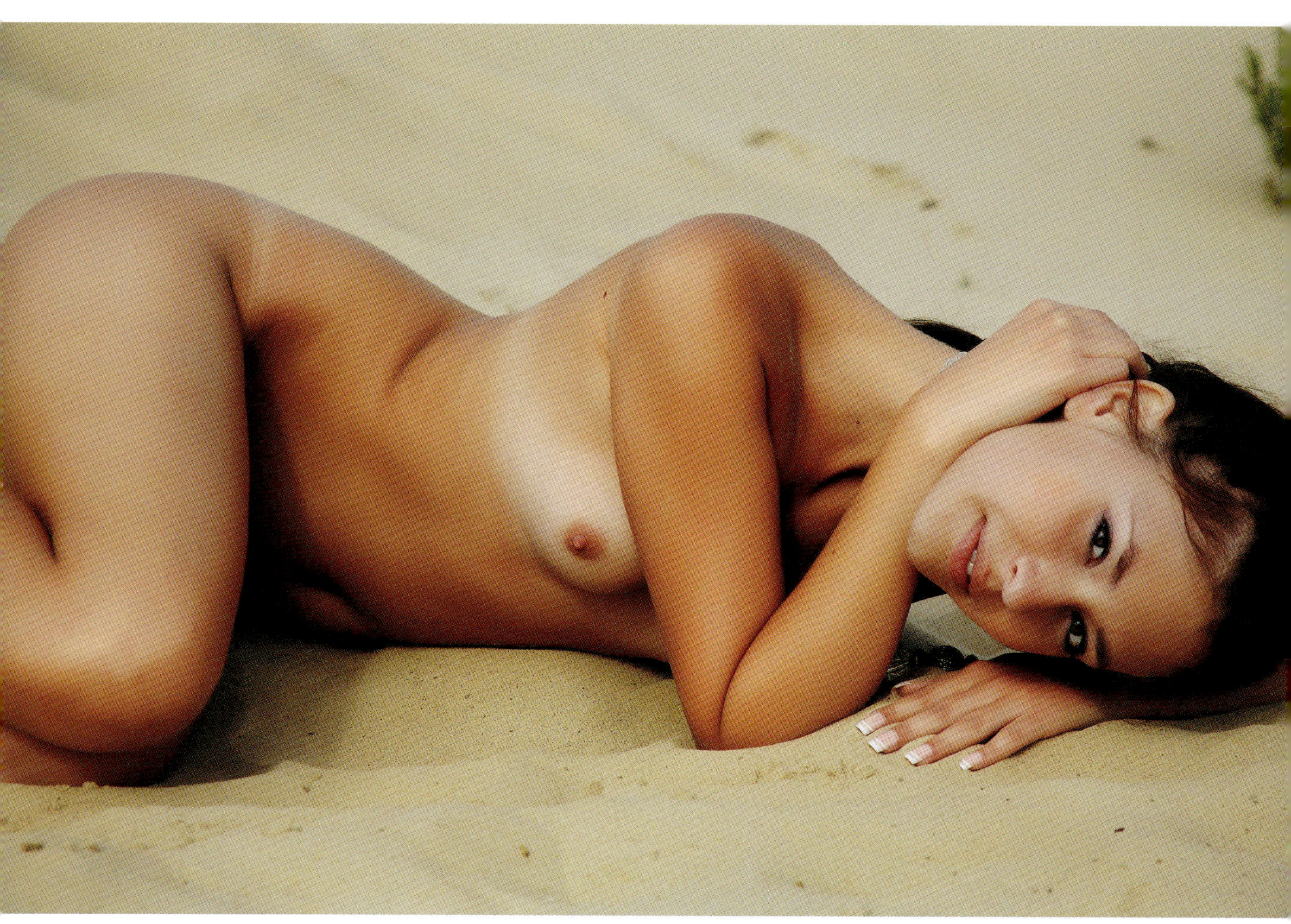

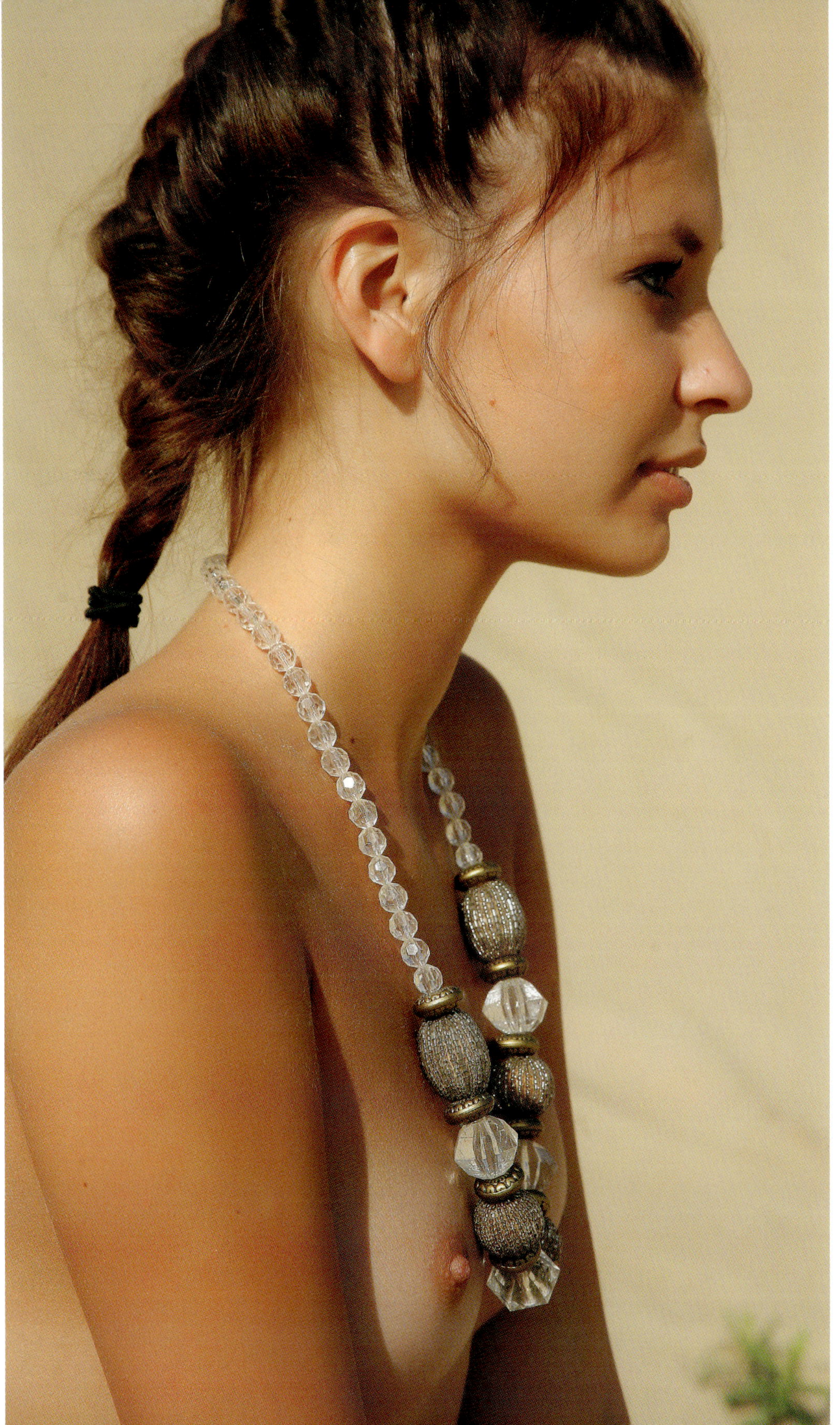

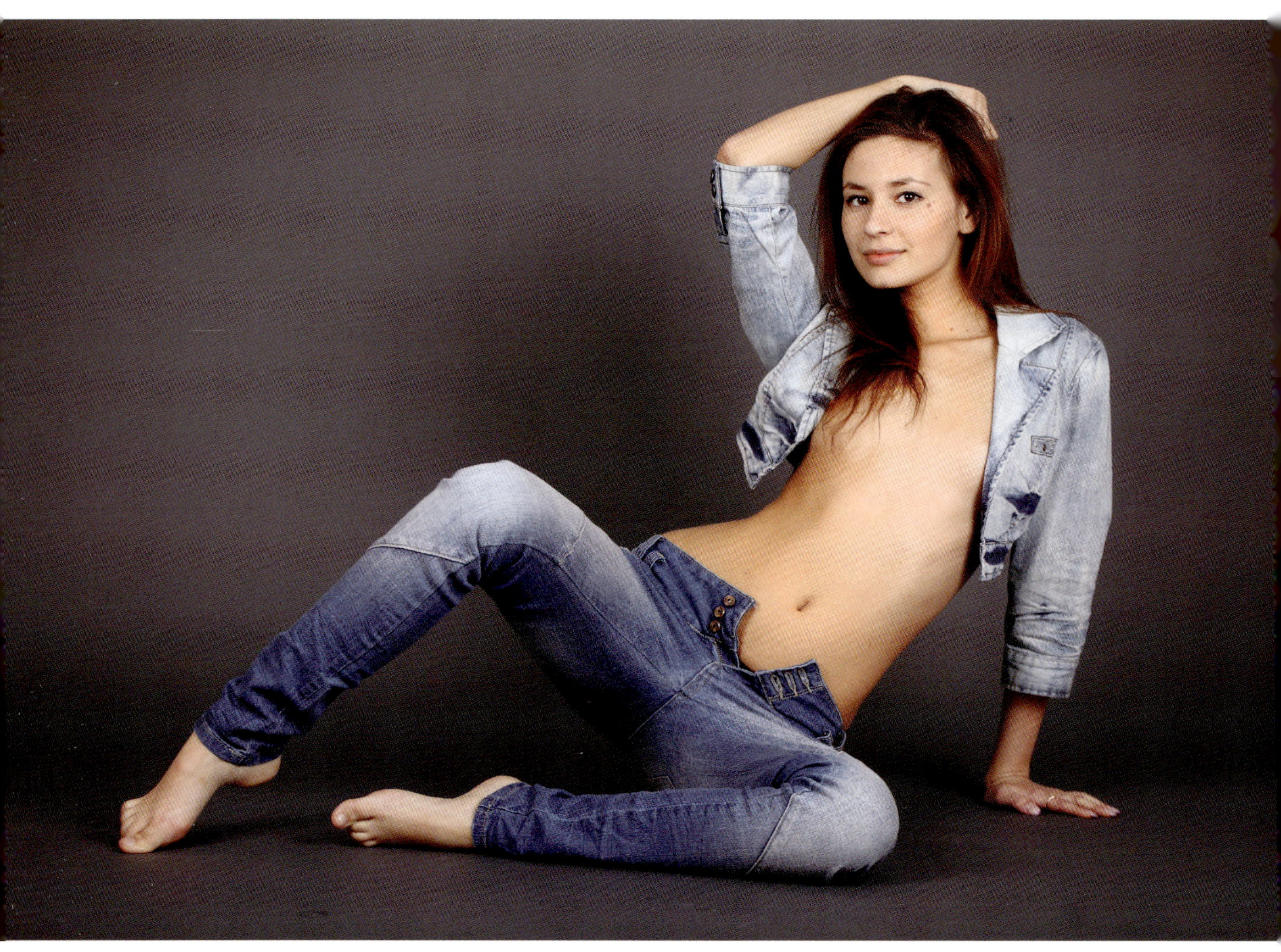

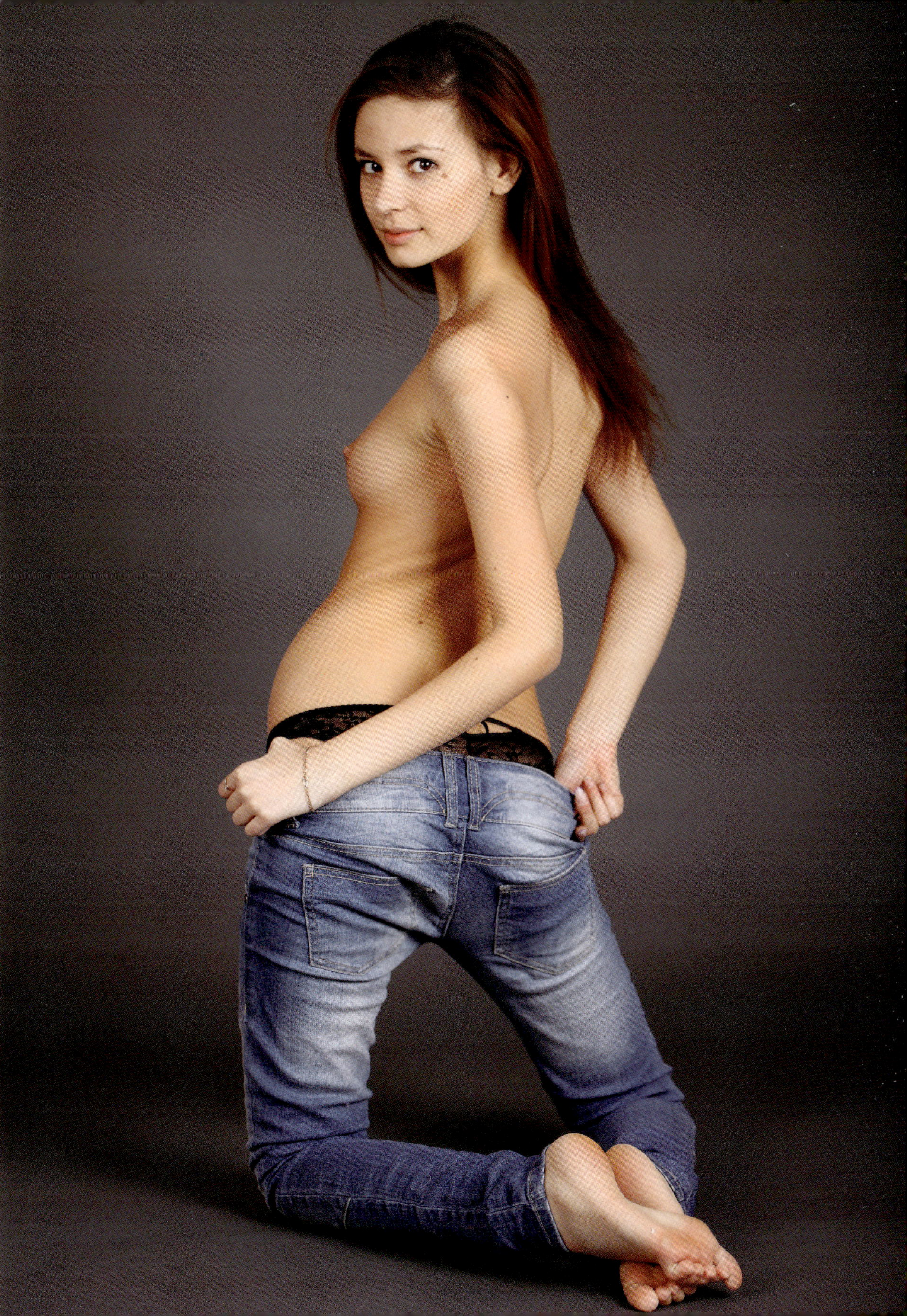

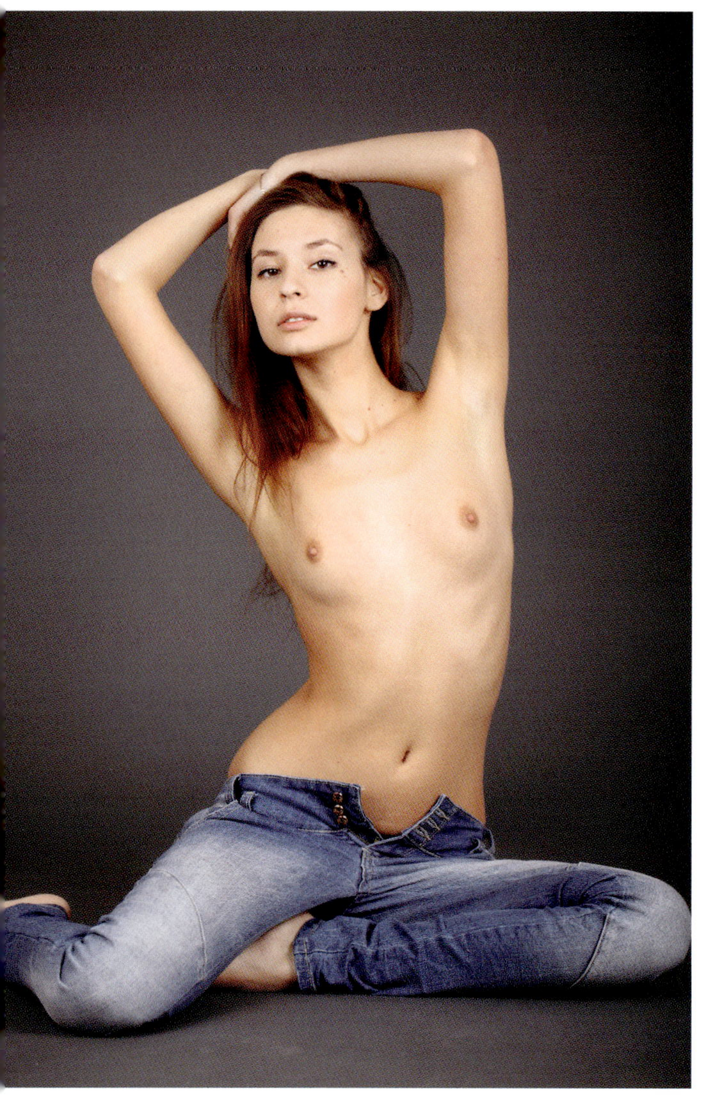
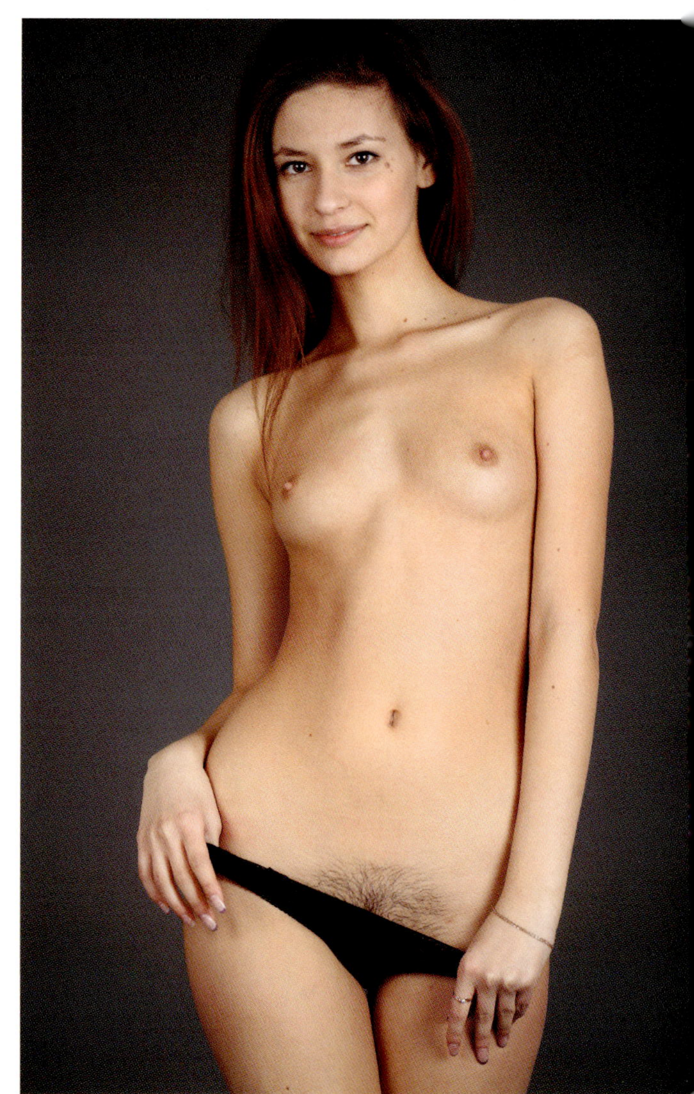

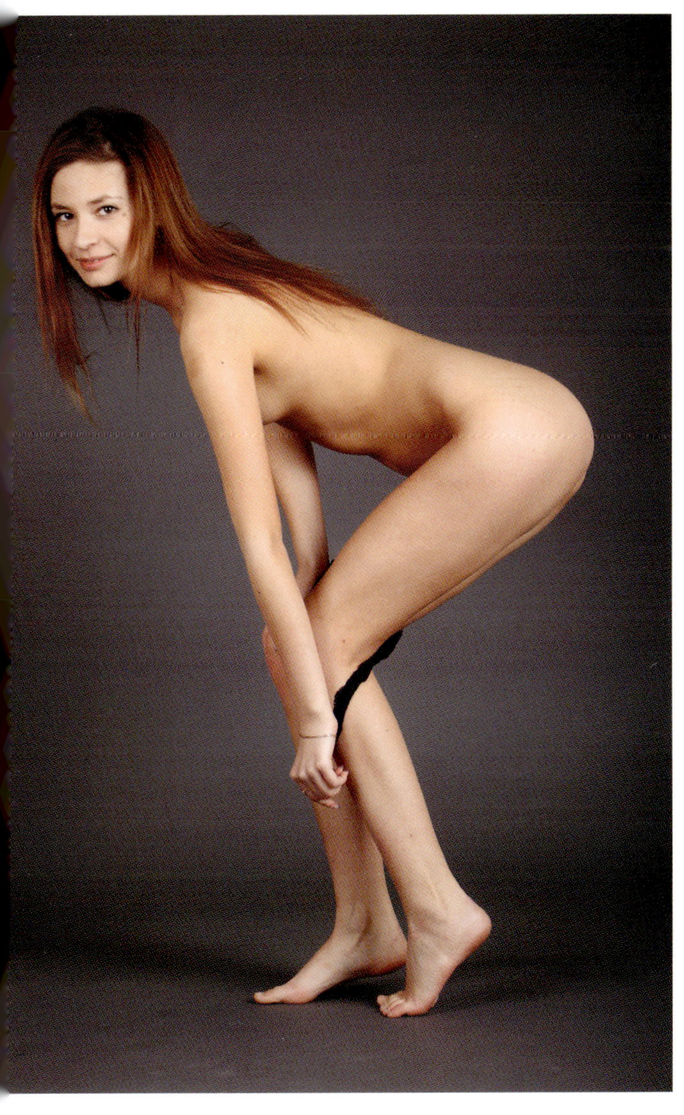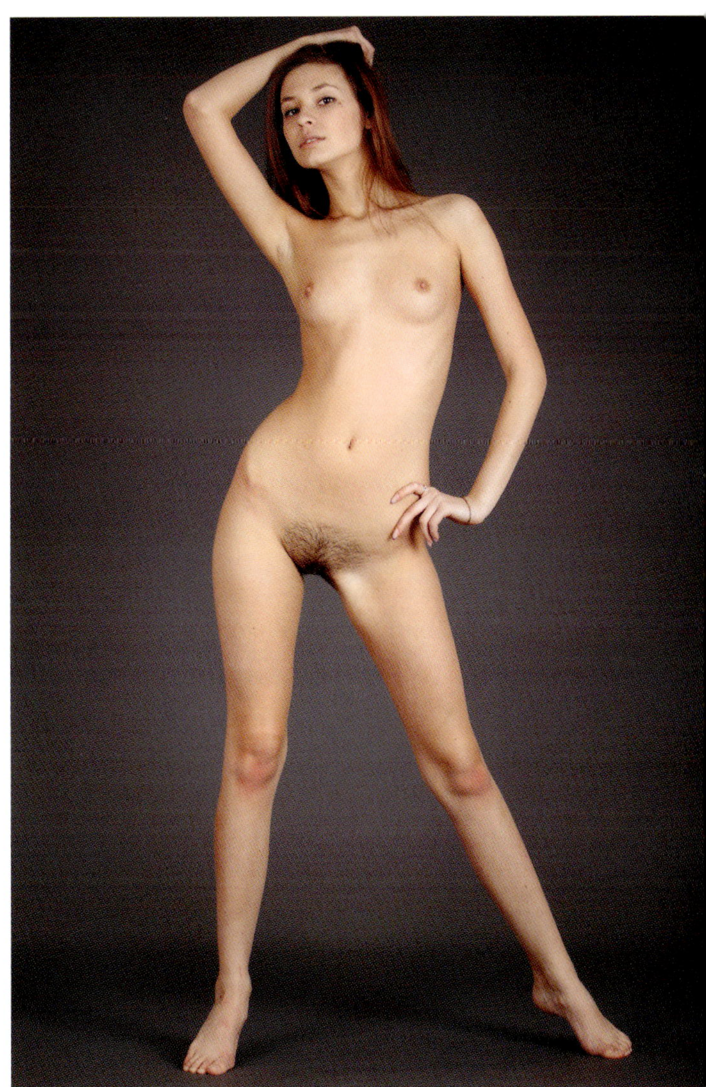

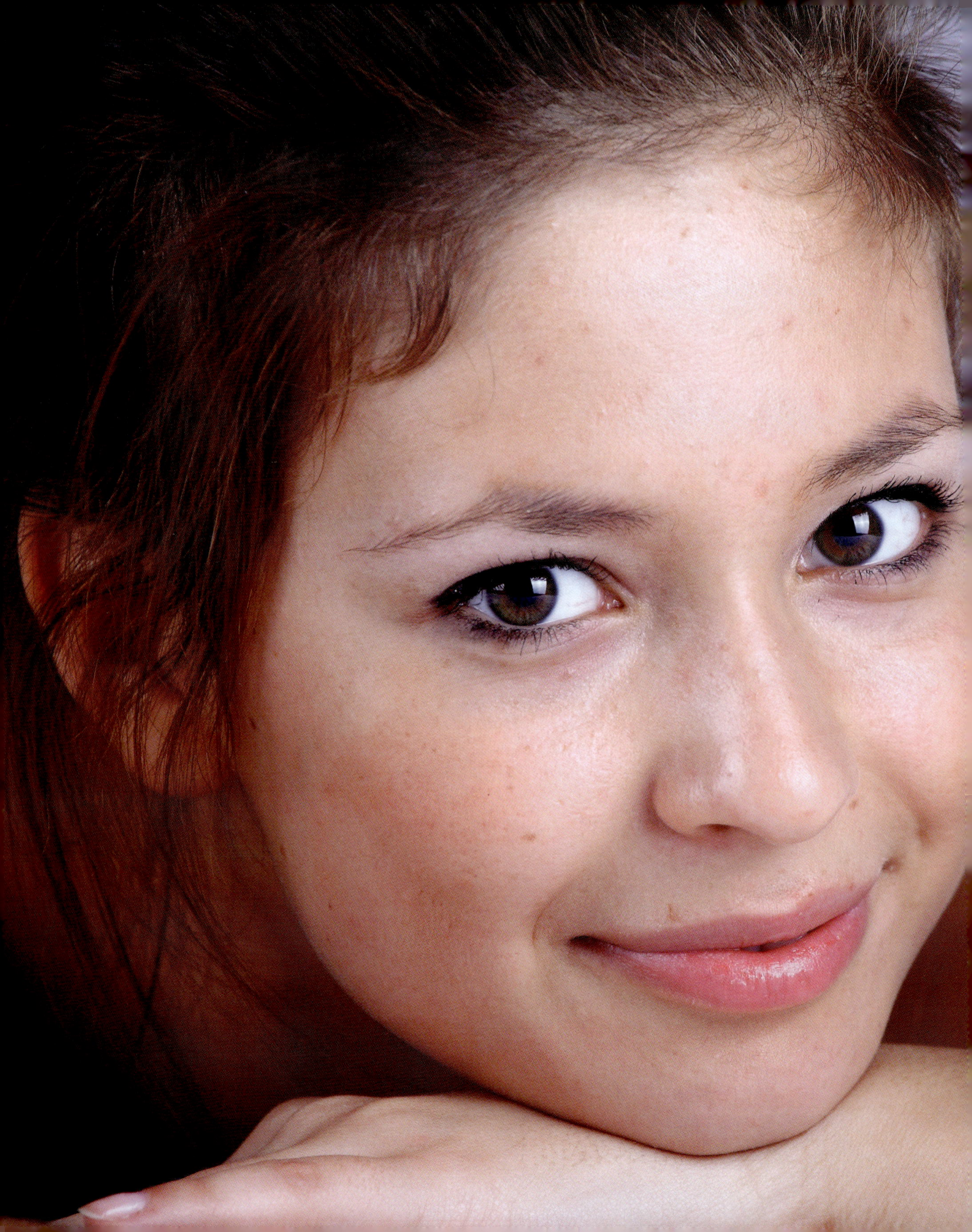

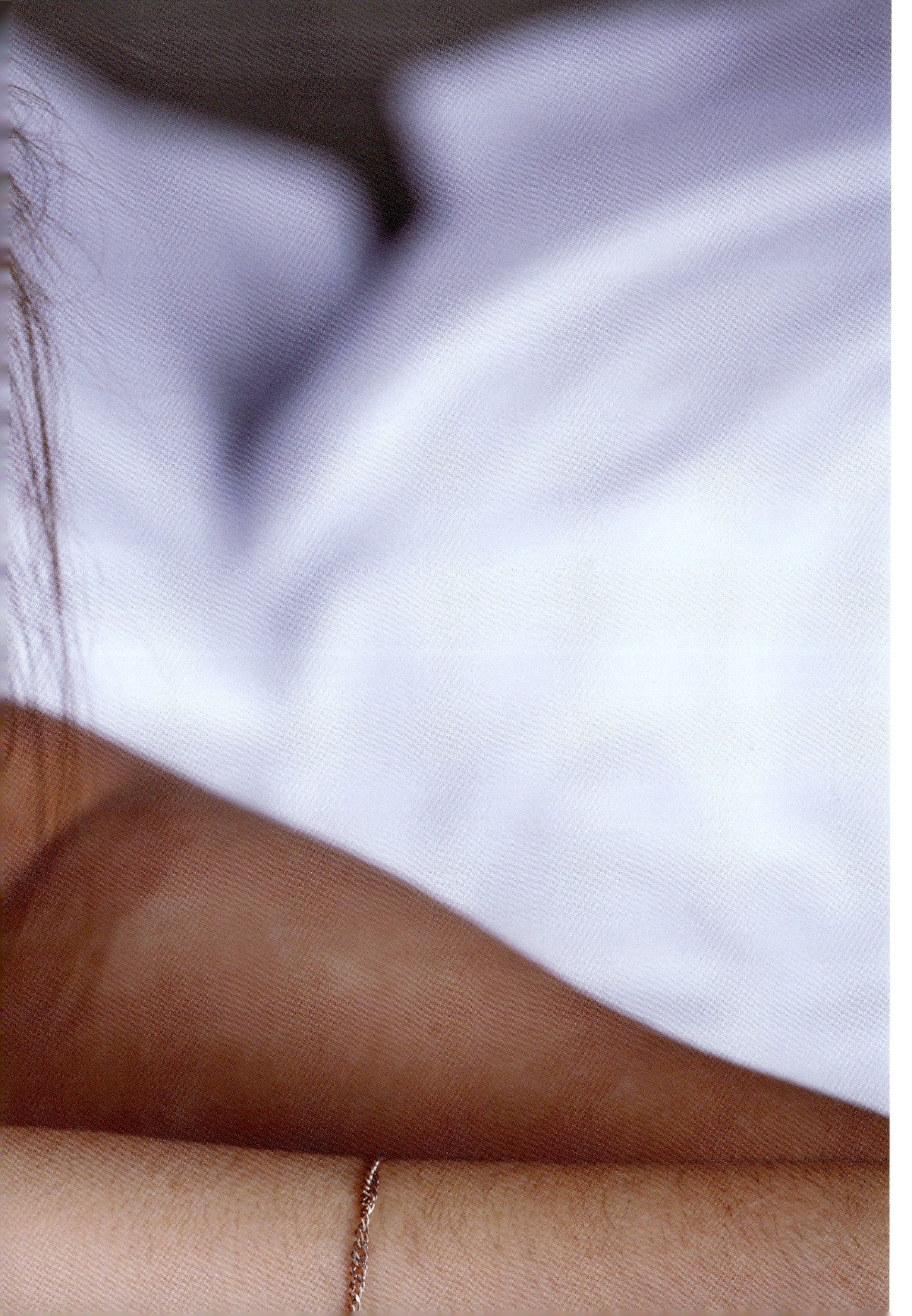

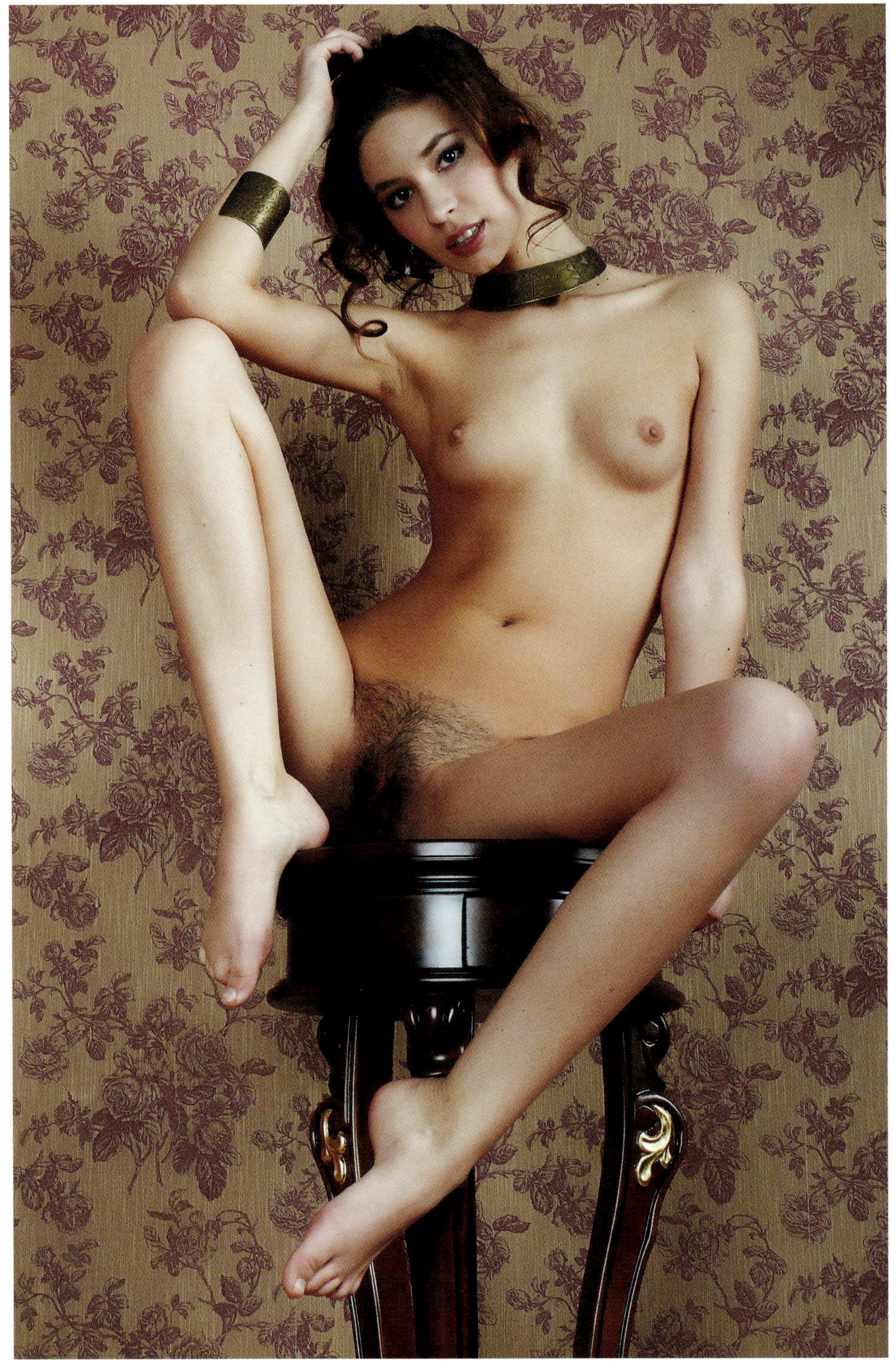

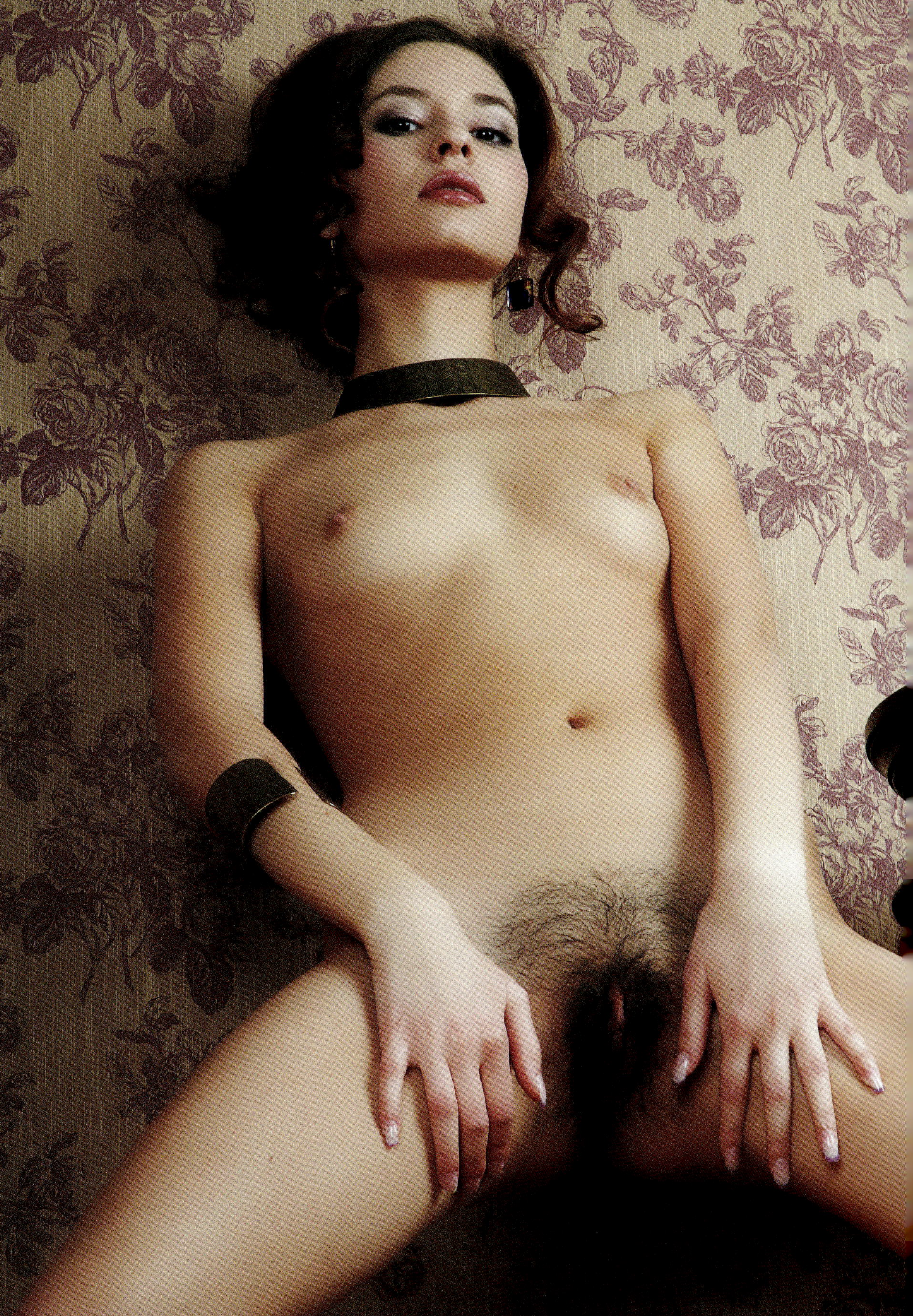

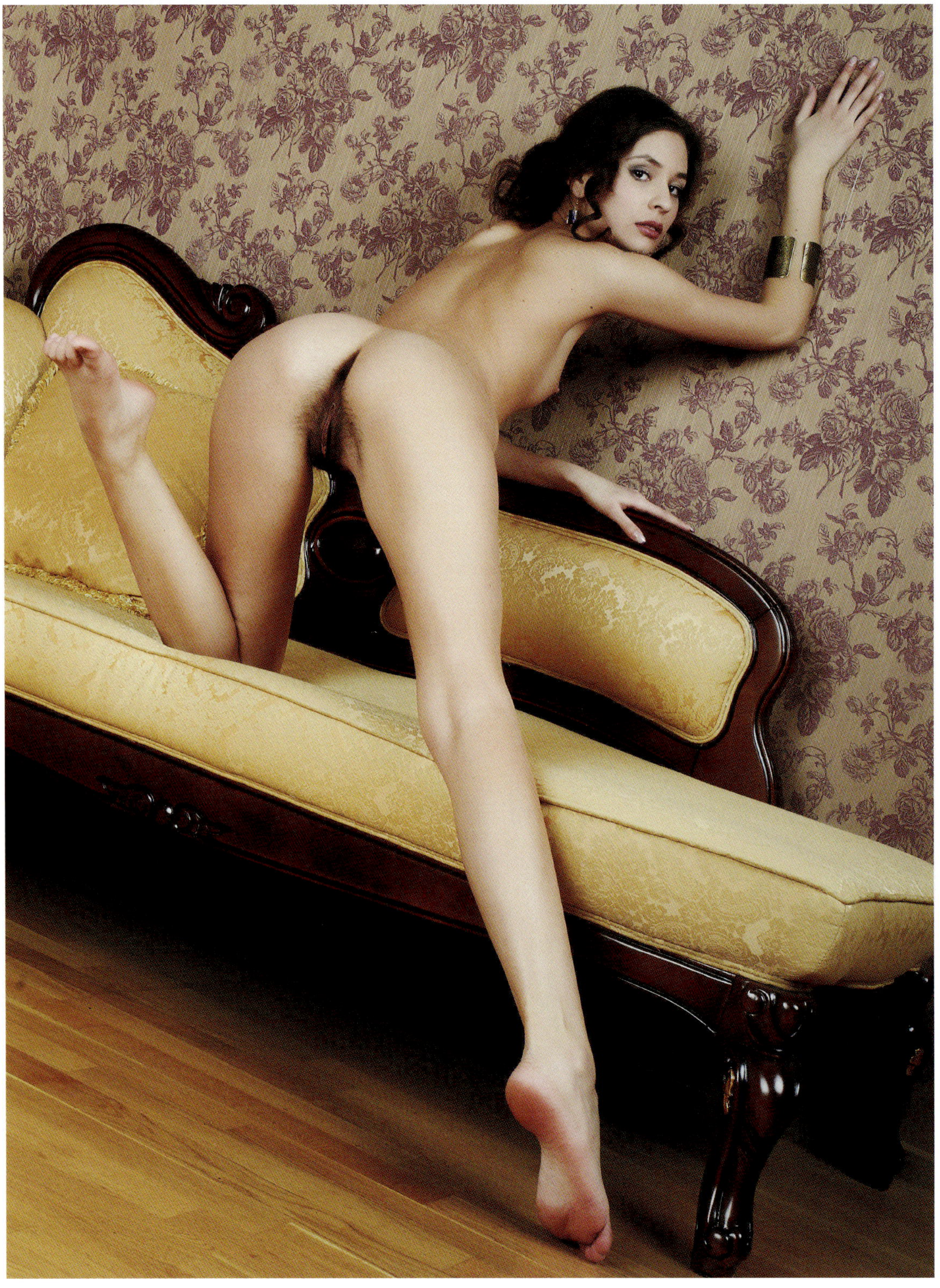

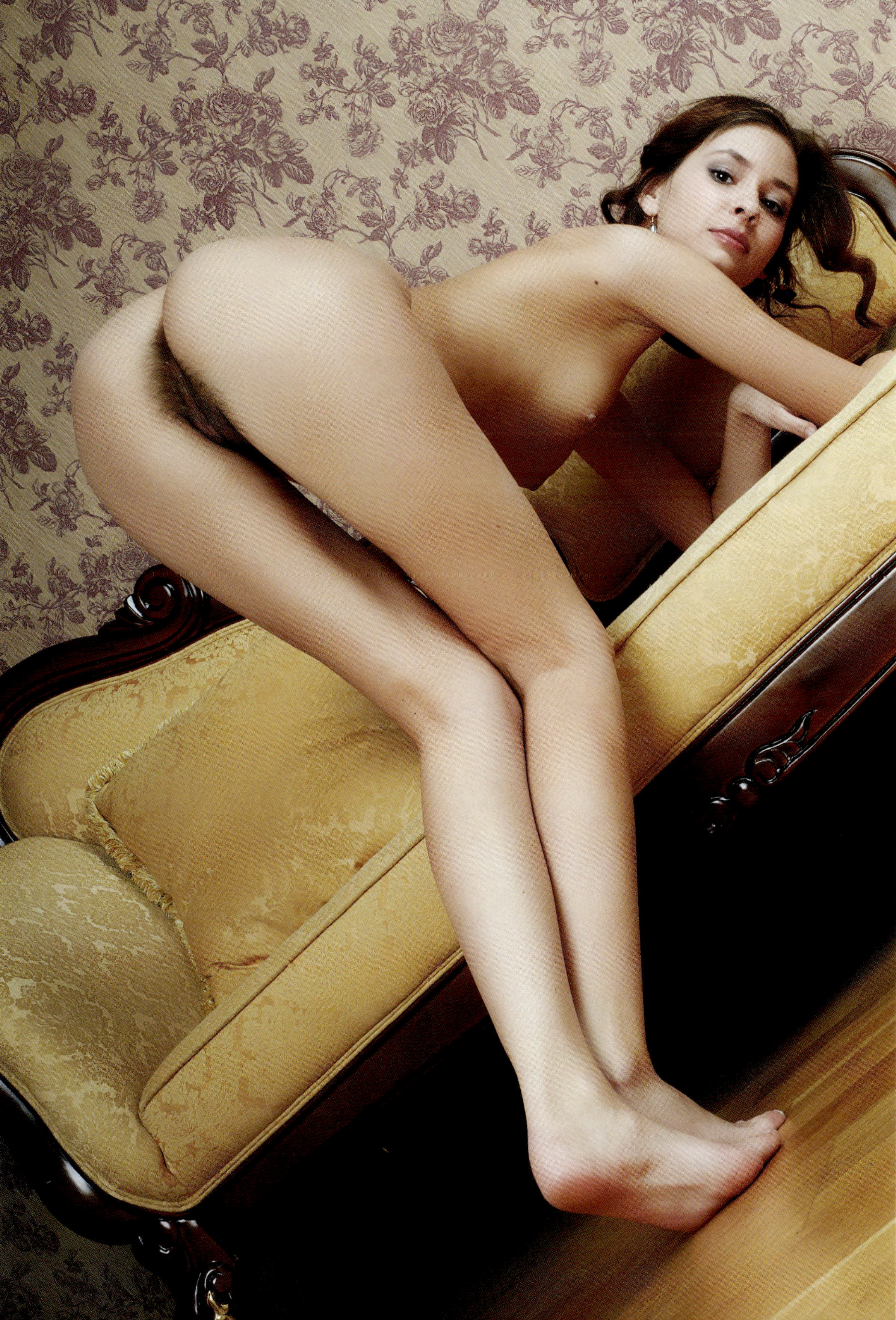

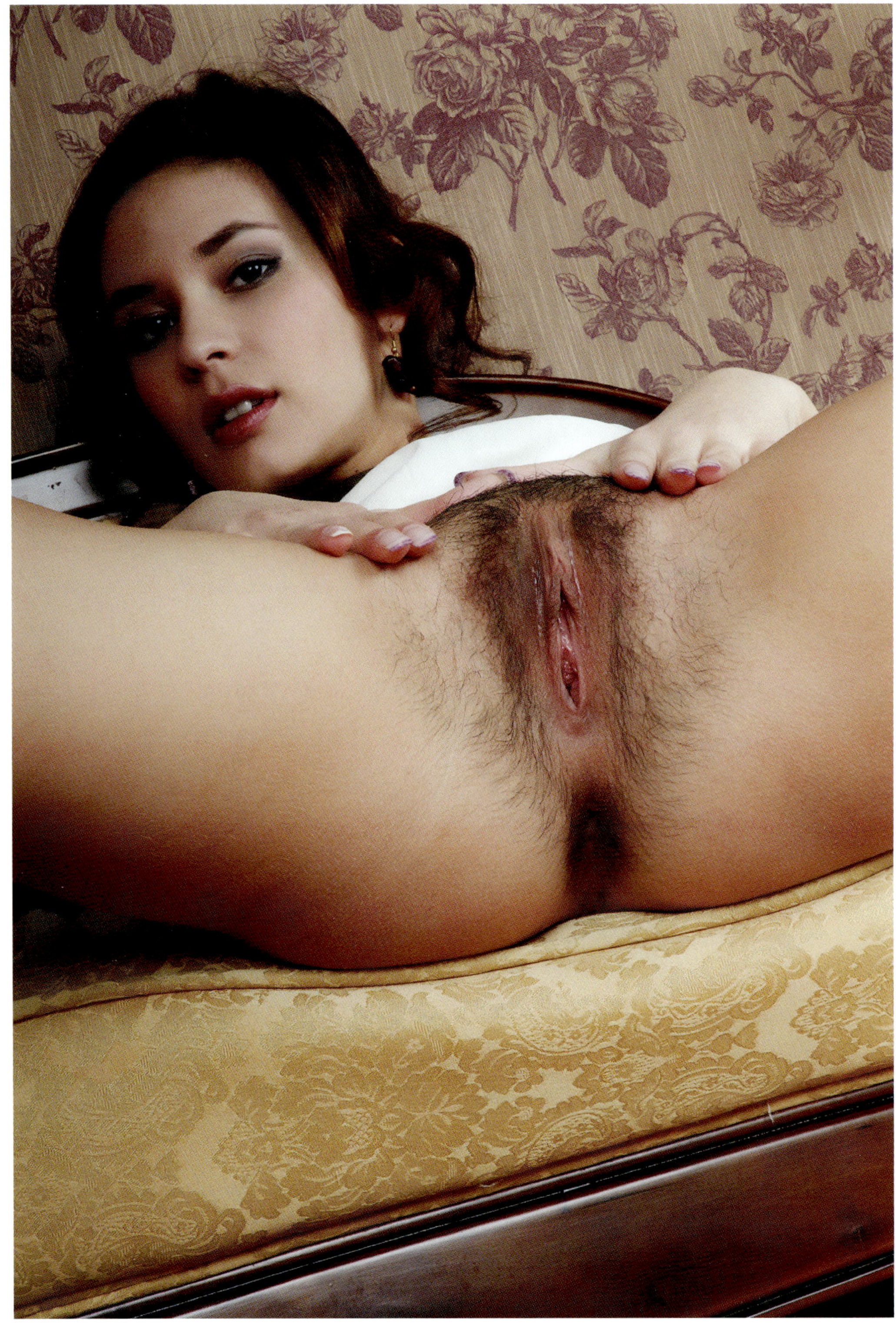

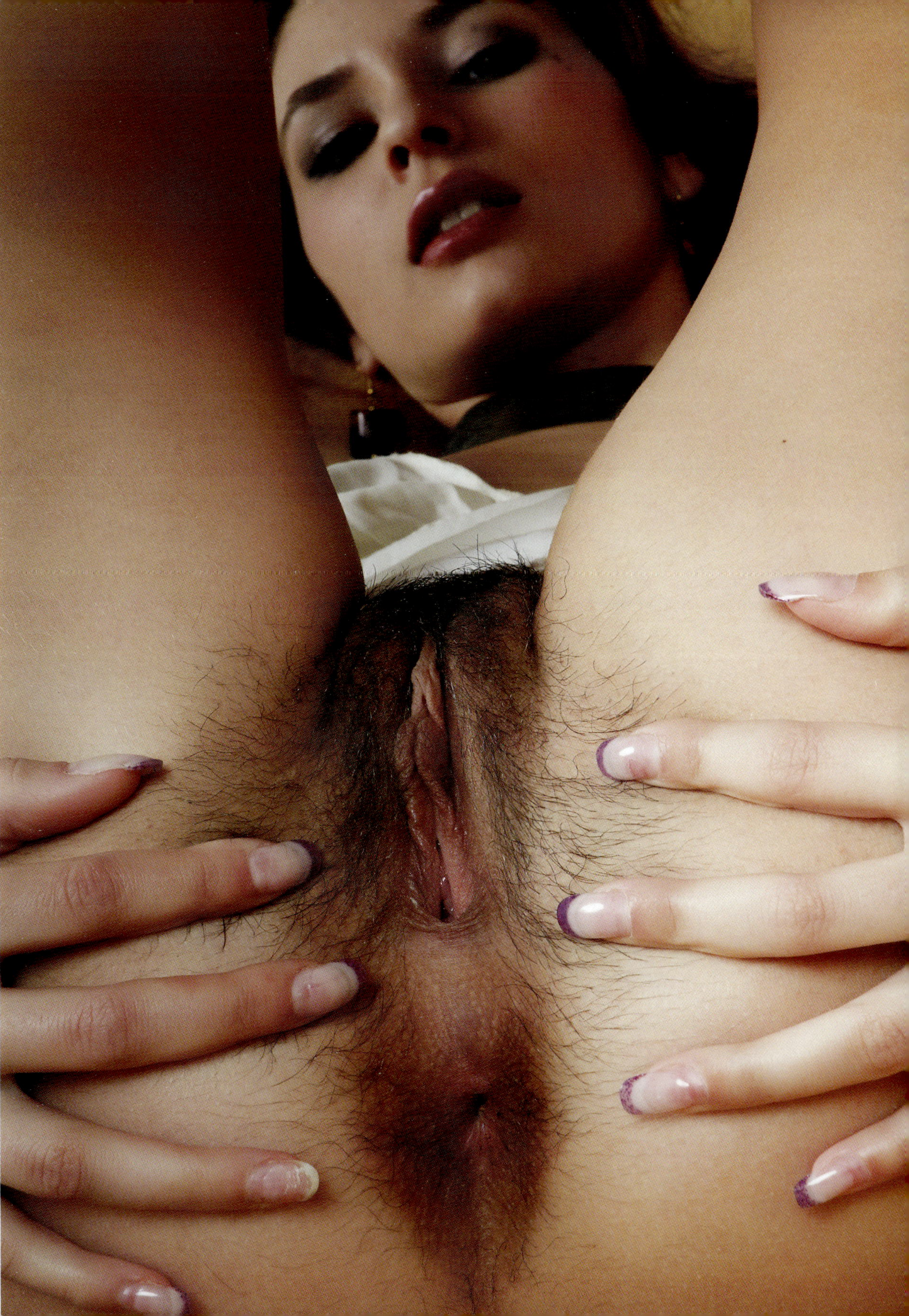

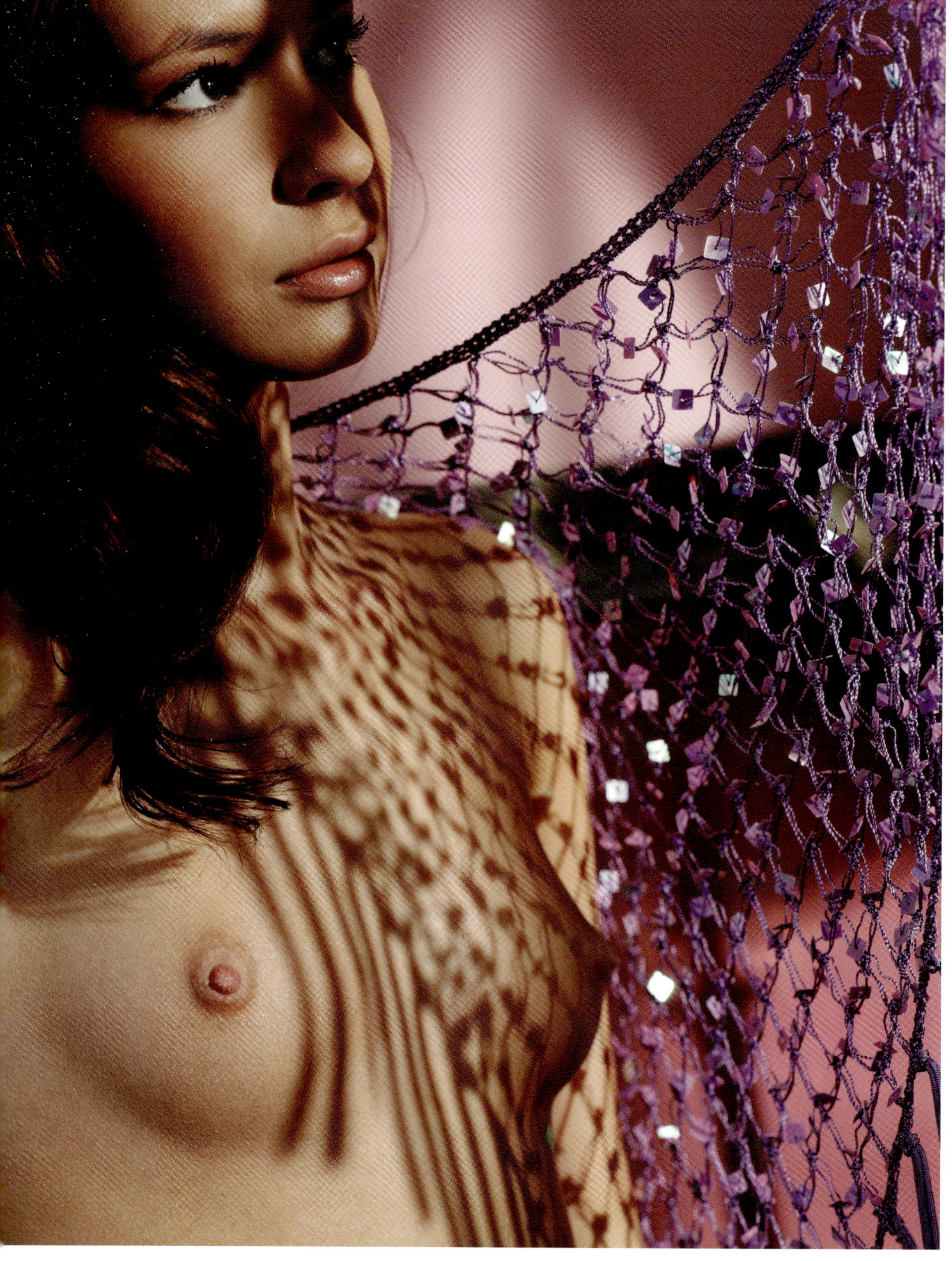

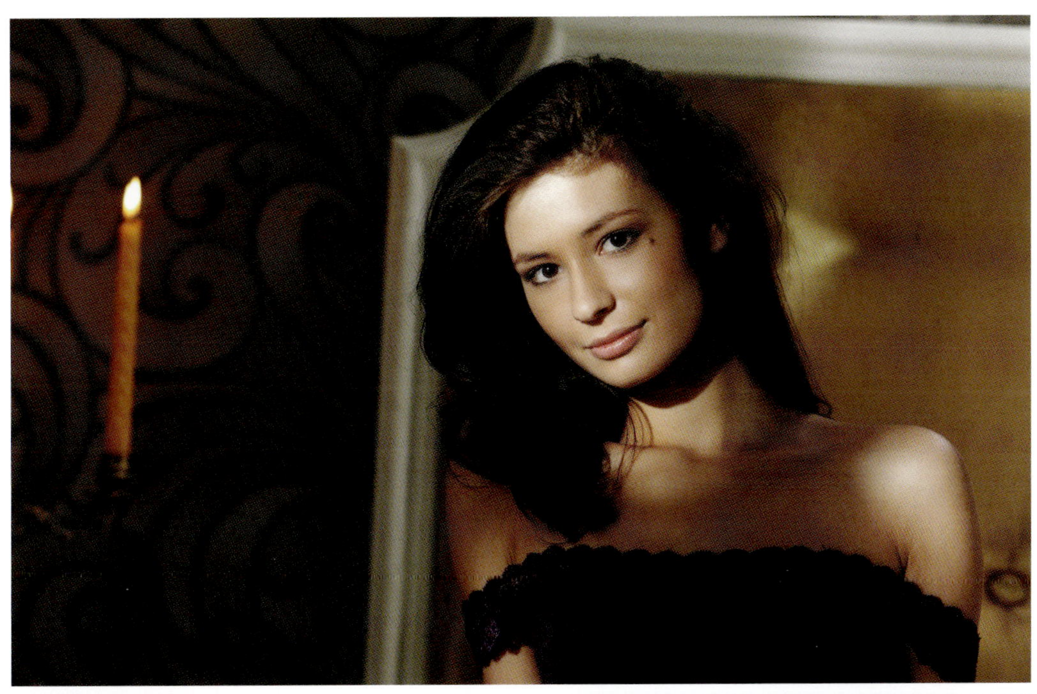

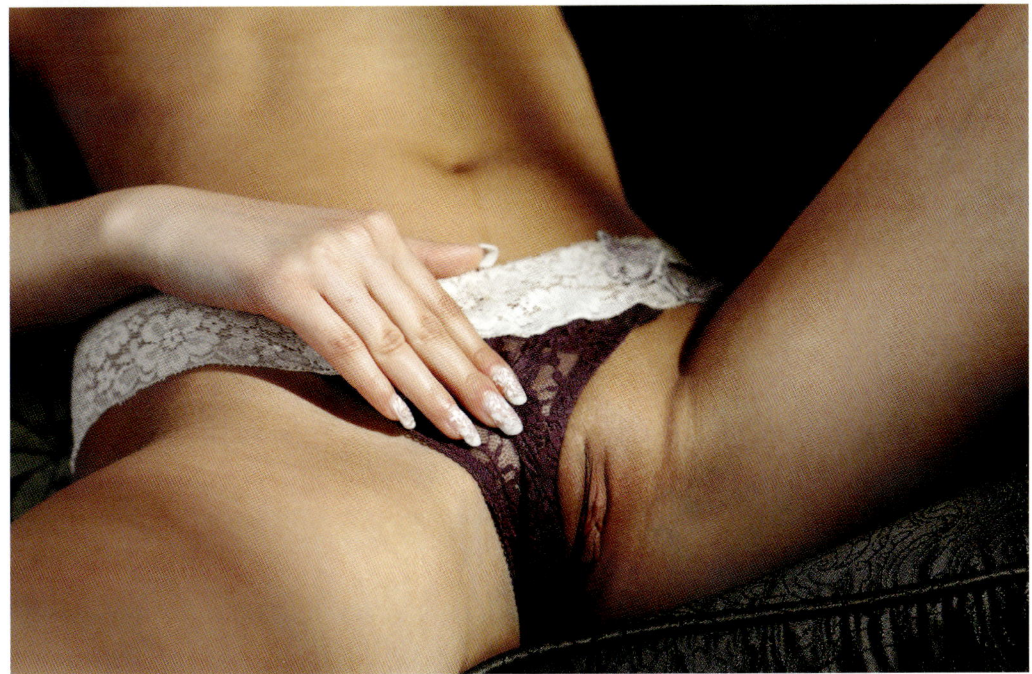

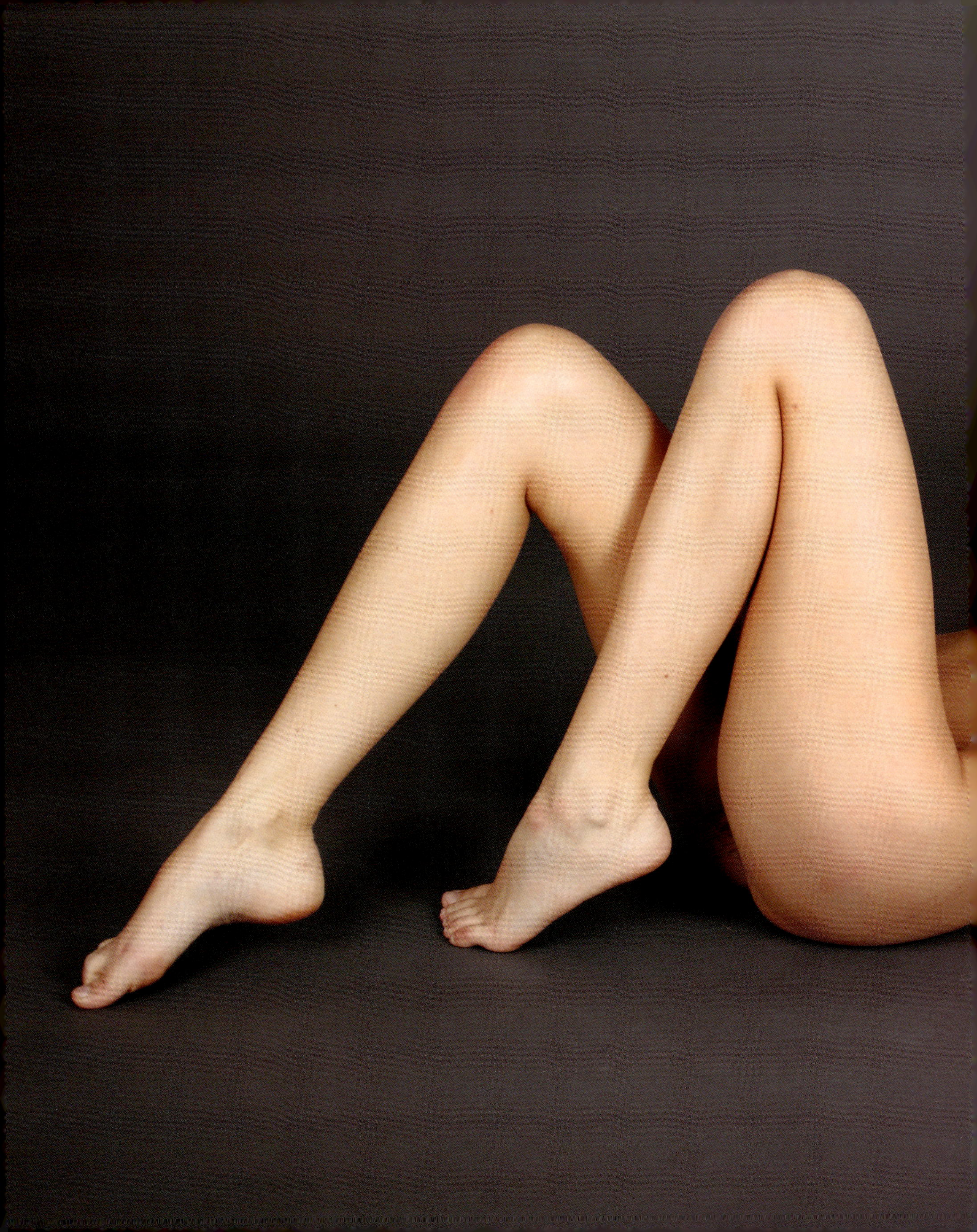

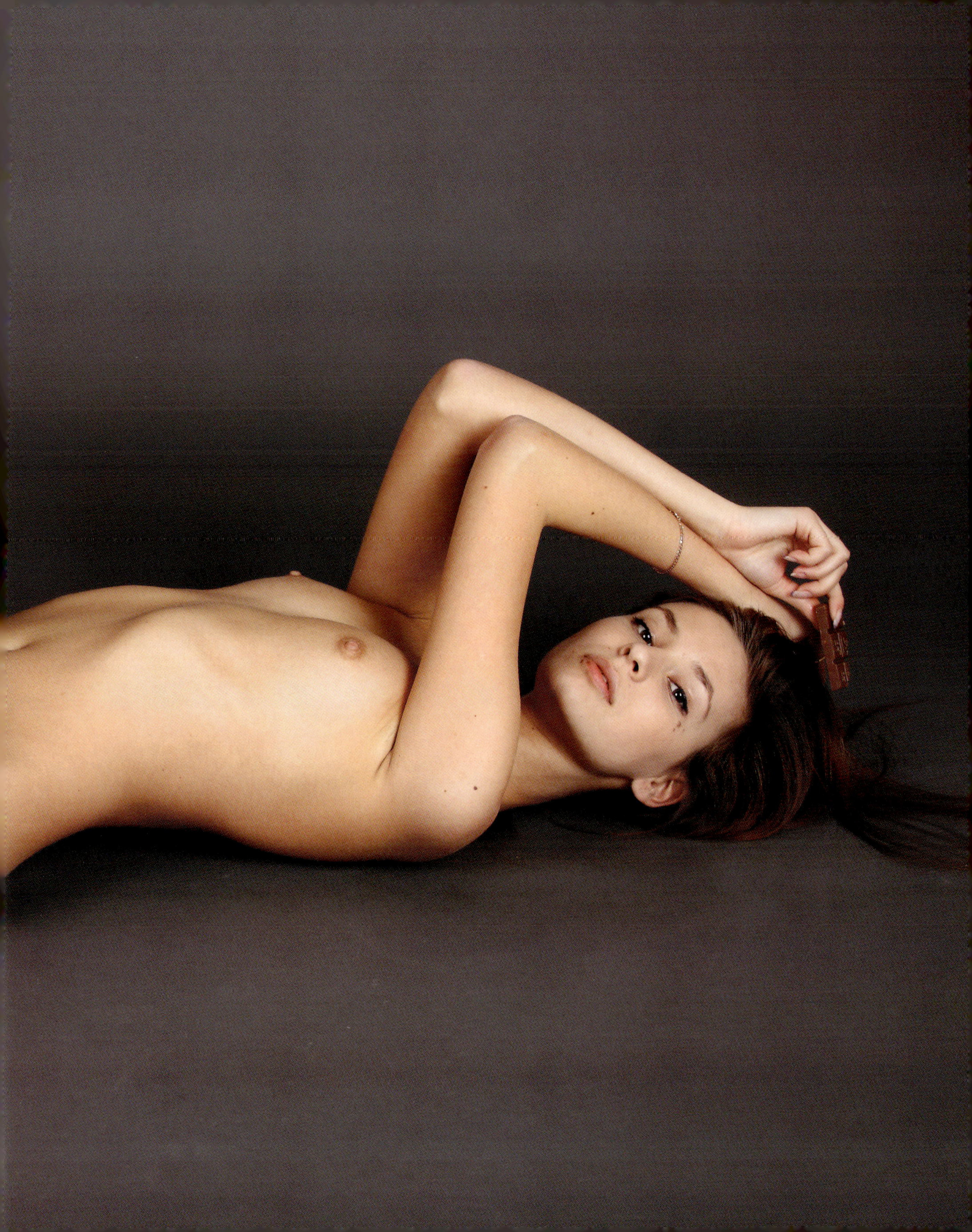

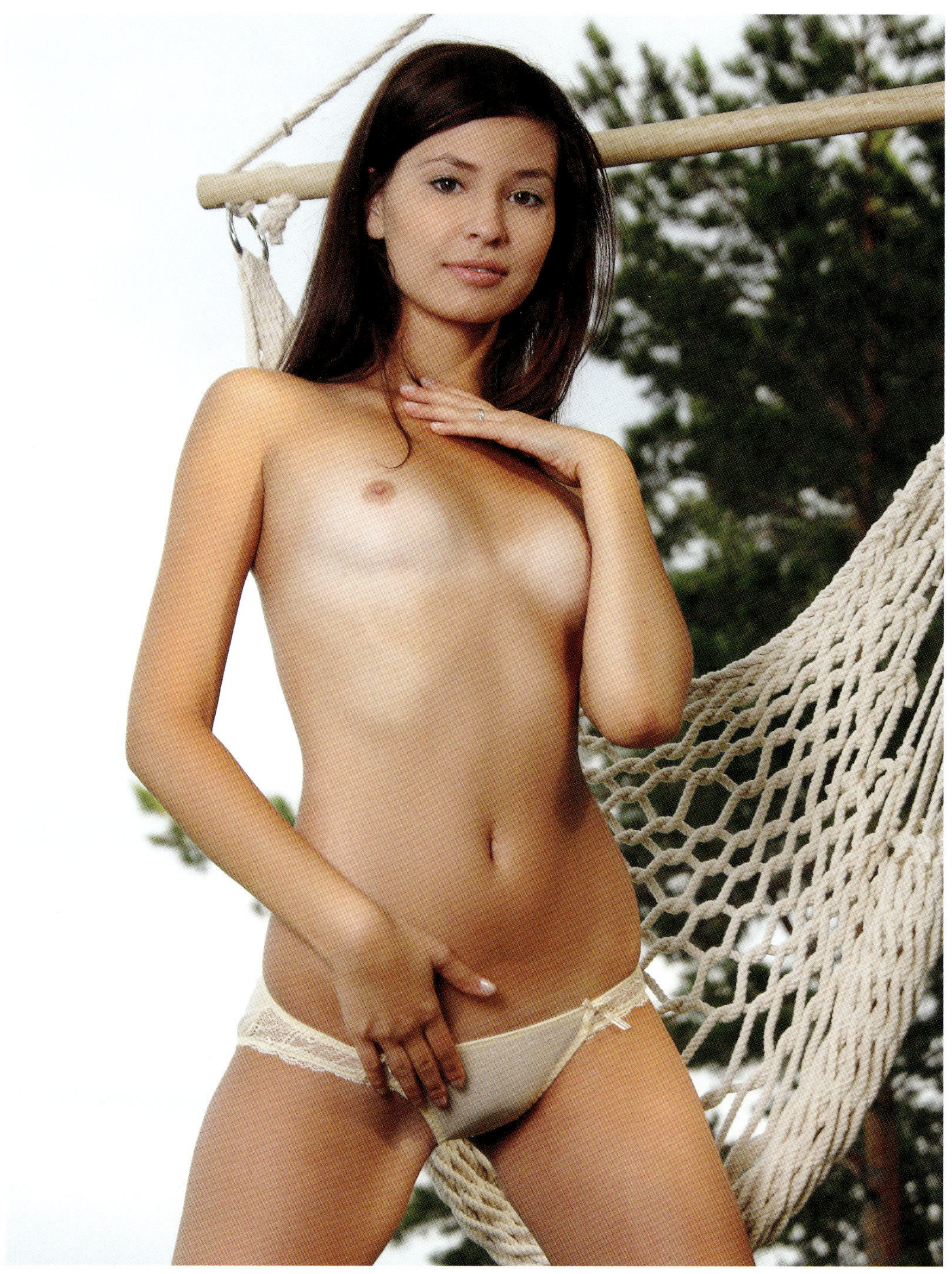

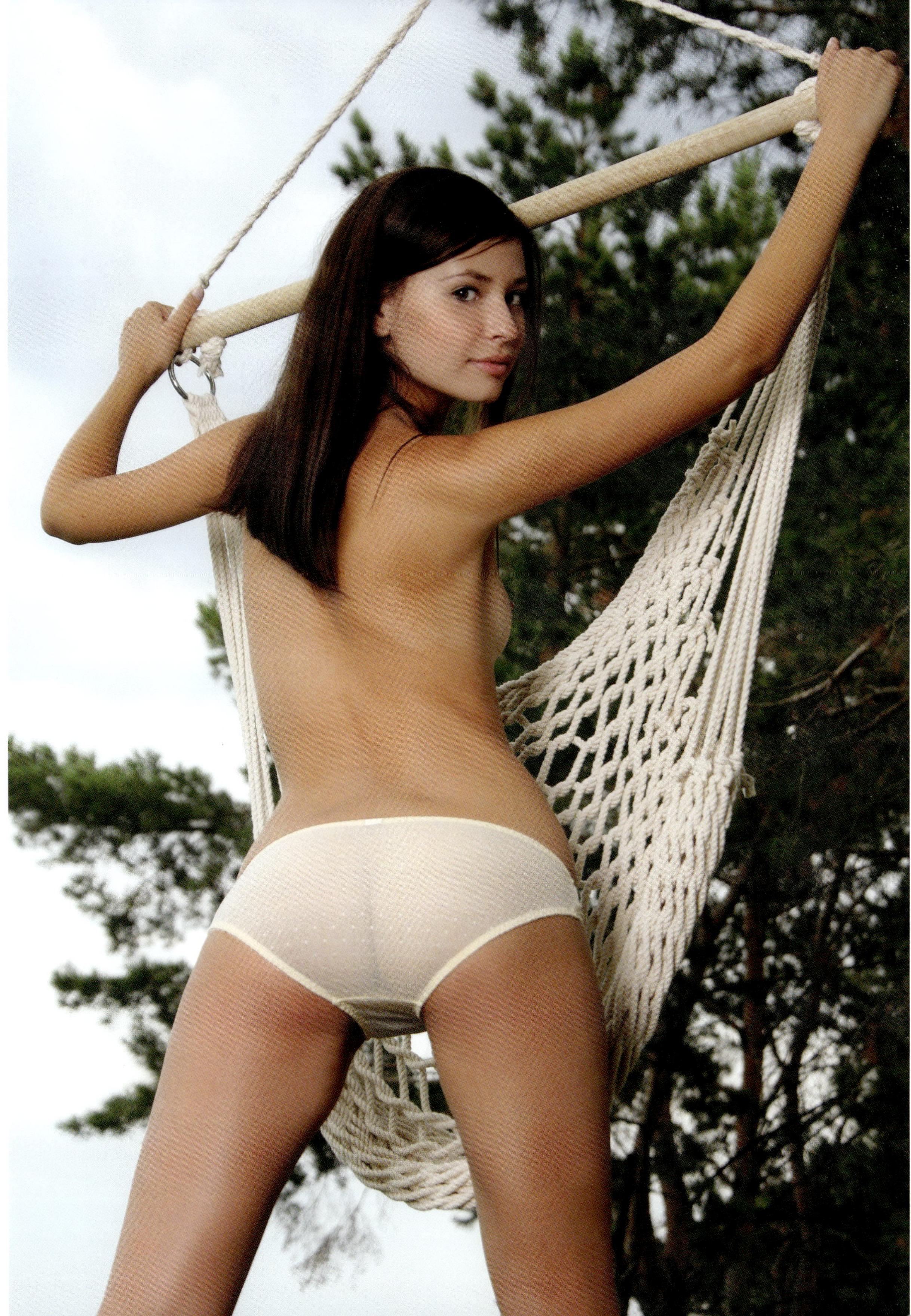

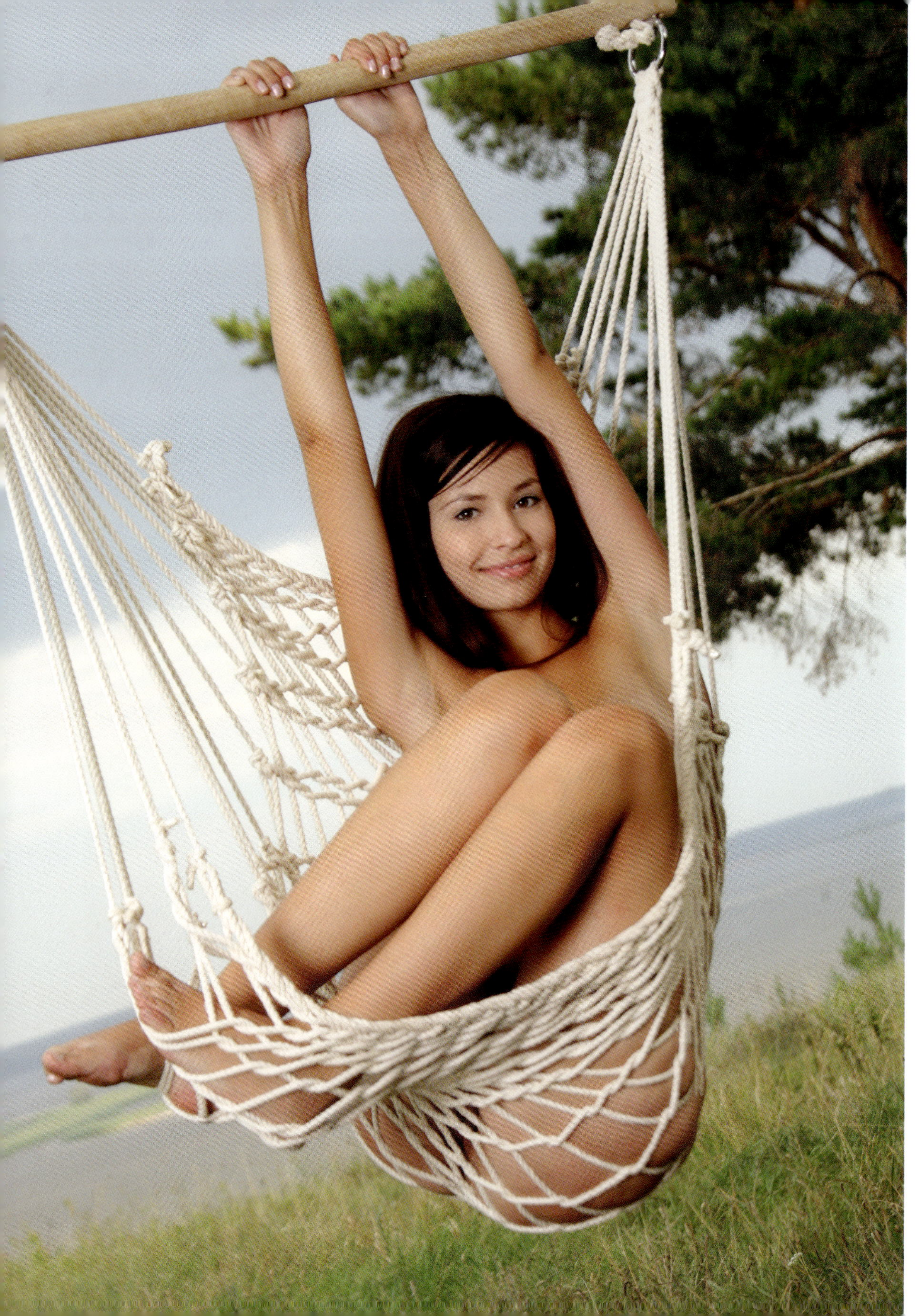

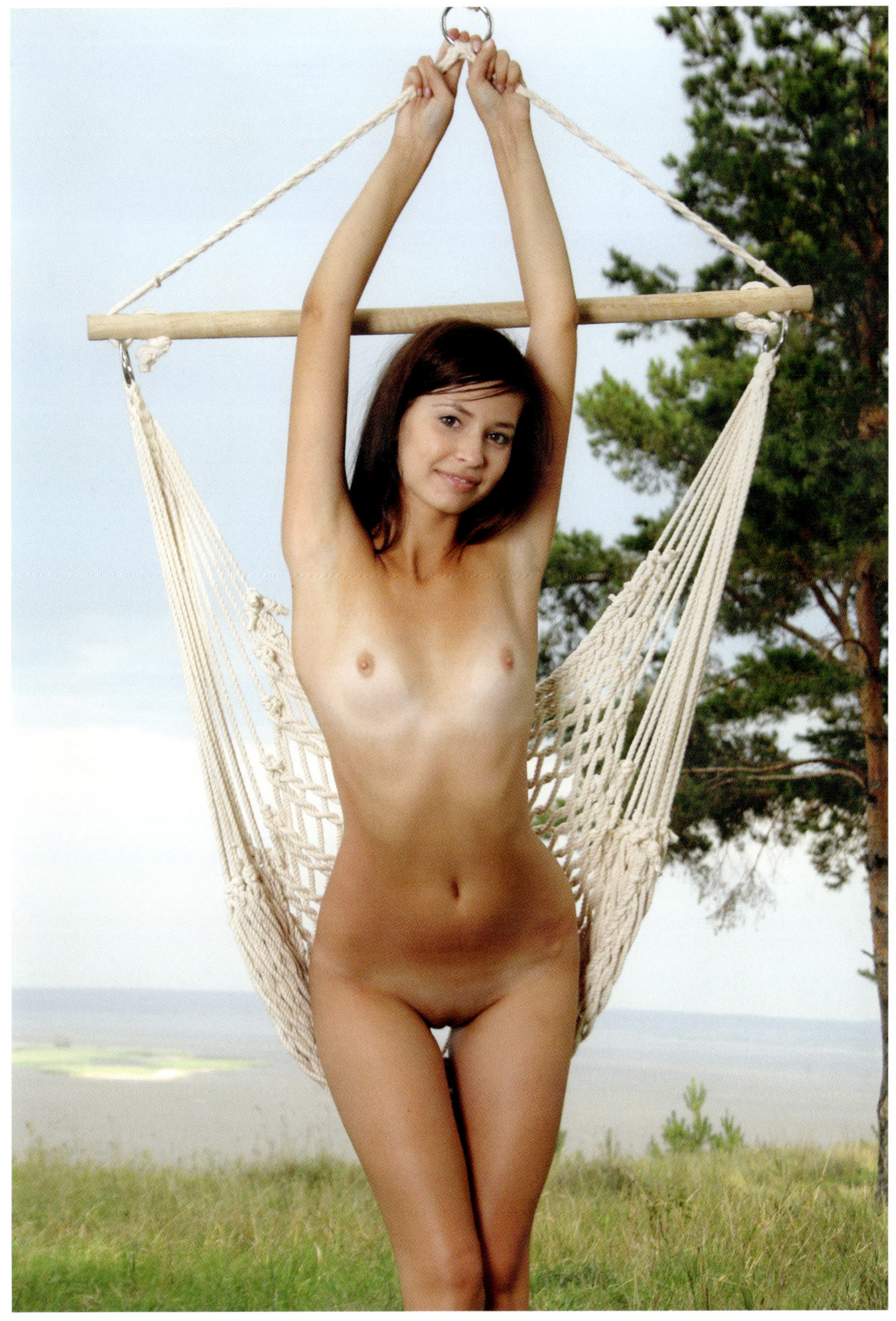

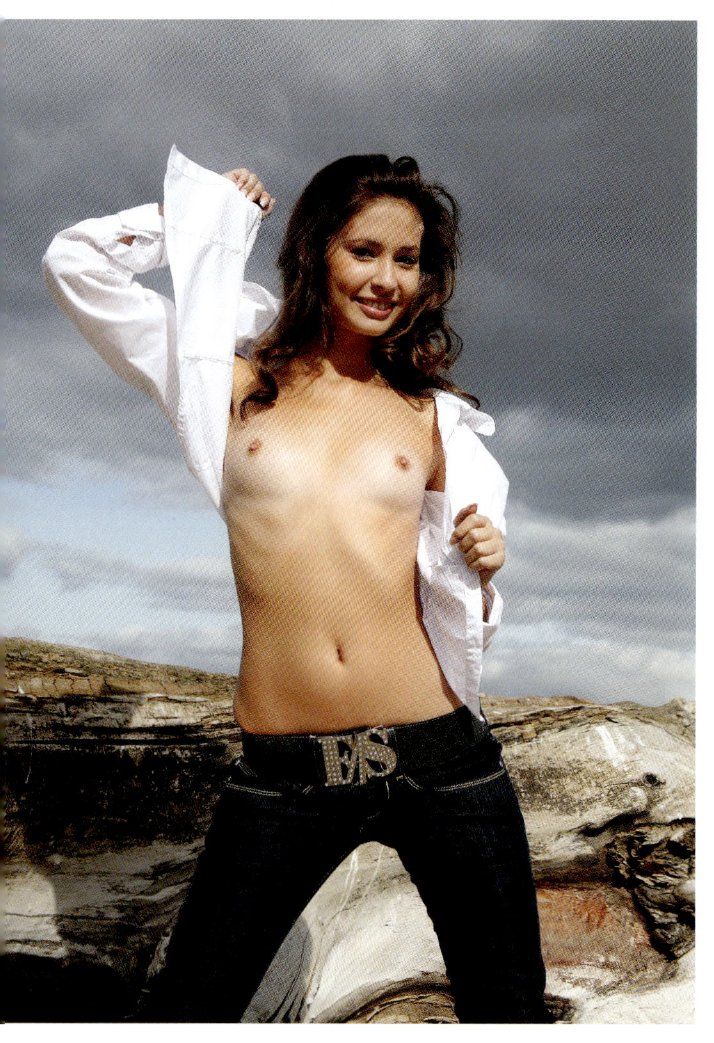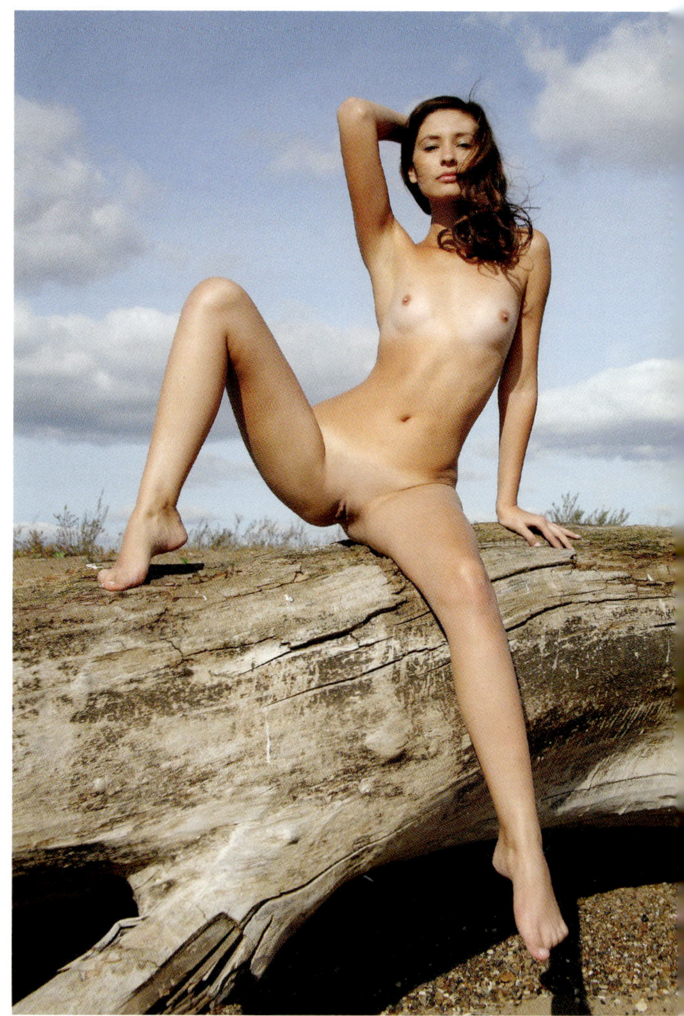

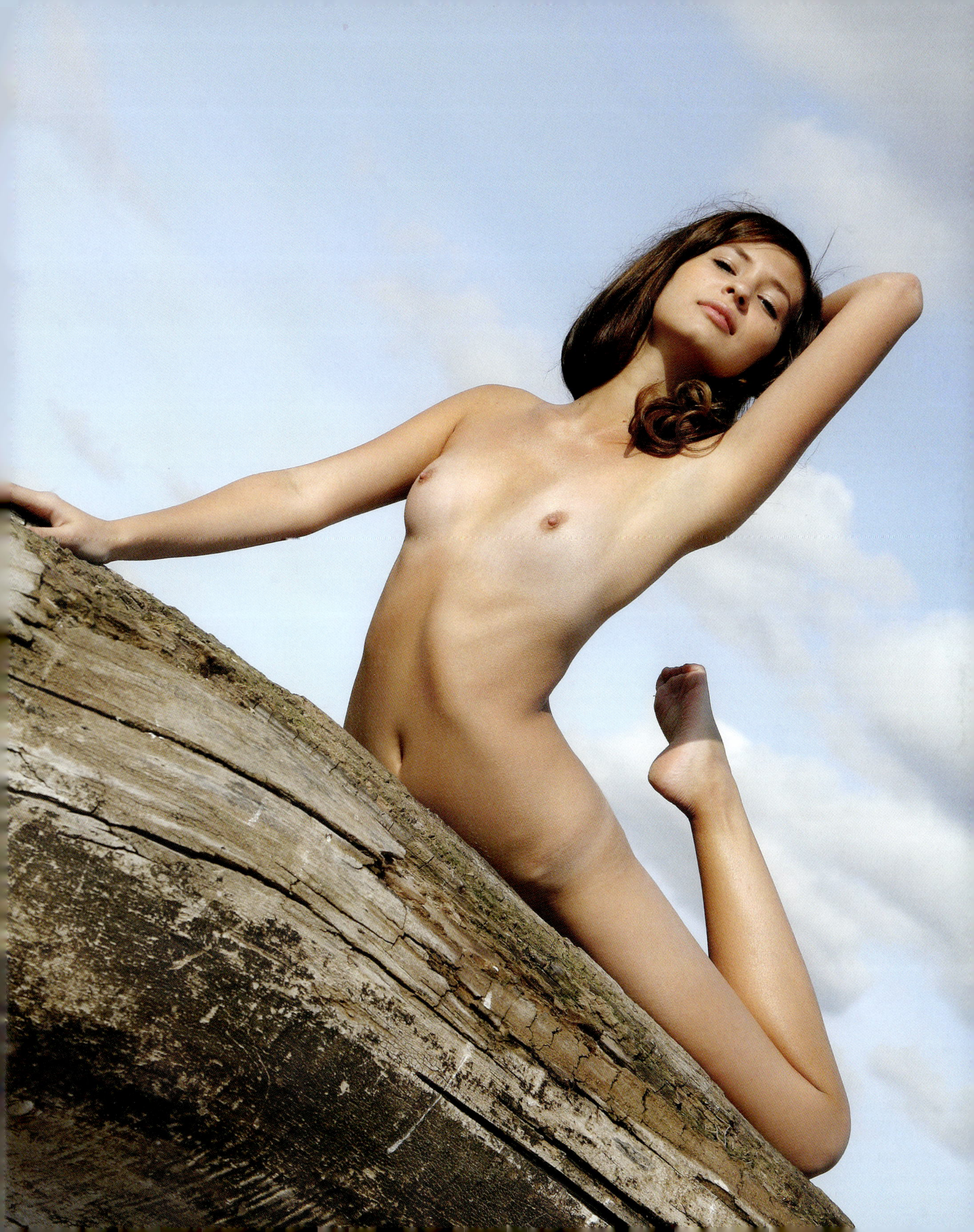

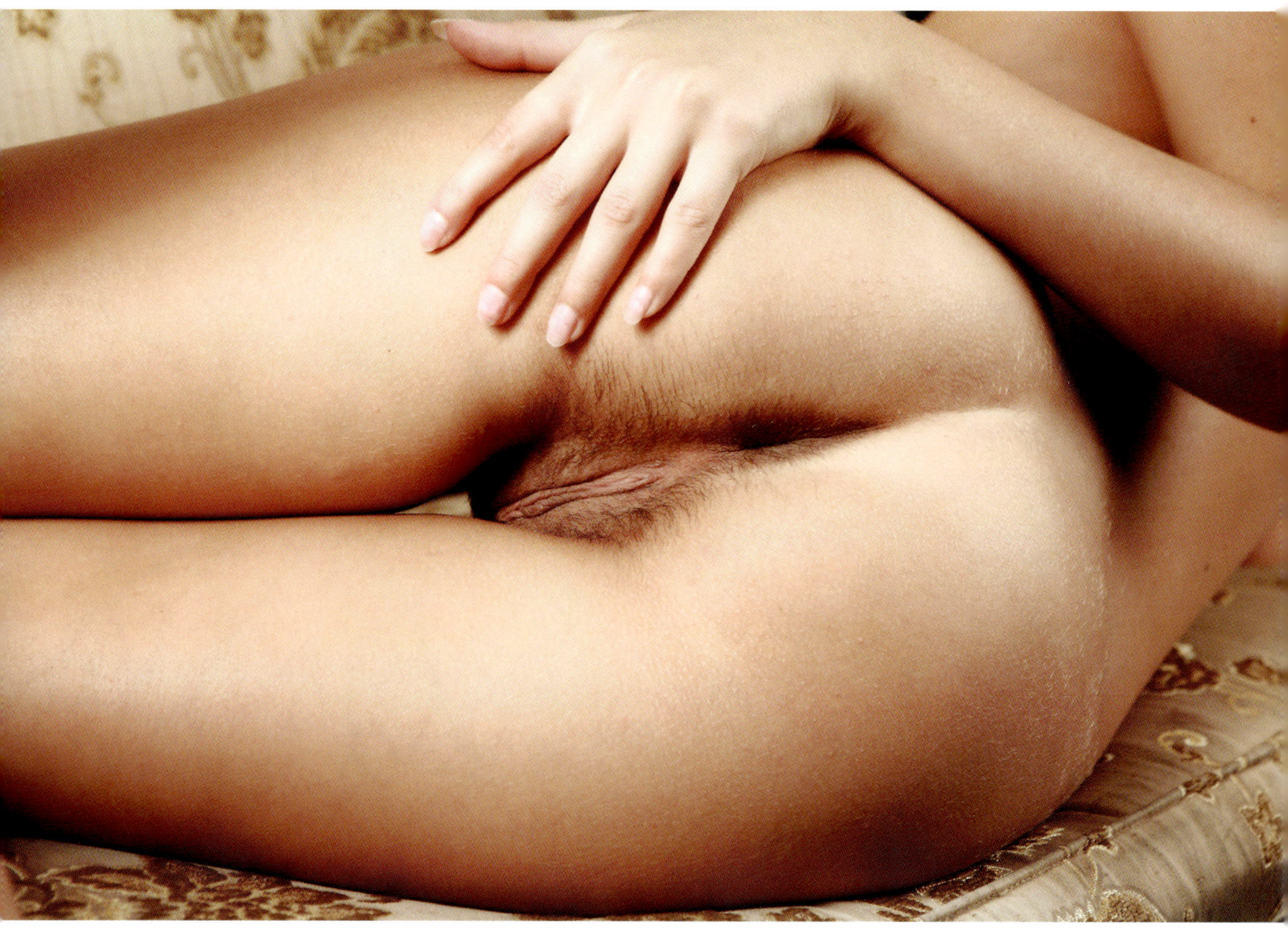

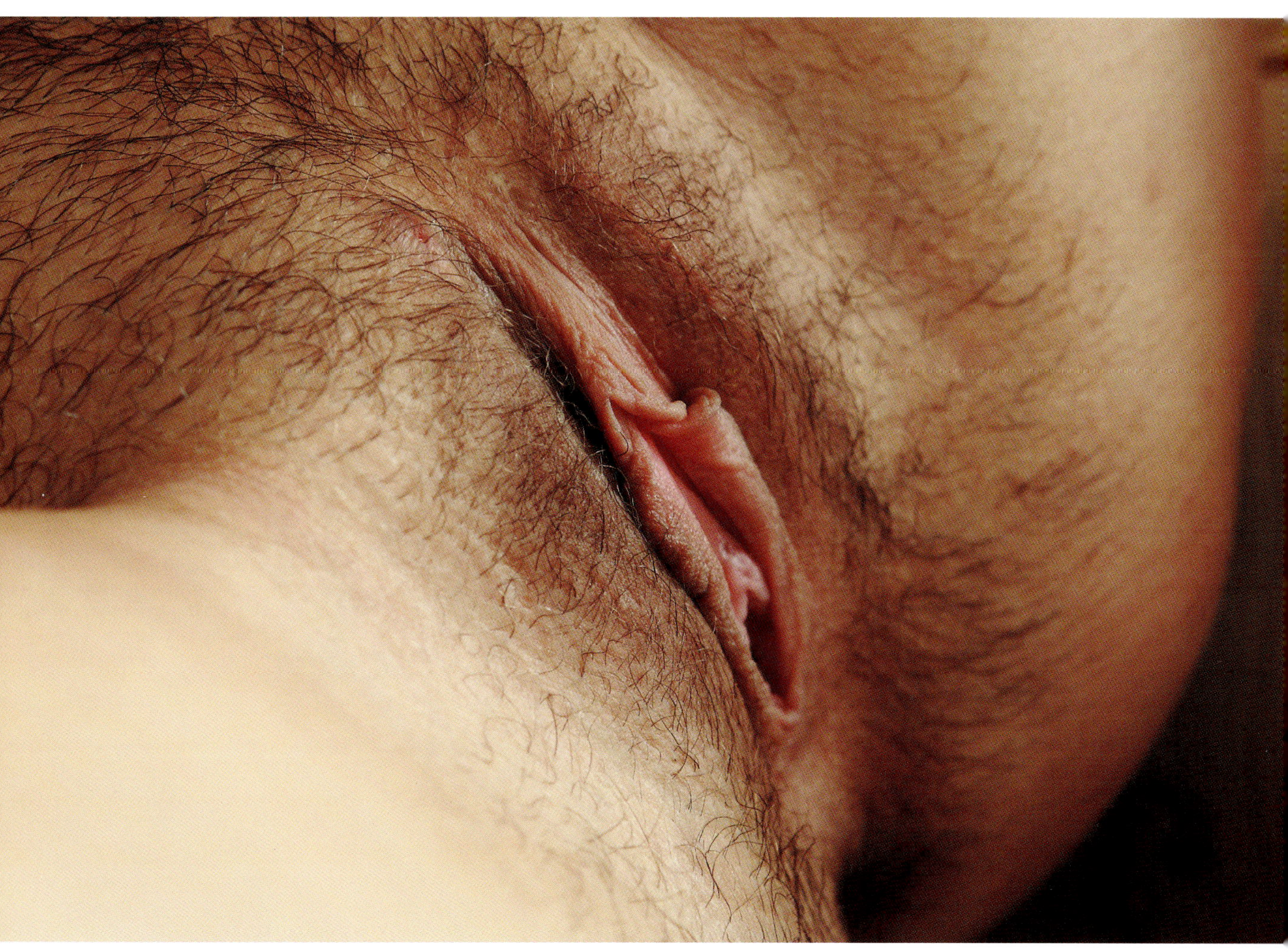

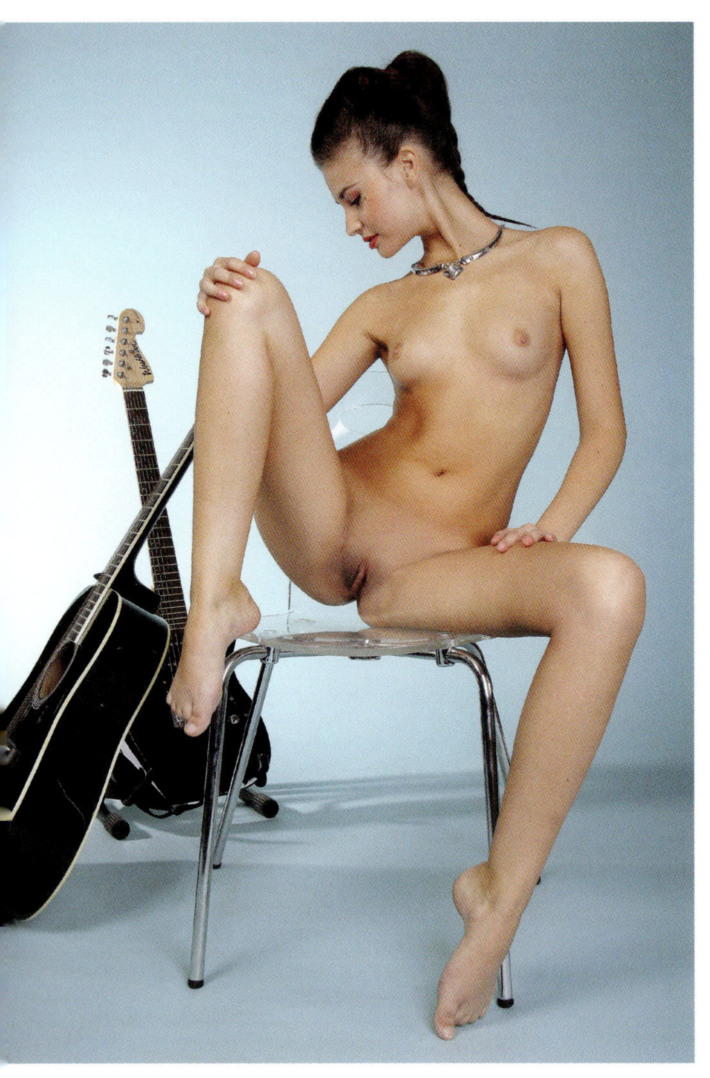
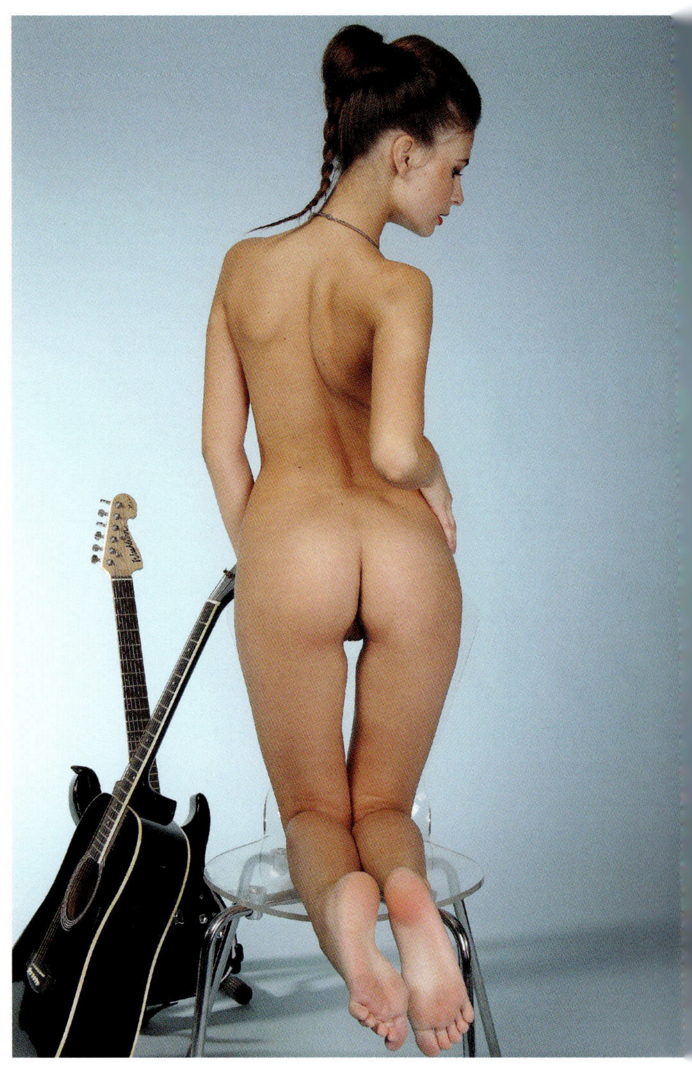

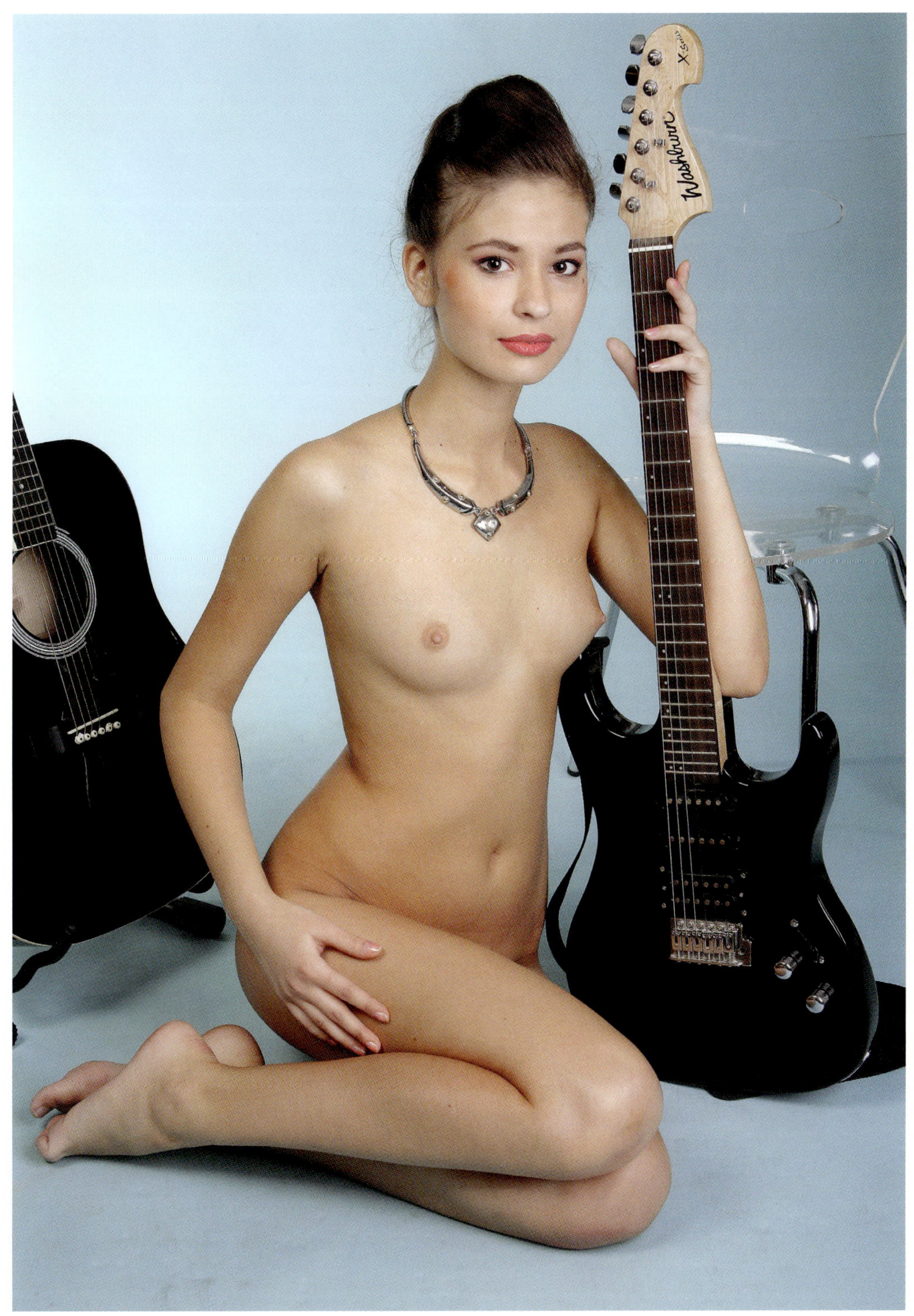

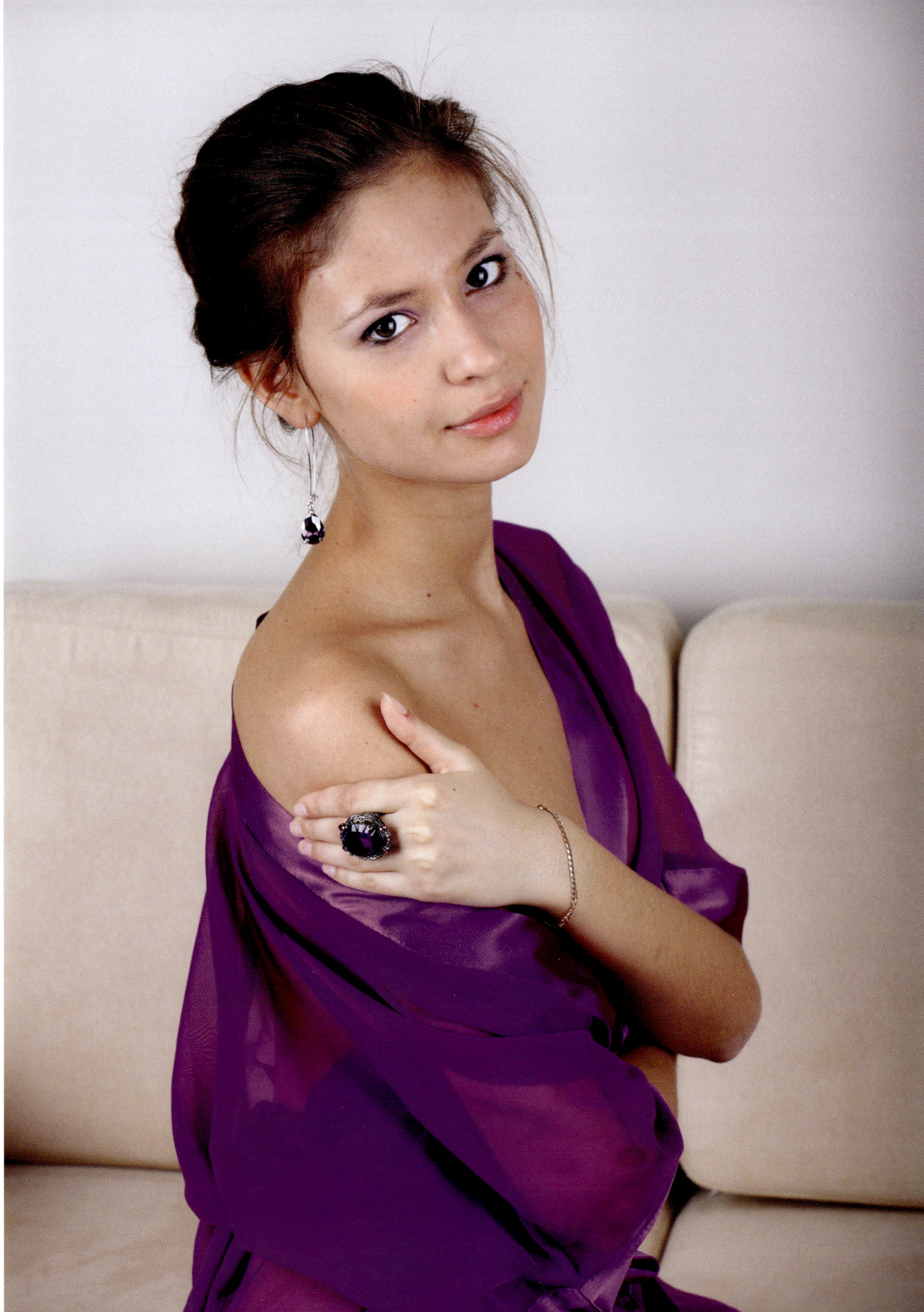

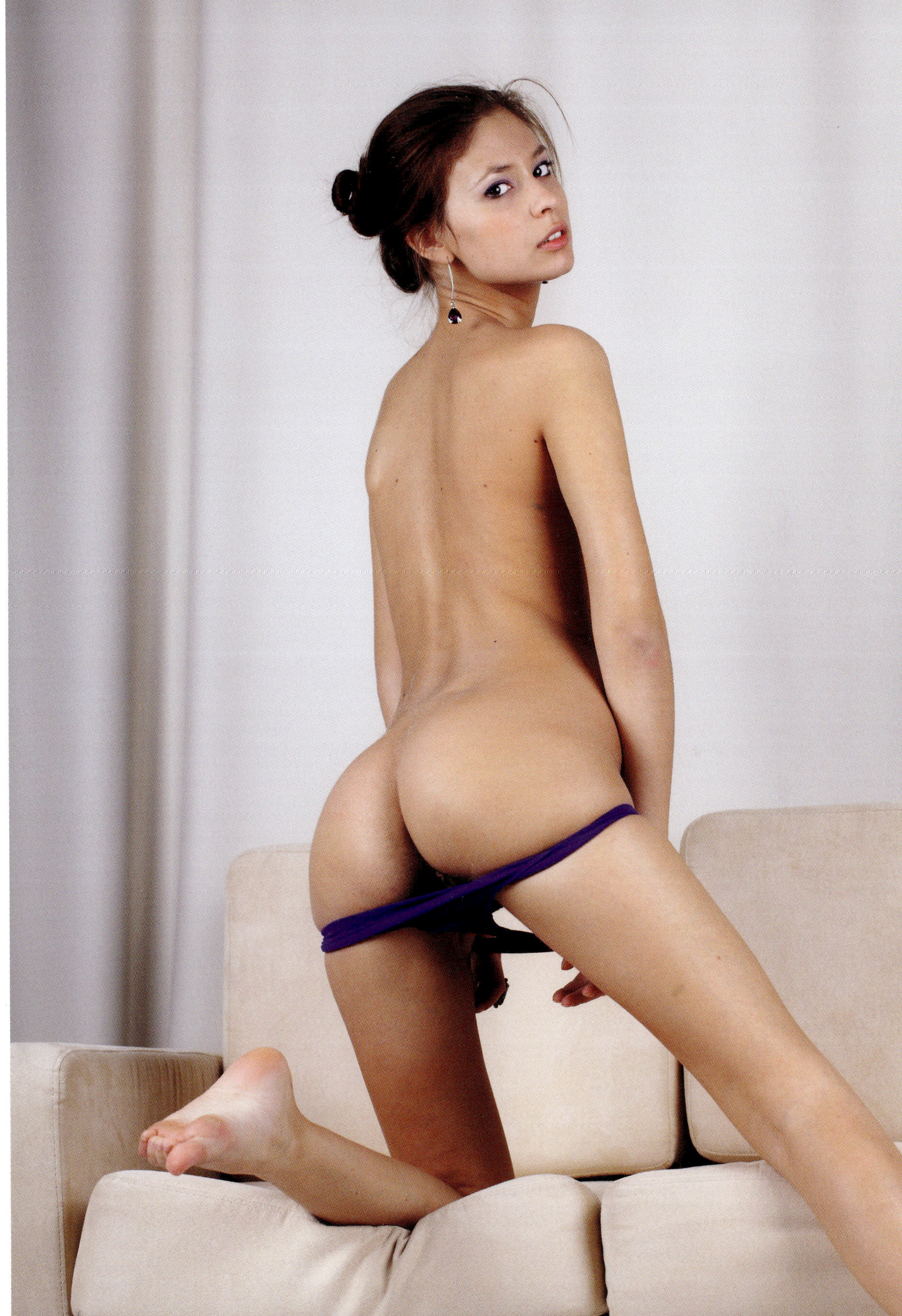

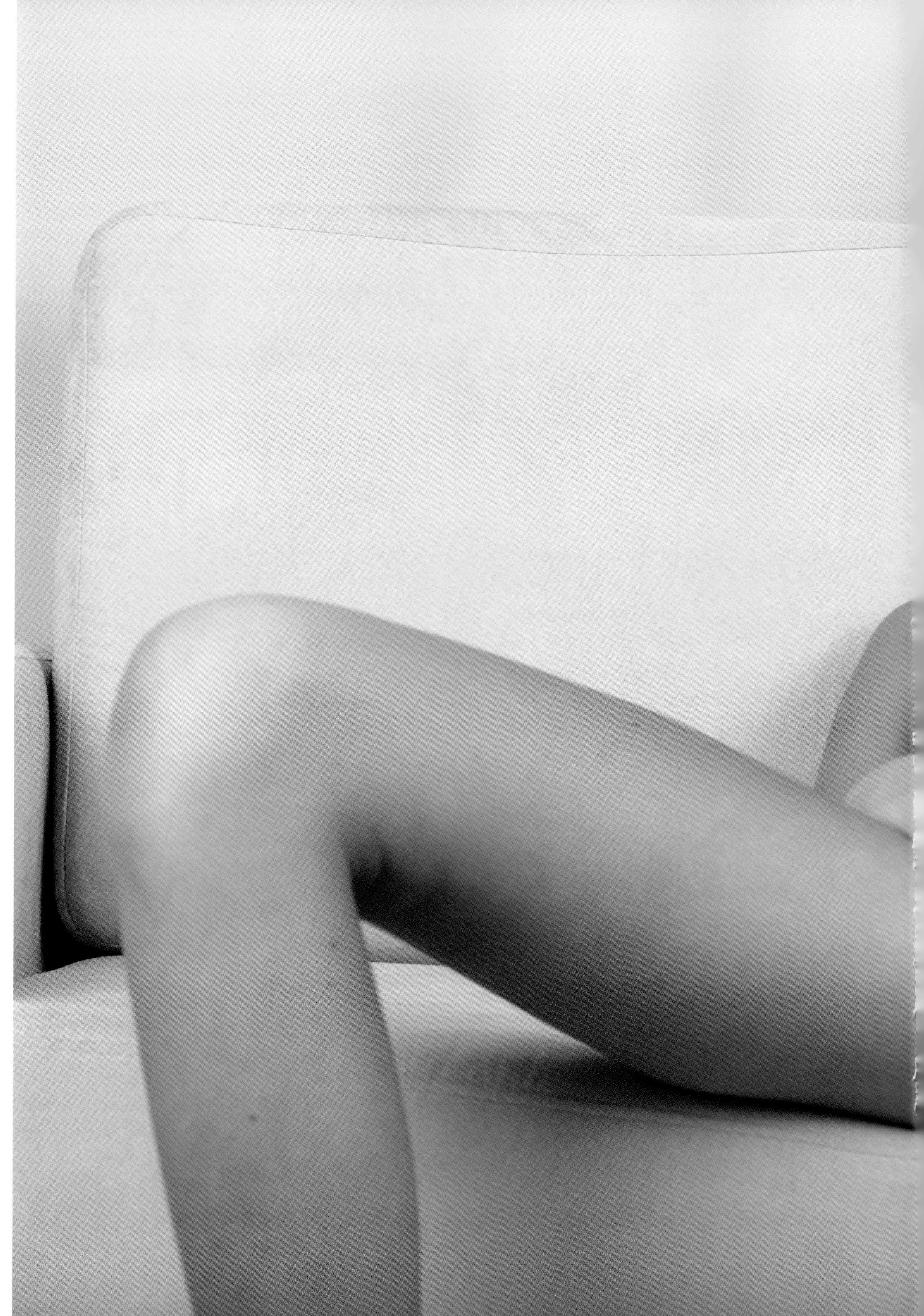

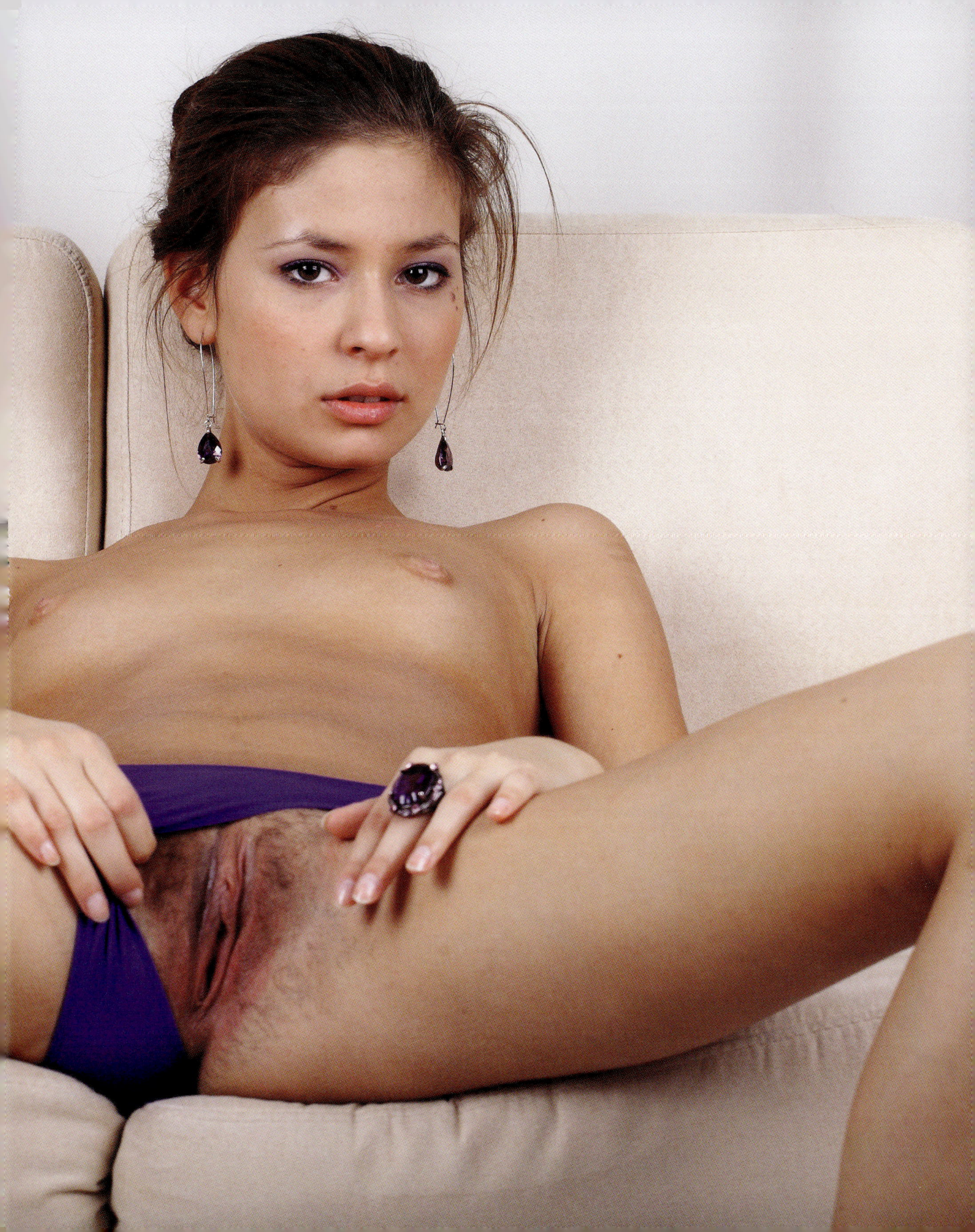

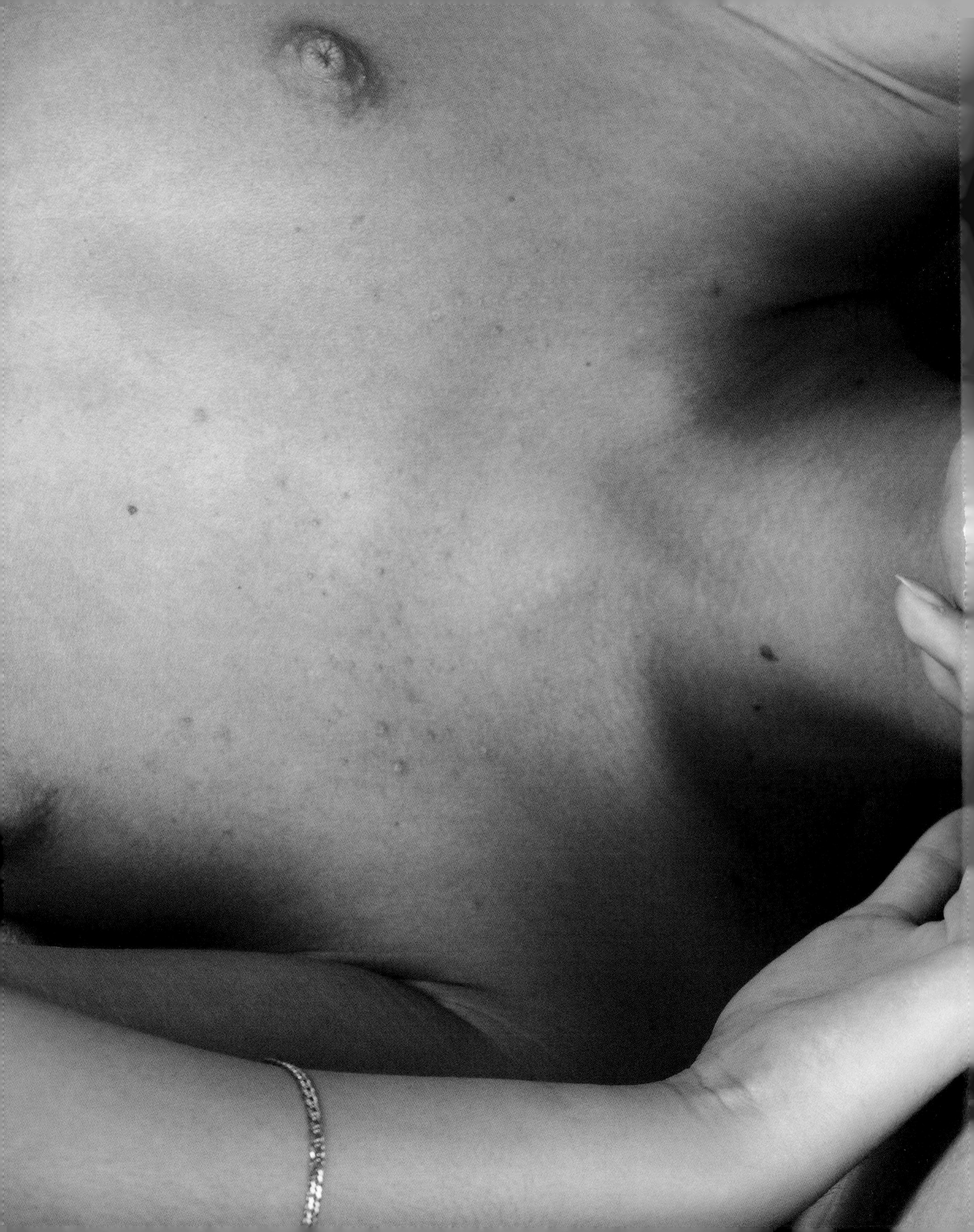

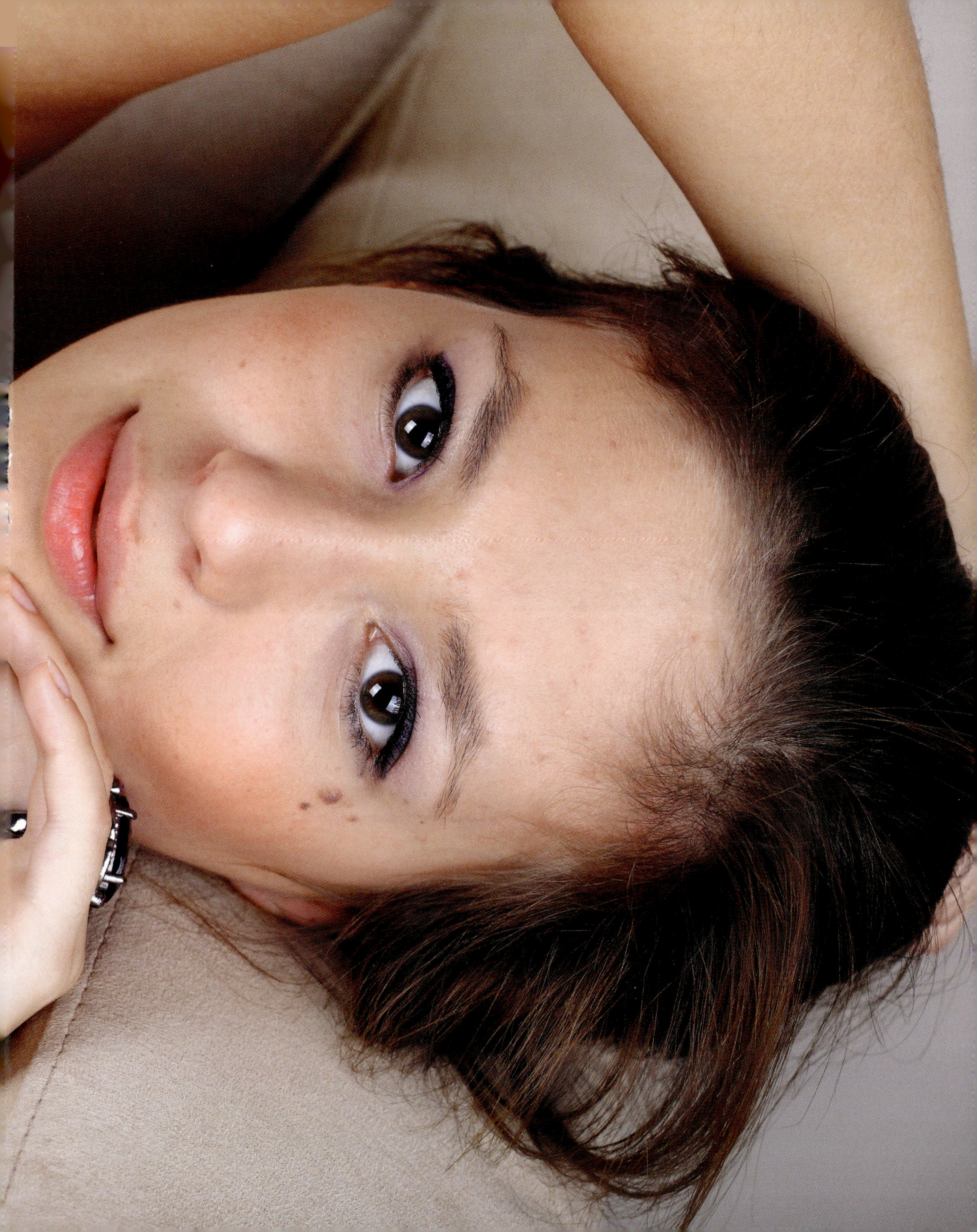

COLLECT THEM ALL: OUR MOST BEAUTIFUL

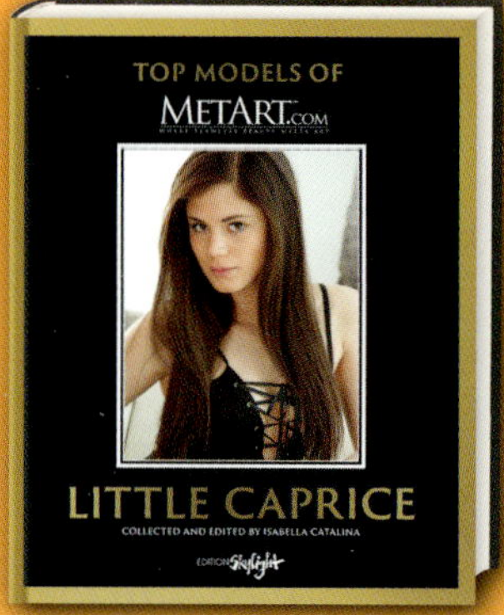

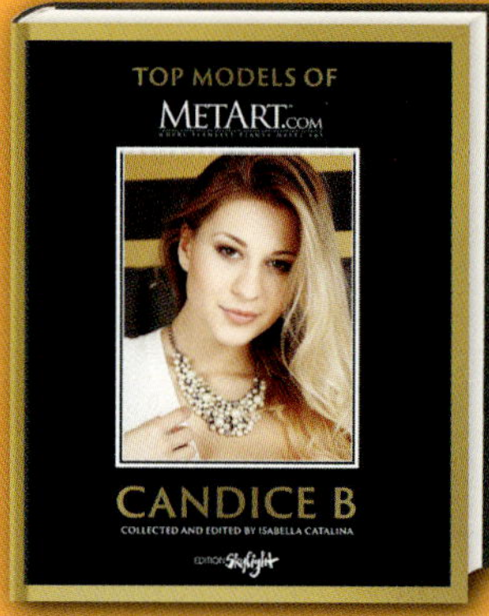

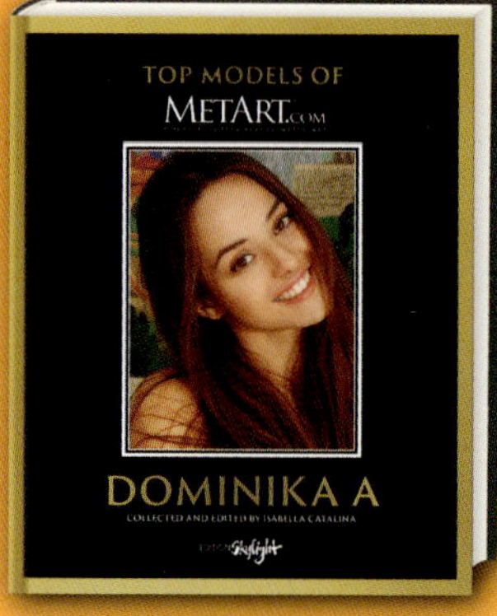

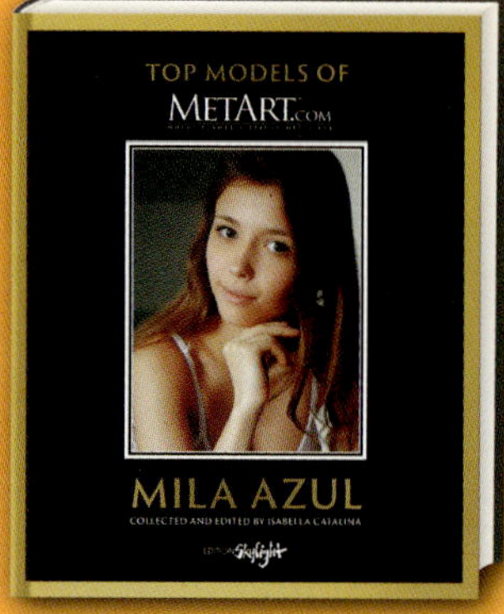

ISBN 978-3-03766-659-3   ISBN 978-3-03766-660-9   ISBN 978-3-03766-679-1   ISBN 978-3-03766-680-7

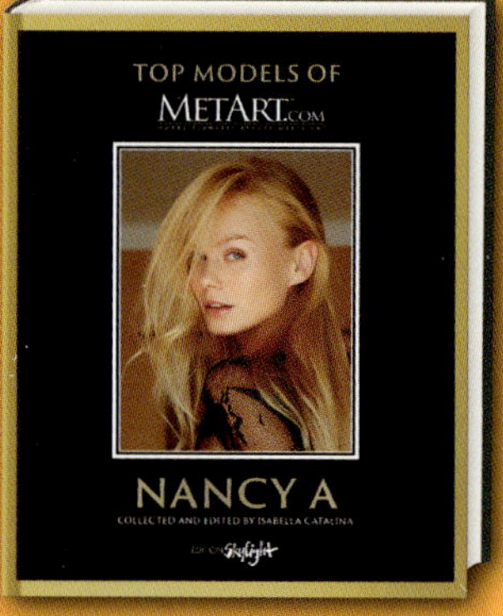

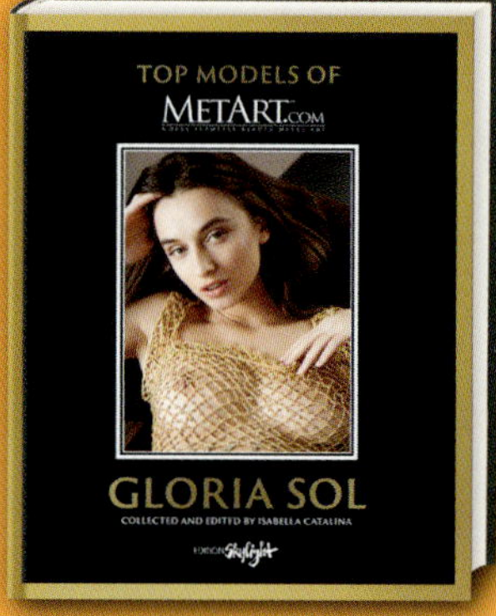

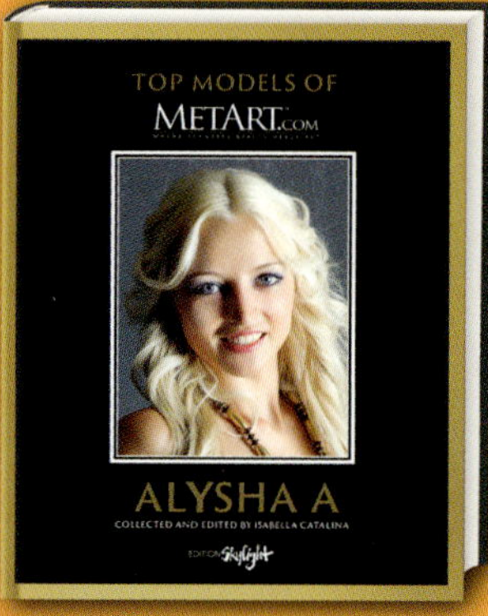

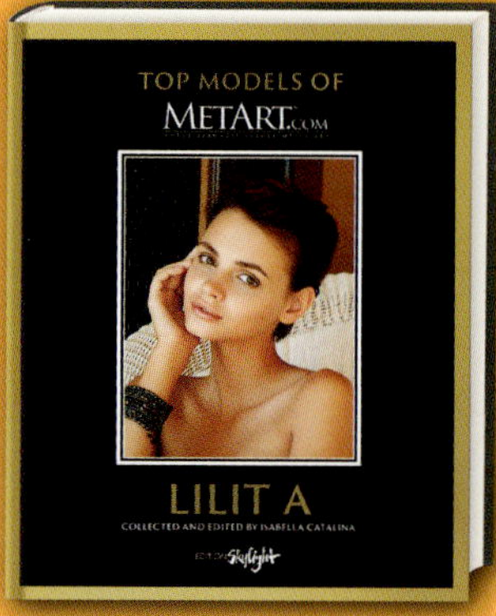

ISBN 978-3-03766-687-6   ISBN 978-3-03766-688-3   ISBN 978-3-03766-692-0   ISBN 978-3-03766-693-7

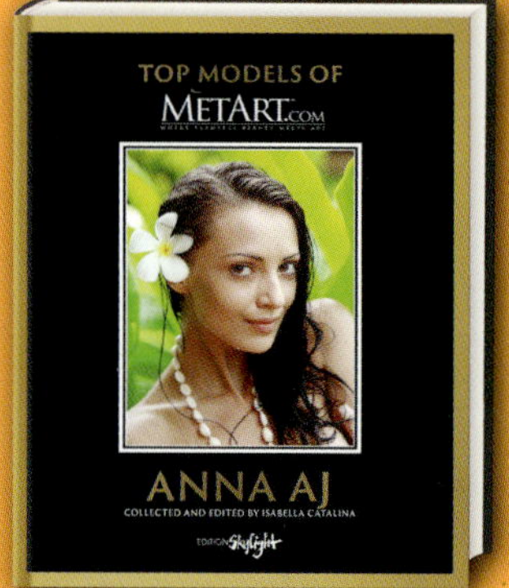

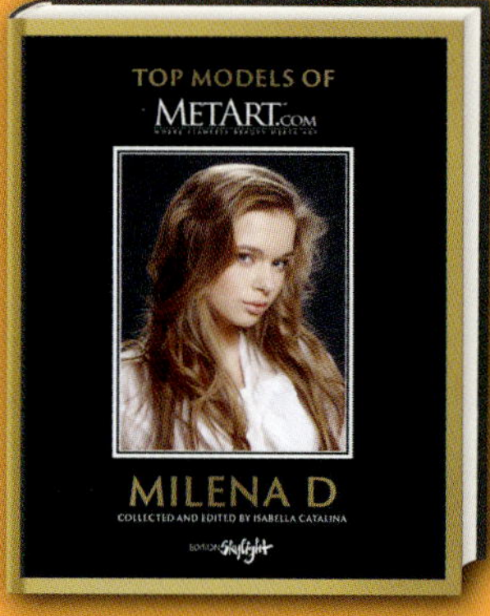

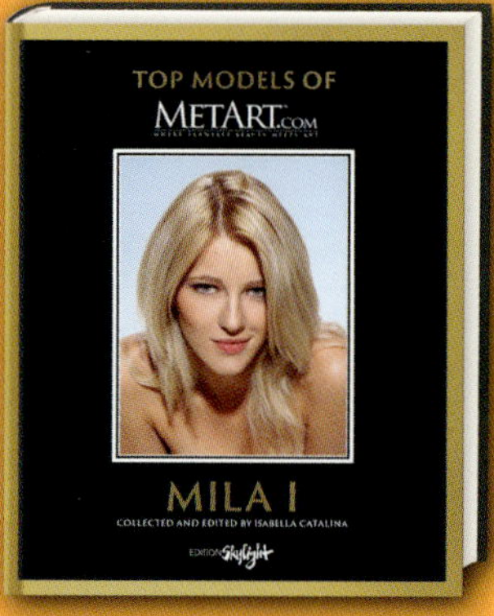

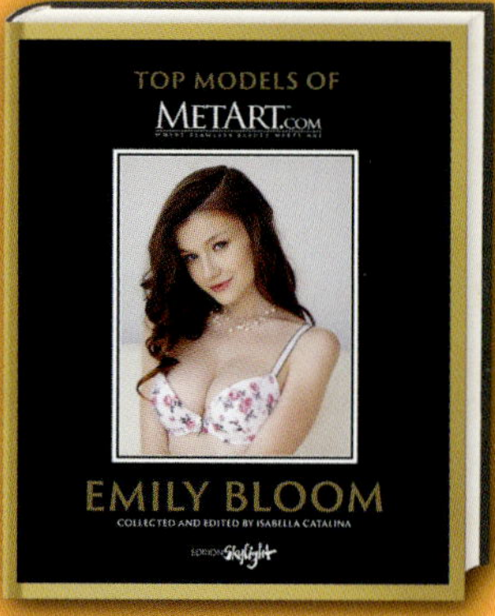

ISBN 978-3-03766-695-1   ISBN 978-3-03766-696-8   ISBN 978-3-03766-703-3   ISBN 978-3-03766-704-0